The Politics of Land-Use Reform

The Politics
of Land-Use
Reform

FRANK J. POPPER

The University of Wisconsin Press

Published 1981

The University of Wisconsin Press
114 North Murray Street
Madison, Wisconsin 53715

The University of Wisconsin Press, Ltd.
1 Gower Street
London WC1E 6HA, England

First printing

Printed in the United States of America

For LC CIP information see the colophon

ISBN 0-299-08530-9 cloth; 0-299-08534-1 paper

To all the other Poppers

The true problem is not to study how human life submits to rules—it simply does not; the real problem is how the rules become adapted to life.

—Bronislaw Malinowski, *Crime and Custom in a Savage Society*

I could have broken up the farm in small pieces and made a fortune—I had an offer that made that possible—and I might have accepted it except for [Dashiell] Hammett, who said, "No, I won't have it that way. Let everyone else mess up the land. Why don't you and I leave it alone?", a fine sentiment with which I agree and have forever regretted listening to.

—Lillian Hellman, *Scoundrel Time*

Contents

Acknowledgments

During the more than four years that I worked on this book, a gratifyingly large and diverse group of people and organizations helped me. It is a pleasure to be able at last to thank them publicly for their contributions.

My earliest debts go back to 1973–74, when I was in Chicago as a staff member at the American Society of Planning Officials, now the American Planning Association. Edmund McCahill and Robert Cassidy, the editors of ASPO's magazine *Planning*, encouraged me to write the articles that led to this book. Beginning in late 1975, the Twentieth Century Fund, a New York City research foundation directed by M. J. Rossant, provided partial financial support, occasional advice, and the excellent editorial work of Judith Jacobson, Beverly Goldberg, and Brenda Shactman. William Nye and Frederick Anderson, respectively the executive director and president of the Environmental Law Institute in Washington, D.C., let me spend much of 1979 as a part-time staff member while I finished the book. The libraries at both the Institute and the American Planning Association have been immensely helpful. Elizabeth Evanson of the University of Wisconsin Press meticulously guided the transformation of the final manuscript into a published book.

In addition to my institutional debts, I have also acquired a large number of personal ones. The following people gave helpful written comments on all or part of the early manuscript: Carol Barker, Charles Geisler, Robert Healy, Michael Heiman, John Rosenberg, Paul Sabatier, Stanley Scott, Jens Sorensen, and William Toner.

Stephen Kahn allowed me to use his Chicago apartment as an office when I needed one. Peter Berle, a trustee of the Twentieth Century Fund, first called my attention to the Adirondack Park Agency, of which he was then a member. Any number of present and former staff members of the Environmental Law Institute and the American Planning Association—particularly Roger Dower, Daniel Lauber, and Richard Liroff—answered questions for me. Julie Aden, Mary Dearing, Christine Edmunds, and Karen Fishman, all of the Environmental Law Institute's staff, helped with various clerical tasks. Approximately two hundred interviewees around the country offered me hospitality, candor, insight, entertainment, and above all, a profound sense of the astoundingly different ways in which Americans care about their land.

My parents, Hans and Lina Popper, always stood by me. They say they know nothing about land use, much less the politics of reforming it. No matter; they know their son. Finally, my wife, Deborah Popper, was consistently this project's most effective critic. Her special skill lay in making me see the larger implications of my findings, and at the same time reminding me that there is more to life than land use. Whatever merit I have managed to give this book would never have been possible without her.

Frank J. Popper

Bethesda, Maryland
May 1980

The Politics of Land-Use Reform

A Regulatory Experiment

In the late 1960s, political activists in what had become known as the environmental movement began working to mitigate the effects that nearly a decade of development boom had imposed on the country's physical settings, social climate, and natural resources. The dominant strategy of this movement was to subject the development process to greater public regulation.

Some of the activists in the environmental movement had a more specific concern: land-use reform. Prior to the 1970s, the role of government in land use consisted largely of local planning and zoning. Local government appeared weak or indifferent to the nation's land-use and environmental difficulties. As regulatory devices, planning and zoning seemed unequal to the problems of land use; moreover, being local, they were inherently unsuited to take into account the broad environmental and social effects of large projects whose impacts transcended local boundaries. Those in the land-use reform movement therefore called for more regulation at higher levels of government—an objective that I shall call "centralized regulation." The movement succeeded in obtaining the passage of a great deal of innovative land-use legislation embodied in new programs of centralized regulation. Most of these programs are administered at the state level, but some are administered at the federal level.

The land-use reform movement and its programs were rooted in an intellectual critique of regulation—not just land-use regulation, but virtually all regulation as it existed in this country in the late 1960s.

3

The most famous proponent of that critique is Ralph Nader. In dealing with a vast range of issues (including land use), he and his associates have argued that regulation of the type that developed during the Progressive Era and the New Deal—which may be termed Rooseveltian regulation—is fundamentally flawed.

Rooseveltian regulation, according to this critique, allows the regulated interests (in the case of land use, development interests, most of which are local) to penetrate and to control public regulatory agencies. The proposed solution is strengthened, nonlocal regulation—centralized regulation—with explicit safeguards to keep the regulatory agencies more responsive to the public at large than to selfish corporate interests. The Nader approach seeks more centralization and regulation to remedy the deficiencies of Rooseveltian regulation. The land-use reform movement can be legitimately identified with this Nader-inspired advocacy of post-Rooseveltian centralized regulation.

This book is a critical assessment of what the land-use reform movement has accomplished. But land-use reform is not just an isolated reform effort in one specialized field or a peripheral skirmish in the broader struggle waged by the environmental movement. This book treats its subject as a case study of the Nader approach as it has actually been applied.

This book examines and evaluates the effects of state land-use programs as instances of centralized regulation. Of course, land-use reform programs may be studied in other ways. For example, the programs, especially those for the coastal zone that have been under way for some years, have been analyzed as experiments in collaborative planning between different levels of government,[1] as citizen-participation efforts,[2] and as examples of the spread of innovative state legislation.[3] The programs have also been studied from administrative perspectives,[4] as well as legal[5] and deliberately eclectic[6] ones.

In addition, the economic effects of the programs—more precisely, the costs they create—have been investigated.[7] But the economic benefits of the programs have received little scrutiny. And no one to my knowledge has ever analyzed the programs as public attempts to make the market deal fairly and efficiently with the spillover effects (in economists' terms, externalities) of urban growth across local boundaries. The actual environmental effects of the programs in terms of, for example, controlling air and water pollution, preserving farmland and scenic vistas, conserving resources, or improving development practices also have received little examination.[8]

But examining the programs as efforts at centralized regulation seems at least as valid and useful as the other approaches, first because it has not been done before; second because the programs' centralization and regulatory functions are their most significant political features; third because the perspective of centralized regulation is broader than most of the alternative perspectives on the programs; and fourth because the United States has had a rich, instructive experience with centralized regulation as a means of reform in a wide variety of fields. Academics and politicians have recently shown a great deal of interest in the effects of all this regulation; centralized regulation has become simultaneously a scholarly and a public issue. Analyses of what has happened to programs of centralized regulation elsewhere are therefore available to shed light on the prospects and problems of land-use reform.

Centralized regulation can be defined as control by higher-level agencies of government over some aspect of the production or use of private goods. The objects of such control are primarily business concerns, but they also may be individuals or other public agencies. The purpose of centralized regulation may be to protect public health or safety, to prevent unfair or destructive business practices, to provide a check on natural monopolies such as power companies, or to moderate business cycles by making them more *regular* and more subject to rules. (The word "regulate" derives from the Latin word *regula*, a rule.) All these concerns have in different ways animated the land-use reform movement.

The centralized regulatory programs fostered by the land-use reform movement are not easy to assess. Most of the state programs are in their first generation and still evolving. Their environmental and economic effects are not yet known. The programs' benefits are hard even to describe.

Other environmental programs can, at least in theory, produce tangible, measurable results: reduced emissions from smokestacks, better overall air quality, and the like. But a land-use program typically consists of a series of complex, ambiguous, conditional regulatory decisions. The results of these decisions cannot be compared to a generally accepted standard of good land use because no such standard exists. Evaluations of land-use programs are for the most part subjective and approximate; many, too, are affected by political predispositions and pressures.

Land-use reform programs almost always encounter heavy opposition, primarily from development interests and the local governments allied with them. This opposition has not succeeded in stopping land-use reform legislation, but it has imposed a variety of pro-developer concessions and compromises on what began as strictly environmentalist bills. The influence of development interests also has deflected actual regulatory practice still further from strict environmentalism. Nonetheless, the programs have held up reasonably well under political attack, mainly because much of the public has come to accept the desirability of regulating urban growth.

The energy crisis and economic difficulties have encouraged many people to regard environmentalism as an unaffordable luxury. These problems also have hindered the implementation of land-use reform programs. But public support for land-use reform has proved sufficient to keep a somewhat abstract altruistic issue alive in the face of more immediate and selfish concerns. Land-use reform has raised the environmental quality of a great deal of development practice; the improvements have not been so extensive or so rapid as some of the movement's supporters might have wished, but they are nonetheless impressive. Land-use reform also appears to have had negative, unintended economic effects that are plainly doing the movement political harm. So on balance, the programs present a mixed picture, one of mingled strength and weakness.

Perhaps an interweaving of accomplishment and inefficacy is the best that any reform effort can achieve. But in general, and especially in the case of land use, I do not think so. Land-use reform programs can be made more effective. For example, Nader has typically—and highly successfully—sought regulation for consumer protection; the land-use movement might work to better effect by representing the interests of the large numbers of people who are consumers of land. Land-use reform advocates also should recognize that the Nader critique of Rooseveltian regulation is not the only possible one, that more centralization and more regulation are not the sole or, necessarily, the best cures for the inadequacies of centralized regulation.

To forestall accusations of hidden bias, I hereby declare myself an environmentalist; I rely on my activist colleagues at the Environmental Law Institute in Washington, D.C., to bear me out. On the other hand, I believe that environmental quality and economic growth are, perhaps with some adjustments on both sides, nearly always compatible. To me, one sign of health in a community is the sound of a developer's bulldozers; another is that the developer complains about the environmental restrictions under which he must operate; and still another is that local environmentalists express dissatisfaction with the lameness of those restrictions.

Certainly, I favor land-use reform. But the deficiencies of the nation's land-use and environmental practices are so many and varied that centralized regulation seems inadequate to deal with them. At the very least, it seems to me, we ought to be trying nonregulatory, decentralized approaches as well.

CHAPTER 2

Land-Use Regulation as a Public Issue

"Land use" is a cool and neutral term that covers a multitude of highly charged and even dangerous matters. Land use affects housing costs, the wealth and ethnic composition of neighborhoods, and the quality of schools and other public services. Land use affects the beauty of one's surroundings, the burden of taxes, and the amount of time and money people spend driving and commuting. Land use affects the severity of pollution, the local unemployment rate, the cost of energy, and the availability and quality of recreation. Land-use decisions that seem trivial, or apparently small procedural alterations in the way land-use decisions are made, can quickly alter the face and feel of a community.

People and organizations struggle to control land because, like capital and labor, it is a factor of production and a determinant of affluence. The primary means of control is ownership. Two out of three American families live in homes on land they own or are buying.[1] Millions of Americans also own business, vacation, retirement, inherited, investment, or speculative land properties. Corporations of various sizes, functioning for various purposes, own vast tracts of the country.[2] Government agencies also have enormous holdings; the federal government alone holds a third of the nation's land, most of it in the West.[3] All landowners care intensely about how their land is used and developed. They also care very much about what happens on adjoining land. Ownership of land implies power, security, independence, fertility, and, above all, wealth. According to one estimate, at the end of 1975 almost 15 percent of the nation's total wealth came from landholdings—about $1.2 trillion.[4] This figure represents the land's resale value; the estimate does not directly include the value of the mineral or agricultural products extracted from the land or the buildings on it.

Land is a commodity, but it also is a resource of permanent importance. The supply of land is limited, especially in urban settings. And most land-use decisions are essentially irreversible. A cornfield, beach, or forest that becomes a suburban development or power plant is not likely to revert to its original use. A polluted river cannot easily or inexpensively be made pure. A highway, airport, or shopping center that blights its surroundings cannot be moved. The results of land-use decisions may be inconvenient, ugly, uneconomical, polluting, or unjust. But such decisions are made every day, and to say that one's grandchildren will suffer from them is to underestimate their reach.

A country's or a state's or a city's land-use patterns—its buildings and roads and spaces, its planes and walls and holes—offer clear physical indications of its priorities and its prospects. The way we cover the ground we are given is endlessly revealing.[5]

The Nation's Land-Use Problems

Until recently, American governments showed little concern for land use.[6] Development pressures in most places were low in relation to the amount of land available. Land use was an obscure technical field. In the 1920s, local governments began to enact planning, zoning, and subdivision ordinances. These laws were supposed to make sure that land development would conform to the community's wishes and needs. But most communities were undemanding, and most regulation was nonexistent, weak, or unenforced. It did not seem to matter.

By the late 1960s and early 1970s, however, rapid growth in the economy and population had produced more people, corporations, and governments with more money, technology, and mobility than ever before. Competition for land increased; therefore, land prices rose. Development rates in the private and public sectors were at record highs. The growth was greatest on the edges of downtowns, on the suburban and exurban fringes of cities, and in heretofore totally rural areas.

This expansion produced a bewildering variety of problems. Development projects of all kinds—not just commercial, residential, and factory complexes but also governmental and energy facilities—were getting bigger and polluting more. Many of them strained local public treasuries and services while destroying unique local amenities. The Interstate Highway System, which was undertaken in the late 1950s and parts of which began reaching completion in the mid-1960s, had created vast new stretches of urban or potentially urban land. Too much of it seemed to be succumbing to formless, costly, energy-consuming sprawl and strip development. Too much good agricultural land was going out of production and into speculation and subdivision. Too many pleasant rural areas were becoming the sites of characterless, often shoddily built leisure home projects. Other rural areas were acquiring ruinous strip mines or polluting power plants. The nation's countryside was urbanizing rapidly and unattractively.

Under these pressures, long-standing deficiencies in the procedures by which local government—cities, towns, and counties—regulated land use became apparent. Most local land-use plans, where they existed at all, consisted of little more than a record of good intentions. The plans were only advisory; they lacked the force of law. Zoning and subdivision regulations were supposed to be consistent with the plans, but a determined developer could almost always get around the intent of a plan by obtaining a variance, especially if he was willing to bribe or make campaign contributions to a few underpaid local government officials.

In most communities, developers had no need to engage in such improper behavior. Development interests—builders, realtors, and their political and financial allies—were heavily represented in local government and ran planning commissions and zoning boards. Many communities competed with one another for all sorts of development projects. They annexed wildly and they uncritically assumed that the short-run property tax revenues and employment produced by development would outweigh any long-run fiscal, environmental, or social costs. This assumption often turned out to be incorrect.

Many relatively wealthy white suburban communities also used their zoning laws to keep out unwanted minorities and the poor. Whether for racial or for economic motives—most often for both— restrictive zoning served to harm the excluded and to raise the prices they paid for the leftover housing they were able to obtain. Such zoning also homogenized the communities that employed it and aggravated the already formidable difficulties of the central cities.

At the same time, various public authorities were undertaking road-building, sewer, and housing projects. These projects, supported by federal grants and influential local political constituencies, such as building contractors and construction unions, were frequently inconsistent with local land-use policies. For example, a highway would be routed through a neighborhood that the local planning department, zoning board, and residents wanted to preserve. Or a sewer system would stimulate growth on farmland that planners wanted to remain undeveloped. But the authorities that ran the projects were autonomous; indeed, they were designed to end-run community or local government opposition.

Local land-use, public-works, and tax policies often had nothing to do with one another or with their counterparts in neighboring communities or at the state level. The states, for the most part, had no land-use policies, and state public works and tax policies were often vague, internally inconsistent, or inconsistent with the policies of neighboring states. The federal government had no real land-use policies either, and federal public works and tax policies represented yet another area of uncoordinated, conflicting government endeavor.[7]

The Reformist Response: Centralized Regulation

The early proponents of land-use reform were a loose coalition of environmentalists (in those days often called conservationists), city planners, land-use lawyers, some state and federal officials, a few progressive business people, and citizen activists of all sorts. They had concluded that the objectionable results of the development boom were caused primarily by zoning, particularly as administered by local governments. So when, in the late 1960s, a larger segment of the public began to perceive the seriousness of the nation's land-use problems, the vanguard of the reform movement had already worked out a solution.

The reformers did not propose to abolish local zoning; they realized that doing so would be politically and administratively impossible. Instead, they sought to supplement zoning with land-use regulation at higher levels of government—primarily the state and regional levels, but also to some extent the federal level as well. This new regulation was to apply mainly to projects that were large or in environmentally fragile areas. In 1973, the Rockefeller Brothers Fund Task Force on Land Use and Urban Growth produced a report, *The Use of Land*, that became one of the best-known documents of the land-use reform movement. It declared: "Important development should be regulated by governments that represent all the people whose lives are likely to be affected by it, including those who could benefit from it as well as those who could be harmed by it. Where a regulatory decision significantly affects people in more than one locality, state, regional, or even federal action is necessary."[8] The pursuit of centralized regulation has always been the hallmark of the land-use reform movement. From time to time, the movement has supported measures other than, or in addition to, centralized regulation.[9] The movement's size, strength, and scope grew dramatically in the late 1960s and early 1970s as its concerns became those of the larger, burgeoning environmental movement. But centralized regulation remained its most characteristic recommendation for the solution of the nation's land-use problems.

Centralized regulation, as the land-use reform movement advocated it, could supplement zoning in several different ways. It might simply take the form of a separate, distinct layer of regulation superimposed on zoning and with no relation to it. Alternatively, centralized regulation might attempt to stimulate more stringent local zoning or to set procedural and substantive standards for local zoning decisions. Centralized regulation might confer entirely new powers on state, regional, or federal agencies. Or it might shift existing powers from local to higher-level governments, sometimes with a promise (and a schedule) of eventually returning them to the local level, sometimes not.

Centralized regulation might mean that higher-level governments would take unilateral action, or it might mean that they would enter into complex partnerships with local governments. Programs of centralized regulation vary in the amount, size, and kind of development regulated and in the relative weight given to planning as against regulation. But the common, defining feature of centralized regulatory programs is that they add regional, state, or federal intervention to land-use decisions that had been entirely local. The programs apply a broad multijurisdictional, heavily environmental viewpoint to decisions that previously were based solely on local and development-oriented concerns.

As the land-use reform movement conceived it, centralized regulation did not enlarge the scope or alter the nature of land-use regulation or planning. Regulation was still a matter of requiring builders of proposed projects to obtain government approval before proceeding, planning still a matter of trying to work out where the projects might best be placed before they were actually proposed. The land-use reform movement did not in general seek to extend regulation and planning to such aspects of land development as prices, profits, advertising or financial practices, mergers, barriers to entry, or economic concentration within the industry. In fields other than land use, government had often regulated such matters. But the land-use reform movement generally focused on the direct environmental implications of development.

The innovative feature of the movement was simply its demand that higher levels of government do more regulating and more planning, particularly from an environmental perspective. The reformers found nothing intrinsically wrong with regulation as a means of controlling land use. They argued simply that, as the sole source of regulation, local government did not have the needed environmental and social sensitivity and seemed unlikely to acquire it.

There never was any doubt that the movement would favor centralized regulation. For one thing, the movement was part of the environmental movement, which has always had a similar penchant for centralized regulation. More important, centralized regulation

accorded with some of the deepest political instincts of both the small
number of land-use reformers and large portions of the wider public.
The advocates of land-use reform, like those of the environmental
movement (and of other reform efforts such as the civil rights,
feminist, and labor movements), have typically been Rooseveltian
liberals who, in dealing with social problems, prefer public to private
initiatives. This preference is inherently centralizing.

The movement's supporters shy away, however, from measures
involving direct government control of the market. The spirit of the
movement is liberal, not socialist. Thus, for example, the Rockefeller Brothers Fund Task Force went out of its way to praise private
property, corporate profit motives, bank lending practices, and large
projects as at least potentially serving, along with land-use regulation, to create "quality development."[10]

Similarly, the movement's supporters have shown little interest in
such issues as the concentration of private landownership, the stew-
ardship of public land, Indian land claims, public development initiatives such as low-income housing, and land reform as the term is
understood in developing countries. These issues do not engage the
movement because doing something about them would mean inter-
fering too obviously, too deeply, with the operations of the market.
For the same reasons, the movement is not usually attracted to such
assertive devices as land banking—the stockpiling, as in some Canadian and Western European cities and provinces with socialist governments, of public landholdings for the specific purpose of controlling development patterns and land prices.[11]

Instead, the movement's supporters incline toward regulation as a
way to mitigate market imperfections, inefficiencies, and injustices.
Regulation will not replace or destroy the market and may not even
disrupt it. Regulation does not directly affect the distribution of
wealth, and it does not, for the most part, have unpleasant ideological connotations. A regulatory mechanism—typically a government
agency with legislation setting out its mandate and a staff to enforce
its rulings on applicants—is the means that the movement's supporters instinctively prefer for reconciling private activity with the public
interest.

As Rooseveltian liberals, the land-use reformers further believed
that higher levels of government, particularly the federal govern-

ment, were superior to lower levels, not only in jurisdiction, but also in ability, efficiency, honesty, and accountability. In short, the movement's supporters inclined toward centralism.

But in historical origin and practical substance, policymaking on land use in the United States has always been obdurately local. The federal government cannot possibly intervene in, much less control, millions of local land-use decisions across the country. It does not have the necessary knowledge, money, or techniques. And many of the decisions are too trivial to justify federal intervention. Physically, psychologically, and politically, the federal government is simply too far away. Therefore, instead of working on getting the federal government to regulate land use, land-use reformers concentrated on getting the state governments to do so.

The reformers considered state government more competent and reliable than local government, more likely to have (or to develop) the environmental and social concerns that had heretofore been missing in land-use regulation. Local government, in the view of the movement, was not to be trusted. "In too many localities," *The Use of Land* concludes,

neither the procedures for determining land use nor the individuals making the decisions have the public confidence. . . . citizens suspect that the people making regulatory decisions are thinking more about themselves and their cronies than about the general welfare. These suspicions are sometimes inaccurate; builders proposing a project and neighbors opposing the same project may both privately complain that the cards are stacked against them. Far too often, though, the suspicions are well grounded.[12]

In addition, state government was in a good position to resolve the competing interests of localities and more inclined than localities to take a broad regional view. *The Use of Land* argues that:

One local government, like one small owner, has only so much turf to oversee and protect, and there is little opportunity (and few incentives) to plan for its use in a scheme that includes neighbors. An ordinary locality will not see a coastal wetland as part of a regional ecological system. . . .

From a regional perspective, it may seem absurd for a locality to fill its portion of a great swamp or to ban multi-family dwellings when workers in its factories cannot afford single-family homes. Moreover, effects of such decisions readily translate into discomfort and inconvenience for neighboring areas.[13]

Land-use reformers could see that in a locally oriented field such as land use, regulation by the states had important advantages over regulation by the federal government. The states were closer to the population at large, more in touch with the on-the-ground specifics and variations of particular local situations, and less arbitrary and bureaucratic. State officials, especially elected ones, were likely to understand and respond to local concerns in a way that federal officials were not. Thus, in the view of the movement, the state governments combined a broad and informed perspective on land-use issues with the ability to apply it to specific cases.

Politically, the movement could more easily focus on the land-use practices of a single state government than on those of hundreds of local governments across the state. And most of the people interested in the movement were more concerned with the particular land-use problems of their state than with the more abstract ones of the nation as a whole. Legally, the movement also was justified in concentrating on state governments. In the 1920s, state governments, acting under their constitutional "police power" to protect public health, safety, and welfare, had begun to delegate planning and zoning to localities. The police power is the ultimate legal basis of land-use regulation; hence, state government was the appropriate focal point for efforts to remedy major systemic defects in local land-use practices.

As a result of these efforts, many state governments acted to take back, qualify, or otherwise alter their delegations to localities. They also established new land-use powers for themselves. The movement has in fact succeeded in getting a great deal of new regulatory legislation passed, most of it at the state level. The laws variously cover all large development projects, particular kinds of large projects (such as power plants or strip mines), or projects in environmentally sensitive locations (such as coastlines or mountain areas).

Moreover, the movement has not been entirely inactive or unsuccessful at the federal level. It has avoided trying to convince faraway, inscrutable federal bureaucracies to change their own land-use practices, but it has increased the centralization of land-use regulation by inducing the federal government to fund some state land-use programs and to set standards for continued funding. The 1972 Coastal Zone Management Act, for example, gives the thirty seacoast and Great Lakes states federal money, contingent on satisfactory state performance, to regulate coastal development. The 1970 and 1977 amendments to the 1967 Air Quality Act and the 1972 and 1977 amendments to the 1948 Water Pollution Control Act provide similar grants for state programs that regulate development.

The broadest piece of federal legislation, however, has not passed. Every year from 1968 to 1976, congressional liberals such as Arizona Representative Morris Udall and Washington Senator Henry Jackson introduced various versions of the National Land Use Policy Act. It would have given the states money to devise comprehensive land-use programs to regulate large developments and other building in environmentally fragile areas. Its high-water mark came in 1974, when the Senate passed it by a wide margin, as it had in 1972 and 1973. But the House defeated it by four votes when President Nixon withdrew his support as a part of an apparent bid for conservative votes to prevent impeachment. The Ford and Carter administrations showed no particular interest in the bill, usually arguing that economic recovery and energy development had to take precedence over environmental protection.

The Nixon and Ford administrations also did not support legislation that would have given states money to regulate strip mining and the siting of new power plants; indeed, President Ford twice vetoed strip-mining bills. But the Carter administration supported these kinds of legislation and, in late 1977, secured passage of a federal strip-mining law, the Surface Mining Control and Reclamation Act. Some version of the power plant legislation seems likely to pass in the next few years.

All the federal legislation demands considerable state action. And on their own initiatives, the states have begun a large number of highly original new programs to regulate land use. But local governments still play an important, probably predominant, role in land-use regulation. In the many states that have not embraced land-use reform, local governments are still the sole source of land-use regulation. In states such as California and Vermont, where the reform movement is strong, local governments still do planning and zoning, take part in state land-use decisions, and rule on the many projects (mainly small ones) that state regulation does not cover. And yet, the local governments no longer have land use entirely to themselves. They must now contend with centralized regulation.

The movement did not have to support both centralization and regulation; in theory, favoring one device does not inherently imply favoring the other. And in practice, the movement has advocated some land-use measures that would increase centralization without increasing regulation—for example, federal and state environmental impact statements for proposed projects, federal or state acquisition of environmentally endangered land, alterations in state tax systems, and state planning mechanisms with no regulatory responsibilities.[14] Conversely, the movement also has advocated measures that would primarily strengthen regulation without adding much more centralization—for instance, state laws requiring local planning or zoning ordinances, statewide minimum procedural standards for the local laws, and stronger citizen-participation requirements at all levels of government.[15]

But the movement has only sporadically concerned itself with plausible measures that neither centralize nor regulate—for example, restructuring local governments by reducing the number of their units, altering their property tax systems, or taking nonregulatory local measures to make local governments more sensitive to the natural environment and surrounding localities. Most land-use reformers have dismissed such options as being difficult to enact or irrelevant to their primary concerns.

Centralized Regulation: The Wider Context

In practical administrative terms, regulation is a straightforward procedure. A regulated interest seeks permission from a regulatory agency for approval of an action it wants to take. The agency, acting under the guidance of its legislation, can approve, disapprove, or approve conditionally. It must then make sure the regulated interest does as it has been told. The agency also has the responsibility of watching over the continuing actions of the regulated interest to make sure it does not violate the regulatory legislation. The regulatory agency and the regulated interest can appeal each other's actions to the courts.

Political maneuvers, legal requirements, or technological ramifications can make particular instances of regulation exceedingly complex. But in principle, regulation is a simple and direct way to influence private-sector and (from higher levels) local government activities, especially those with effects that cross local or state boundaries. Consequently, it has been used in a large number of fields.

Such venerable federal agencies as the Interstate Commerce Commission (the first of the federal regulatory agencies, established in 1887), the Civil Aeronautics Board, the Federal Aviation Agency (now part of the Department of Transportation), the Federal Communications Commission, the Federal Trade Commission, the Food and Drug Administration, the Securities and Exchange Commission, and the Federal Power Commission (now the Federal Energy Regulatory Commission, part of the Department of Energy) do nothing but regulate the interstate markets of the private goods in question. Other federal agencies—for example, the Nuclear Regulatory Commission, the Occupational Safety and Health Administration, and the Environmental Protection Agency—also have important regulatory functions.

Most of these agencies have counterparts at the state level. State governments also are active in regulating utilities, banks, insurance companies, some common carriers (such as trucking companies), and the professions. And local governments regulate other common carriers (such as taxis), occupations, building construction practices, and, through the mechanism of zoning, land use.

Regulation, particularly centralized regulation, is thus one of the prime endeavors of American government, and it is expanding. The federal government has, according to one estimate, established between two and five major regulatory programs every year for the last decade. The number of regulations generated by federal agencies has been increasing by 20 percent every year.[16]

Centralized regulation has its virtues. It deters some of the worst abuses and excesses of corporate and individual self-aggrandizement. It meets legitimate social needs and wants. It improves the overall health, safety, and welfare of the population. It tends to become objectionable only when applied to oneself; everyone is usually for regulating what someone else is doing. Even corporate executives have come to admit that in an ever more complicated, interdependent world, regulation is not an unmitigated evil. As Stanley Marcus, head of the merchandising Neiman-Marcus Company, told a business audience at the University of Nebraska in 1975:

> We almost drool at the prospect of arriving at the millennium when every businessman can do as he damn well pleases; when all regulations will be declared null and void.
> All of them?
> Do we really want to eat meat that hasn't been inspected by a federal agency?
> Or use an airline that isn't controlled by FAA flight regulations? . . .
> Let's not be simplistic about the whole matter of regulation. Let's understand what we're talking about.
> The fact is that regulation is not just some monster dreamed up by 20th Century advocates of big government. Regulation of commerce was one of the few specific domestic powers that our wise founding fathers reserved for the federal government in the Constitution. The interstate commerce clause of Article I provides that: "The Congress shall have power . . . to regulate commerce with foreign nations, and among the several states. . . ."
> The more complex and impersonal our society became, the more regulations were required. . . .
> Let's face the obvious fact that regulation is a necessary part of our modern society and is always going to be with us.[17]

Of course, centralized regulation inherently constitutes governmental infringement on private markets, local government, and individual life. During the 1930s, when public confidence in the market and in local government had been shattered, centralized regulation became widely accepted as a solution for a multitude of problems. But at present, big government, large bureaucracies, and Washington in general are widely distrusted. Recently, politicians of various stripes have sought, for whatever reasons, to distinguish themselves from conventional New Deal liberals of the school of the late Hubert Humphrey.[18]

The three strongest contenders in the 1976 presidential race—Jimmy Carter, Gerald Ford, and Ronald Reagan—all in different ways ran against centralized regulation and Rooseveltian liberalism, as did the most successful dark horse, Jerry Brown. Presidents Ford and Carter sought to weaken the grip of centralized regulation by, for example, loosening federal controls on oil and natural gas prices, substantially deregulating the airline, trucking, and railroad industries, and examining the paperwork requirements and financial costs created by other forms of federal regulation. Several governors, notably Brown in California, Richard Lamm in Colorado, and Hugh Carey in New York, have also made efforts to deregulate some activities. In the 1980 presidential race, none of the contenders seemed willing to defend centralized regulation. Even Edward Kennedy, Humphrey's heir as the standard-bearer of contemporary liberalism, endorsed, for example, further deregulation of the airline and trucking industries.

Centralized regulation also has come under heavy intellectual attack from both the right and the left as well as from the liberal center, which might have been expected to support it.[19] The attacks from the right are identified primarily with University of Chicago economist and Nobel laureate Milton Friedman.[20] Those from the center can be associated with consumer advocate Ralph Nader and his public-interest research organizations.[21] Those from the left are exemplified by a less well known but still influential figure, Cornell University political scientist Theodore Lowi.[22] All three schools of thought see centralized regulation as the characteristic governmental device of a liberalism that had its heyday during the Progressive Era (1887–1917) and the New Deal (1933–41). Centralized regulation is, they argue, incapable of dealing with the problems of the late-twentieth-century American economy. The problem with centralized regulation, as they see it, is the tendency of regulatory bodies to be influenced and even controlled by the economic interests they are intended to restrain. And although centralization came into favor originally as a means of avoiding corruption by local interests, the critics maintain that more centralized bodies tend to be less accountable than local agencies to the public at large and more vulnerable to subversion by powerful economic blocs.

Thus, centralized regulation, according to its critics, produces higher prices for consumers and less competitive markets. It fosters distant, cumbersome, self-absorbed bureaucracies. It keeps newer or cheaper ways of doing business from being introduced. It harms small businesses and the poor. It does not guide or shape markets in the long-term public interest but deforms them, usually under the influence of short-term private perspectives. The Friedman, Lowi, and Nader schools agree that centralized regulation, for all its faults, is not about to disappear. They differ sharply, however, in their analyses of the sources of its defects and what should be done about them. As a result, they also differ in the land-use initiatives they would suggest to remedy zoning.

Milton Friedman, taking a position on the right—typically the Republican right—argues that government regulation is inherently objectionable because it interferes with the market. Left alone, Friedman argues, the self-interested forces of the market will over time, in the manner of Adam Smith's invisible hand, achieve the best possible resolution of economic and social problems. If government meddles, its various regulatory bureaucracies will, deliberately or not, tend to ignore what the market and the public want, to crush private initiative, and to leave nothing useful in its place. Incentives, productivity, profits, and investment will suffer; economic growth will dwindle. The private forces will naturally attempt to defend themselves against these possibilities by infiltrating the regulatory agencies. Thus, Friedman wrote: "Every regulatory commission you can name, whatever may have been its origin, has sooner or later been taken over by the industry it is supposed to regulate and largely conducted in the interest of the industry."[23] Having reviewed a large number of studies of the impacts of regulation in a variety of fields, University of Chicago law professor Ronald Coase wrote that these studies "all tend to suggest that the regulation is either ineffective or, when it has a noticeable impact, that, on balance the effect is bad, so that consumers obtain a worse production or a higher priced product or both, as a result of the regulation. Indeed, this result is found so uniformly as to create a puzzle: one would expect to find, in all these studies, at least some government programs that do more good than harm."[24]

Society would be better served, Friedman and his "Chicago School" associates argue, if heavily bureaucratic higher-level governments would stop imposing centralized regulation on the market. A Friedman approach to land use would therefore emphasize non-regulatory alternatives to zoning. It might, for example, involve private agreements among landowners regarding permissible land uses or perhaps steep taxation of socially undesirable uses. It might in many cases advocate the abolition of zoning. It would certainly resist shifting powers to regulate land use upward from the local level or creating new land-use regulatory powers of any kind.[25]

Theodore Lowi is not a Marxist, but his condemnation of inequality in American society, his analysis of its political and administrative causes, his dismissive opinion of the powerful, and his wintry view of the present political prospects for American liberalism clearly place him on the left. Lowi's position virtually ignores the market and stresses governmental forces. According to Lowi, the ruling philosophy of American government is "interest-group liberalism"—heavy, often dominant representation of organized, established interests in the interior workings of public policymaking. These interests, however, are typically opposed to one another; so in drafting legislation, they usually produce compromises and avoid confrontation of the issues dividing them by delegating discretionary power to administrators. Liberal regulatory initiatives voice a concern and tell a bureaucracy to deal with it but say little about how it should do so. Regulatory initiatives consist of "statues without standards, policy without law" and "yield pluralism and bargaining throughout the system."[26] Lowi wrote: "No present-day liberal is prepared to propose that a government of laws is impossible or undesirable, just as no politician would propose that we do without the Constitution. But the system the present-day liberal would build is predicated on just such propositions."[27]

Inevitably, the decisions generated by interest-group liberalism will favor the politically stronger interests. Pluralism may mitigate or mask this outcome but cannot by itself produce fair decisions. Furthermore, even if the stronger interests wish to be benevolent or to promote change, the regulatory programs of interest-group liberalism will fall short because of legislative vagueness. "A grant of broad powers to administration," Lowi stated, "is not a grant at power to all. It is an imposition of impotence."[28] Regulation will have little effect on, or may actually benefit, the more powerful regulated interests. Lowi wrote:

Government by and through interest groups is in its impact conservative in almost every sense of that term. [It results in] weakening of popular government and support of privilege . . . in other words, two aspects of conservatism. It is beside the point to argue that these consequences are not intended. A third dimension of conservatism, stressed here separately, is the simple conservatism of resistance to change. . . . If this is already a tendency in a pluralistic system, then agency-group relationships must be all the more inflexible to the extent that the relationship is official and legitimate.[29]

Analyzing the disappointing performance of the federal regulatory agencies, Lowi quoted Harvard law professor Louis Jaffe: "Much of what the agencies do is the expectable consequence of their broad and ill-defined regulatory power."[30]

A Lowi approach to land use would therefore attempt to give zoning less administrative discretion and more legal specificity. Like Friedman, Lowi would favor nonregulatory alternatives to zoning. The zoning laws themselves would set forth precise physical standards and policies for permissible development. The laws also would contain clear procedural standards providing for frequent administrative rule-making so as to prevent the case-by-case bargaining that, according to Lowi, benefits the stronger interests. Lowi would not object to giving higher-level governments more powers to regulate land use; he sees many unexplored possibilities for constructive action by state governments in a variety of fields. But he would insist that their new land-use programs have clear standards and policies.[31]

Ralph Nader may be considered the major intellectual force behind the land-use reform movement. Nader specifically advocates land-use reform. Unlike Friedman and to a lesser extent Lowi, Nader considers centralized regulation a useful tool of government, and for that reason he belongs in the center of the political spectrum. Nader's is essentially a liberal Democrat's position. He supports regulation in theory but objects to the manner in which it has been implemented—more precisely, he objects to the large representation of regulated interests on regulatory bodies and to the way these interests use the agencies for their own ends.

Nader maintains that the problems of regulation result from corporate wrongdoing and corporation-promoted government collusion in it. Nader finds flaws in Rooseveltian regulation but does not believe that the cure is to abandon regulation. He also does not believe that effective regulation must lead to direct government control of the market. His alternative to Rooseveltian regulation is a citizen's movement for more extensive and stringent regulation, with particular attention to attenuating the links between regulators and the regulated interests.

In the introduction to a 1973 study he sponsored of California land-use practices, Nader wrote:

> The corporation's ability to separate power from responsibility or accountability received recognition as far back as the first half of the 19th century. The rapid growth of the railroad, timber, and oil companies was met by a countervailing force in the form of government regulation and the populist-progressive movement at the turn of the century. This force temporarily curbed some overt abuses but soon exhausted its energies. The burgeoning ability of the corporations to develop new practices and acquire new resources enabled them simply to circumvent and outstrip the reach of these reforms. The land interests in California, to a significant extent, have bought, intimidated, compromised, and supplied key officials in state and local governments to the point where these interests govern the governors. . . .
>
> Underlying all the specific reform proposals which Mr. Fellmeth and his associates lay before the reader is the principle of accountability, a principle continually undermined by the institutions of corporatism and private government . . . the laws as presently constituted and administered virtually guarantee that social myopia and profiteering are securely wedded; the bond is corporate irresponsibility and nonaccountability.[32]

To Nader, both centralization and regulation are needed to promote corporate and governmental responsibility. The Nader California study, for example, terms local regulation of land use "the developer's best friend."[33] It goes on to make proposals for stronger, more active state planning and environmental agencies; tighter enforcement by state regulatory bodies of existing laws; and more demanding lobbying, campaign-finance, and conflict-of-interest laws.[34] A Nader approach to land use at both state and local levels would restrict the conditions under which variances could be obtained from regulatory boards, limit the number of members of the boards who could have connections with the development industry, make sure that environmentalists are strongly represented on the boards, increase citizen participation, and strive for maximum corporate and governmental accountability to the public.

The Nader approach is to revamp traditional Rooseveltian centralized regulation without changing its essential thrust. It tries to modernize and extend the approach of the New Deal in light of subsequent experience.[35] It calls for additional centralized regulation, often in areas that did not previously have it at all. Richard Babcock, a lawyer who has been one of the key figures of the land-use reform movement, has—probably hypothetically—argued that

if one were really serious about growth management instead of playing games, you would—in addition to land banking—say to the state legislature, "There is going to have to be legislation on large-scale development that permits the public to inquire into the prices that are being charged by the developer; that looks into the prices that are paid for the land; the prudence of the investment; the quality of the service that he is going to provide; and the financial stability". . . . If such powers were established, no one would dream of giving them to local government. . . . So it means state participation in the decision-making.[36]

Babcock is a prominent corporate lawyer, a leader of the Chicago bar; yet here he seems to be advocating what many people would consider socialism. Babcock's is an extreme position, and he appears not to believe it completely himself. But in its stress on consumer protection, in its flirtation with, but ultimate rejection of, direct government control of the market, and above all in its emphasis on additional centralized regulation, his statement shows the intellectual debt the land-use reform movement owes to Nader.

The story of the land-use reform movement provides a clear example of what will happen when the new kind of centralized regulation inspired by Nader is introduced in a field, such as land use, and at a level, such as state government, where it did not previously exist. Moreover, the land-use reform movement provides a real-world context for the examination of public issues that are sometimes treated as abstractions. By examining the movement's activities and effects, it is possible to attach specific meanings to such general terms as corporate power, government responsiveness to citizens, the conflict between the environment and the economy, the organization of local and state government and the federal system, the growth of bureaucracy, the competing claims of private property rights and the communal public interest, and the opposing virtues of preservation for the few as against access for the many.

CHAPTER **3**

The Birth of an Issue

The 1970 census showed that during the 1960s California had moved ahead of New York to become the nation's most populous state and that the nation's suburbs had grown larger than its central cities. At about the same time, what may have been the biggest public works project in history, the coast-to-coast Interstate Highway System, was completed. The condominium and the fast-food franchise were becoming fixtures of the landscape, and parts of Wyoming and Vermont were beginning to look distinctly urban. One day, Miami nearly ran out of water because of overbuilding throughout south Florida.

The year 1970 also was notable for Earth Day, a remarkably effective display of grass-roots environmental concern primarily focused on the specific problems of air and water pollution but with some attention to the complex of problems described as "land use." In the late 1960s and early 1970s, a feeling was widespread among Americans that something had gone wrong with how we were using the land. We were losing an older America, and the newer America that was being built seemed, despite all the wealth and the social and geographic mobility it generated, to be impairing more than enhancing what was called the quality of life. In late 1971, Russell Train, then chairman of the Council on Environmental Quality and later administrator of the Environmental Protection Agency, wrote of "the urgency we feel with respect to land use as the most important environmental issue remaining substantially unaddressed as a matter of national policy."[1]

27

The New Growth

The nation's metropolitan areas, especially in the South and West, were expanding voraciously, filling up their centers and reaching out into what had previously been hinterland. In spread-out complexes, such as Tampa–St. Petersburg, Phoenix, or San Diego, a car had become a necessity to get to the five separate downtown areas (one of which might not have existed a few years before) that a big city was likely to have. Plenty of northeastern suburbs, too, had mushroomed as fast as the Sun Belt metropolises since World War II and had fostered a similar dependence on the automobile.[2] Nationally, the suburban explosion constituted one of the largest migrations in the country's history; between 1950 and 1970, over 35 million people, the population of more than ten Chicagos, moved to suburbs.[3] The suburban and Sun Belt explosions produced similar physical results; the large new towns on the outskirts of New York, Boston, and Pittsburgh bore a surprising resemblance to the center of Houston.

But the new growth was not confined to big cities and suburbs. Beginning in the late 1960s, nonmetropolitan, rural, and small-town areas with previously declining populations experienced startling spurts of growth. Each year from 1970 to 1975, 131 people moved out of a metropolitan area of more than 50,000 people for every 100 who moved in. During the same period, nearly two-thirds of all nonmetropolitan counties, as compared with only one quarter in the 1960s, showed net migration gains.[4]

Many communities far from large cities, especially in attractive areas such as the Rockies, the Ozarks, northern New England, southern Appalachia, and the Pacific Northwest, found themselves receiving a rapid and unexpected influx of new, previously urban people: retirees; business, professional, and academic people who found they could pursue their careers in the country; hobby farmers; long-distance commuters; weekenders; seasonal residents; even romantics who were "returning" to the land. The influx had many causes: the new decentralization of many industries (especially service industries), disenchantment with the city and its suburbs, the spread of retirement communities outside Florida and the Southwest, the low cost of living in rural areas, the construction of large new branches of many state university systems, the improvements in transportation and communication that brought the city and the country physically and socially closer to each other, and a widespread desire for a slower pace of life closer to nature. Yet rapid expansion sometimes transformed the small, settled old communities that it hit.[5]

Developers, speculators, and some civic boosters rejoiced in all this growth, metropolitan and nonmetropolitan, but others were uneasy about it. For instance, in the early 1970s, Richard Lamm, then a member of the Colorado House of Representatives, opposed holding the 1976 Winter Olympics in the state. He wrote:

> The economic and environmental problems caused by growth have been accentuated in Colorado by its suddenness. The State's population increased by 25.8 percent in the last decade, twice the national average, and the rate is increasing. This increase is distributed poorly; a string of cities along the eastern foot of the Rockies, the Front Range, experienced a population increase of 37.1 percent in the last decade, while 32 of Colorado's 63 counties, most of them rural, actually lost population over that time. Denver's smog is now the sixth worst in the country because of unfavorable atmospheric conditions and the highest per capita ownership of automobiles in the Nation. Land development is following an exponential rather than a linear curve; in 1965 30 new subdividers registered in Colorado; 45 registered in 1968, 103 in 1969, and more than 300 in 1971. In sum, Colorado is being plowed under, paved over and polluted at an ever-accelerating rate.[6]

Lamm's opposition was successful. In a 1972 referendum, Colorado's voters by a 3-to-2 margin rejected the 1976 Olympics which instead were held in Austria. The referendum passed in ski resorts, steel towns, Chicano districts, rural areas, and both wealthy and working-class parts of Denver.[7] In 1974, running on a growth-control platform, Lamm was elected governor.

The rate, location, and appearance of much of the new growth were disconcerting enough, but the sheer size of some of the new developments was disturbing, too. Near St. Augustine, Florida, a development subsidiary of International Telephone and Telegraph Corporation was planning a new city that was intended eventually to have about 750,000 people. Its 100,000 acres would take up a third of the land in a county whose population was 4,500. Elsewhere in Florida, between 1950 and 1970 Fort Lauderdale's Broward County had had an astounding annual population growth rate of 9 percent, compared with a national annual growth rate of well under 1 percent during the same period.[8] By 1980, Broward seemed likely again to double its 1970 population of 800,000. At least three of the county's developments under construction were designed to serve populations of over 100,000.[9]

In New York State's Adirondack Park, mostly mountainous and forested wilderness, second-home development projects of thirty or forty square miles apiece were under way. Projects of similar size were being built in the lush forests of Hawaii, the deserts of Arizona and Nevada, and throughout California. In the New Mexico desert, a group of utilities was building the Four Corners complex of seven giant coal-gasification plants, each at a cost of $400 million. The Arizona strip mine that supplied them with coal was to grow from four to nearly fifty square miles. It was already the largest in the country.[10]

Many other new communities, factories, power plants, mines, airports, highways, office centers, universities, stadiums, theme parks, tourism complexes, and agribusiness developments were only slightly smaller. The large projects were not inherently bad. But their environmental, social, and economic effects would be of incalculable magnitude.

The Disappearance of Amenities

By 1970, these changes had damaged or destroyed some irreplaceable natural settings. Because of filling and diking for residential and industrial development, San Francisco Bay had shrunk by more than a third since 1850.[11] Large bodies of water, such as Florida's Lake Okeechobee and the Ohio portion of Lake Erie, seemed to be approaching biological death. For the first time, Vermont had more people than cows. Smog was no longer a unique feature of southern California; it had become a metropolitan affliction throughout the nation. Across the country, strip mining was scarring land, polluting water, killing fish, eroding soil, clogging streams, and causing floods. In countless places, development was encroaching on wilderness, closing off shorelines, endangering valuable wildlife, paving marshes, or raising prices of desirable land so high that governments could not even consider purchasing it for public enjoyment.

Some losses were not so much environmental as visual and social; many of the newly proliferating works of man were ugly, boring, and inconvenient. These included the expressways and the huge ubiquitous developments: glass-box office buildings, uninviting suburban shopping centers, and leftover downtown areas that, partly because of the shopping centers, were deserted after dark. Lifeless new communities and subdivisions had been named after natural features that were obliterated, bland, or nonexistent. And it was becoming impossible to get around even middle-sized cities on foot or by public transportation; one had to drive—in large cities, sometimes for hours. A Sunday drive in the country often became a ride into exurbia; suburban growth had put real country out of reach for a day trip.

Moreover, the new neighborhoods, although not all located in suburbs, possessed many of the features that had made suburbia a byword. They lacked a recognizable center and had little sense of community; there were few adult males during the day, no comfortable taprooms, stores, or parks, and no "public characters" to keep the sidewalks safe, friendly, and interesting.[12] Often there were no sidewalks at all; developers saw no need to provide for pedestrians. Getting groceries became an automobile expedition, and many housewives spent their days as chauffeurs. Distances were conceived not in miles but in travel time by car. These arrangements were especially hard on the poor, the elderly, the young, and the handicapped. The new urban growth often seemed designed more for cars than for people. In many cities, automobile-related land uses—expressways, streets, parking lots, driveways, garages, gas stations, repair shops, and car dealerships—together accounted for more than half the city's land. In Los Angeles, freeways alone took up, by one estimate, a third of the city's 464 square miles.[13]

Ultimately, what was being lost was a sense of secure settlement and rooted distinctiveness. The nation had always been building. But now, development pressures were changing the country's face with a rapidity that, as the revived historical preservation movement showed, many people found disturbing. The stable rural and small-town communities of the past were disappearing. Rural and urban vistas whose permanence had been taken for granted were being decisively disfigured. Familiar cities were suddenly acquiring unfamiliar skylines. Socially valuable buildings and neighborhoods were falling into the hands of developers and speculators. By 1974, over a third of the 16,000 structures described in the Historic American Buildings Survey of 1933 had been destroyed.[14]

It was not just the rapidity of the new construction that jarred one's sense of place. The results were disturbing, too. The dingy chaos of strip development, the functional lifelessness of the office tower, and the static pall of most residential construction were creating a nation that looked essentially the same from coast to coast. Places as varied as Philadelphia, Minneapolis, and New Orleans were being reshaped in a mold that was turning out to be that of the southern California suburb. A homogenized national suburban sprawl culture, whose twin architectural symbols were the McDonald's and Holiday Inn arches, was flattening distinctive urban, small-town, and rural cultures.

The feeling of loss was strongest, of course, in what had been the most pleasant places. For example, Miami, according to Ben Funk, an Associated Press writer who came to the city in 1951, was "one great place to live" because of its white sands, unhurried pace, amazing trees, lack of crowding, and extraordinary wildlife. But soon, Funk wrote:

The drumbeaters were busy. Resort owners and land promoters, cities, airlines, counties, and the state were spending huge sums of money to lure people to this unique corner of the continent. They were coming in rapidly growing numbers. . . . More and more people meant more garbage, more trash, more sewage, more hotels, more automobiles. Human wastes poured in an ever-increasing flood into the canals, the Miami River, the bay, and ocean. Fumes from automobile exhausts and jet planes fouled the once pure air. Hammocks were flattened by bulldozers. Dredges mangled the shoreline. Mile after mile, hotels and motels marched up the beaches—gaudy monuments to the tourist dollar—hiding the oceans behind a concrete wall. . . .

And one day we took a good look around. Suddenly we knew that we had kissed the good life goodbye.[15]

The "concrete wall" now lines virtually all of the more than sixty miles of coast—it is called the Gold Coast—from Miami north to Palm Beach. Hardy Matheson, a former county commissioner in the Miami area, told *Science* writer Luther Carter, "This was a pleasant place to live in the 1930s, even though we were all broke. Now we are affluent and nobody wants to live here."[16]

Highways and Other Growth Shapers

Large public works projects such as highways often had a decisive influence on the loss of amenities. These capital-investment projects frequently determined whether and where other new growth would occur. They made particular areas more or less desirable for development, and thus could profoundly alter local economies, environments, and social settings. Whether a community remained rural or became suburban or urban often depended on whether or not it lay in the path of an expressway or sewer system.

The problem, at least from the local standpoint, was that local priorities had little to do with these decisions. They were primarily made in state capitals or by the federal government, which provided the bulk of their financing. Federal funds, for example, pay for 90 percent of Interstate Highway System construction and up to 80 percent of mass transit construction costs, 75 percent of interceptor-sewer and sewage-treatment plant investments, and 70 percent of non-Interstate highway costs.[17]

To the extent that localities were represented in the making of these decisions, the local representatives were public works departments and development interests, which inevitably favored the largest projects possible. These groups generally were far more influential in local politics than local planning departments or citizens' groups. The head of the local highway department, for example, was typically an unelected official but one with a strong constituency of his own (contractors and construction unions) and much patronage to dispense to it. He often was nearly as powerful as the mayor. He and his constituency found influential allies at the state and federal levels; the head of the state highway department, for instance, also was an unelected official with a distinct constituency and patronage of his own, and he, too, frequently was almost as powerful as the governor.[18]

The results are familiar to anyone who has traveled on suburban highways. Huge public facilities were scattered all over the landscape. They attracted private developments, sometimes in a fashion the local community could handle, but usually too rapidly for it. Strip development, sprawl, and speculation often had unforeseen or unprevented environmental, economic, and social consequences. The community could seldom do much about them after the buildings went up and could seldom mobilize to deal with a problem beforehand.

Highways, especially Interstates that opened up vast areas of countryside, had enormous effects on local growth. A consultant's report for the Council on Environmental Quality points out that "until the expressways were constructed, poor access to the open land ringing Atlanta confined new housing to the city limits and parts of nearby DeKalb County. The Interstate system permitted Atlanta to expand to a seven county metropolitan area encompassing over 2000 square miles."[19]

Similarly, when Route 128 near Boston was built in the late 1940s, it was intended to be a beltway around the city by which long-distance travelers and truckers, as well as travelers between suburbs, could avoid heavy downtown traffic. But it attracted so much industry, especially computer and electronics firms, that it quickly became an essential part of Boston's business district. The highway simply spread the city's congestion to previously distant suburbs. A whole new highway, Route 495, had to be built farther out to perform the beltway function. The beltways around Washington and Baltimore have induced similar growth, and may also eventually become the problem they were supposed to prevent. Moreover, the advent of the beltways contributed to the economic decline of center cities and reduced ridership of energy-efficient mass transit. In some cases, feeder highways for the beltways or other long-distance roads knifed through and ultimately destroyed what had previously been perfectly healthy long-settled city neighborhoods.[20]

In rural areas, the completion of the Interstates produced land booms and serious environmental damage; the highways made Vermont and the Adirondacks accessible with only a four-hour drive or less for nearly 40 million people. On the other hand, many towns bypassed by the Interstates turned into backwaters or suffered economically, even if they were on perfectly usable roads.[21] And competition from the Interstates undoubtedly hastened the decline of the (energy-saving) railroads.

Other public works projects had similar effects. A new sewer system with excess capacity relieves developers of the necessity to build their own sewers and septic tanks. So sewers open up new land for development. The construction of sewer systems has contributed to the feverish and speculative growth of communities as diverse as Fairfax County, Virginia; Tulsa, Oklahoma; and Lake Tahoe, Nevada.[22] In the late 1950s, the opening of Chicago's O'Hare Airport, then and now the country's busiest airport, led to the establishment of a new, and chaotically growing, business district on what had been the city's fringe. Today, construction of the Dallas–Fort Worth Regional Airport is having the same effect, and the airport will eventually have a larger capacity than O'Hare. Mass transit systems, bridges, dams, state facilities (such as universities and office complexes), and federal facilities (office complexes, research facilities, and military bases) have frequently stimulated growth that has also turned out to be destructive.[23]

The Economic Effects of Development

The soaring land prices generated stiff economic competition among land uses: urban development, agriculture, energy facilities, public works, recreation, and so forth. The most frequent winner of the competition was new commercial and residential construction. Its developers argued that it would be an economic boon for its community because it could do more than alternative uses could to stimulate business, reduce unemployment, and produce new public revenues, especially from the property tax, the basis of local public finance. Local officials, sold on this view of development, sometimes made crazy-quilt land annexations to get it.

But increasingly often, especially when the residential housing in question was below the outright luxury class, the claim turned out to be false. The development might or might not help business, but it would almost always cost the local taxpayer money and increase local taxes—not just the property tax, but all taxes. The problem was that the development always needed additional local public services—mostly schools, but also roads, police and fire protection, garbage collection, hospitals, utilities, and a controlling administrative structure. Sometimes the new residents in previously rural areas would demand entirely new services: paved roads, street lights, garbage pickups, big libraries, parks, golf courses, tennis courts, parking lots, and the like. The new or additional—essentially urban—services always cost more than whatever the rural locality had provided previously.

Some communities made the developer provide some of these services; the developer would then pass the costs on to his customers. But most localities unthinkingly assumed that the new property assessments and tax revenues would more than cover the new public costs. Over the long run, many of these localities were mistaken. The new development drove up land prices further, and speculation became more prevalent. Assessments and taxes had to rise to pay for the new services. And even if tax rates remained constant, as they did in relatively few localities, property taxes based on them still rose because of the climbing land values.

As the price and tax increases began, the established community residents found themselves subsidizing the new residents. The landed poor were the hardest hit. In one well-publicized case, most of the 236 moderate- and low-income residents of Hardenburgh, New York, a small town in the Catskills, were so angered by the rapid tripling and quadrupling of their property taxes that they obtained mail-order divinity degrees so as to get ministers' exemptions from the taxes.[24] But in most towns, when the tax imbalance became large enough, the poorer residents were forced to sell out (admittedly at high prices) and move. The sales accelerated the development process and raised land prices further. By accepting a lot of growth, many rural communities were forcing out both the smaller farmers, ranchers, loggers, or fishermen who gave the place its cherished character and the other economically insecure native residents, such as those on fixed incomes. Lower-middle-class urban neighborhoods that became targets of high-rise residential or office development similarly lost some important kinds of residents. The urban displacees, most of whom moved to the suburbs, were such people as the grocers and drugstore owners who gave the neighborhood informal meeting places and the resident policemen who kept it safe. The public costs created by the new development were often surprisingly large. In 1971, consultants for Palo Alto, California, found that the city would actually do better to buy up the land in its undeveloped (and not especially large) foothills area at its full market value than to allow it to become an "addition" to the local tax base through development. Even $80,000 houses (at 1971 prices) would not pay for themselves. Developing the foothills—and getting property taxes and other revenues from them—would cost each resident of Palo Alto about $17 each year. The annual per capita cost of buying up the land and keeping it open was less than $12.[25] A more detailed 1974 citizens' study for Santa Barbara concluded that the city could minimize local taxes most effectively by minimizing population growth.[26]

The new development also created unexpected private costs. Development that generated construction jobs did not always give the jobs to local or neighborhood residents. The local people often were not skilled or specialized enough; the developers therefore brought in their own construction workers. Similarly, in commercial or industrial development, the new jobs might go not to existing residents but to more educated new ones.

The influx of newcomers increased the demands on local public services (thus raising local taxes and assessments), tightened the local housing market, took jobs away from local people (often further depressing a local job market that, especially in some rural areas, was already depressed), and raised prices in local stores because of the higher purchasing power of the newcomers. The private costs of the new development, even more than its public ones, consistently displaced or impoverished economically marginal local residents who often gave the community its desirable flavor in the first place. Few local officials realized what was happening before it was too late.[27]

Energy Development

Big energy facilities, such as power plants and strip mines, posed serious land-use problems that the 1973–74 oil embargo exacerbated. Electric utility companies, for instance, already had the largest capital investment of any American industry,[28] and it promised to get bigger fast. Energy projects, like other massive developments, degraded the environment, transformed local economies, destroyed local cultures, and in general amounted to an urban invasion of rural areas. But the new energy projects were larger, more concentrated, and more disruptive than other forms of development. They used (and polluted) water at a rate that, for example, seriously strained the chronically short water supplies of the West. The rights-of-way for their electrical transmission lines consumed hundreds of square miles of land; they often crossed public lands, such as national parks and state forests, or impinged on Indian or Eskimo settlements. The safety of nuclear power plants in particular became a major political issue.

The quadrupling of energy prices produced by the oil embargo intensified all these problems. It made economically feasible the strip mining of western coal on a scale that promised to be more destructive than anything that had happened in Appalachia, where most strip-mined areas had comparatively fertile soil, high rainfall, temperate climates, heavy vegetation, and mild or absent slopes. Few of these conditions, which made the land relatively easy to reclaim, prevailed in the western areas to be stripped.[29] Meanwhile, the coal companies contemplated intensive restripping of Appalachia.[30] The energy crisis also hastened offshore oil and natural gas drilling on the Outer Continental Shelf and in effect overrode environmental objections to the Alaska Pipeline.

Even if the embargo had never occurred, the country would still have needed more energy. Its energy needs were growing in large part because its cities were growing. In particular, sprawl and strip development consumed disproportionate amounts of energy, requiring people to drive more. Scattered buildings with many windows—particularly single-family homes and small business establishments—were more expensive to heat, cool, light, and power than were more densely clustered dwellings.[31]

Now the country's energy needs would have to be met increasingly from domestic sources. In his 1975 State of the Union address, President Ford said that approximately "640 new electric generating plants must be in operation by 1985 . . . [including] the equivalent of 200 1000-megawatt nuclear plants and 150 new 800-megawatt coal-fired plants.''[32] The energy pressures were naturally greatest in the areas of highest growth. For example, the Florida Energy Committee, an advisory body to the state government, projected that even if the state undertook serious energy conservation measures, by the year 2000 it might still need fifty new 1000-megawatt plants and 1150 miles of transmission lines.[33] The proposed new energy facilities for the nation, according to an estimate by the Congressional Research Service at the Library of Congress, would require a land area the size of Missouri.[34]

Such figures probably overestimate, if only because many existing power plant sites have room for additional installations.[35] But one new 1000-megawatt power plant may now cost $1 billion and take up several square miles. The most economical and safest place to locate a power plant is in a flat rural area with comparatively cheap, flood- and earthquake-free land, and nearby sources of water and coal, oil, or nuclear fuel. (Much land with these features is near public lands or Indian reservations.) Building the plant may employ a skilled construction crew of at least a thousand highly paid workers for four or more years. When the crew leaves, perhaps a hundred highly paid professionals operate the plant. The construction phase provides only a few dozen semiskilled jobs for local people, and most of these jobs last only for the duration of construction. For nuclear power plants, these figures are perhaps 30 percent higher.[36] Power plants of all kinds generally remain in operation for thirty or forty years.

This process sounds straightforward enough. In fact, it is probably a formula for disaster. It has already produced some of the most virulent contemporary examples of pathological urban development. Most power plant sites are located in or near small towns or underpopulated areas where comparatively small numbers of new transient workers and their families will create frenetic growth during construction of the plant. Operation of the plant will then increase air and water pollution. (In the case of a nuclear plant, operation can also add radioactive emissions, as well as wastes that are difficult—perhaps impossible—to dispose of safely.) Finally, the plant will become obsolete, leaving the surrounding communities whatever agricultural or ranching remnants and whatever natural beauty it has not destroyed. The cycle of forced boom and nasty bust is likely to transform many healthy communities into ghost towns. In the course of American history, gold, copper, and oil discoveries; homesteading; and construction of canals, railroads, dams, roads, and military installations have been associated with similar cycles.

The classic recent case is the town of Rock Springs, in southwest Wyoming's Sweetwater County, now on the steep upswing on the energy boom.[37] In 1970, the town had a population of 12,000 and was a sleepy ranching settlement. But then two utility companies, Pacific Power and Light and Idaho Power, bought up or leased much of the local land to build the 2000-megawatt, $400 million Jim Bridger Power Plant. Big strip-mining and oil companies set up installations to supply it. Big chemical companies began mining and refining the large local deposits of trona, a valuable mineral that, when converted into soda ash, is an ingredient of many consumer products (glass, detergents, plastics, paints) and industrial chemicals. The area's rich supplies of coal, oil, oil shale, and natural gas were suddenly a magnet for development. Rock Springs would never be the same again.

By 1974, its population, growing at an annual rate of over 21 percent, had reached 26,000 and was projected by some observers to increase to nearly 60,000 by the early 1980s—a decade-long annual growth rate of roughly 15 percent. Already, Rock Springs had an overloaded sewage system, high prices, large new bonded indebtedness, traffic congestion, deteriorating schools and roads, a water shortage, and a high crime rate with particularly unpleasant drug, prostitution, and racketeer problems. No housing was available. The affluent construction workers were sleeping in tents, campers, and trailers in a climate where winter brought subzero temperatures for weeks at a time. Rock Springs had virtually no recreational facilities.

The town's mental health caseloads had increased tenfold, and its per capita suicide rate was the third highest in the country, behind only San Francisco and Las Vegas. In 1978, the town's police chief went on trial for murder, charged with having publicly shot between the eyes an undercover narcotics investigator he had hired; he was finally acquitted in late 1979. A special state prosecutor and grand jury were probing numerous charges of political corruption, and most local officeholders were choosing to retire rather than to run again.[38] Small ranchers were being squeezed out of business, and large new open-pit coal and uranium mines were on the way.[39]

Much of Rock Springs had become as dangerous, ugly, and unpleasant as any urban ghetto. Rock Springs and Sweetwater County were developing public services sufficient for the new residents, but by the time the facilities were ready, most of the construction workers would be gone, and the permanent residents would have to absorb the costs of what would then be excess facilities. Sweetwater County was paying the price of rapid energy development. And as increasing amounts of western coal were stripped and coastal oil and gas drilled, more communities would pay it as well.[40]

Leisure Homes

In the late 1960s and early 1970s, about 5 percent of the families in the country owned second homes.[41] Roughly half again as many additional families owned rural land on which they planned to build a home, perhaps for retirement. Some of this ownership—the isolated fishing shack, for example, or the single lot on which nothing would be built for many years—presented no particular land-use problems. However, an increasing amount of leisure home construction was taking the form of large developments, some of them occupying dozens of square miles. These developments produced all the usual environmental, economic, and social problems associated with massive projects in rural areas, and some special problems as well. Moreover, leisure home development naturally gravitated toward beautiful areas—northern New England, the Poconos, the Ozarks, the upper Great Lakes, south Florida, the Rockies, the Southwest, and the California coast. It went directly for the prettiest, most ecologically fragile parts of the country.

Some of the special problems of leisure home development arose where lightly capitalized "developers" sold bare lots with few or no improvements. They bought some marginal land, chopped it into lots, advertised nationally, asked for low down payments, and sold to investment-minded but often gullible buyers who had never seen their property, and probably never would see it. Vast empty subdivisions of southwestern deserts or Florida swamplands were acquired by Michigan or New Jersey owners. Some of the subdivisions had barely adequate roads, but they often entirely lacked water (especially in the West), and any other improvements were out of the question. The raw land had no resale value, could not be reassembled, and became worthless.

The few owners who tried to occupy their land were disappointed, if not shocked—especially if they could not obtain improvements in public services for their parcels. All the owners tended to fall behind in paying their property taxes or not to pay them at all, depressing the treasuries of local governments, some of which had counted on these revenues. Sometimes the local governments acquired the land for free as a result of tax delinquencies, but the parcels remained essentially useless and provided the localities only with an unwanted responsibility. These conditions gave rise to numerous charges of consumer fraud.[42] In early 1977, the Federal Trade Commission (FTC) ordered the Great Western Union Corporation to refund $4 million to buyers of lots in its California, Colorado, and New Mexico leisure home developments that had been marketed with deceptive sales techniques. It was the largest consumer refund in the FTC history.[43] In 1979, in another case, the FTC approved a refund of up to $14 million to the buyers of lots in six Colorado projects.[44]

Some developers with more capital put in some improvements, but not enough to prevent considerable environmental damage. In Virginia's Warren County, near Shenandoah National Park, the George Washington National Forest, the Appalachian Trail, and the crest of the Blue Ridge Mountains, I saw leisure home developments that were bulldozed up the sides of mountains or located in areas prone to flooding. Siltation from the projects damaged miles of trout streams. In one project, roads were cut on a steep slope and then lightly filled in over tree stumps. A moderate rain turned the roadbed into an impassable drainage ditch with the stumps sticking out. In another project, the extensive removal of water-absorbing trees increased flood dangers for both the project and its surroundings, including a good deal of national park land. Some projects have gone bankrupt, making their expensive siltation, road, and flood problems the undesired joint concerns of the project residents and local government.[45]

At the high-priced end of the leisure home spectrum, developers built whole new resort communities that gave good value to their buyers. But precisely for that reason, they, too, caused problems for their surroundings. The buyers, especially retirees, moved in permanently in unexpected numbers, filling up projects that had been intended to be only partially occupied at any one time. The vacation or retirement havens often suburbanized just as frenetically and haphazardly as the farmland ringing a fast-growing big city, and with the same unappetizing consequences.[46] The devil's-bargain economics of rapid growth expelled many long-established residents, drove them out of business, or forced them into trailers. A public-interest group study of a northern Vermont town found that 88 percent of the full-time, year-round jobs produced by skiing-oriented leisure home development went to people who moved in after the development began.[47]

The newcomers to these communities were usually wealthier and better educated than the natives. Those who were retirees also had more free time. The populations of the large retirement developments of Arizona and Florida, which often constituted self-contained de facto cities, sometimes outnumbered those of the surrounding communities. The retirees, especially those from northeastern urban settings, did not hesitate to form political machines to defend their own interests. For example, they consistently voted down new school-bond issues, a practice that did not endear them to the natives.[48] In addition, the big new leisure home developments looked artificial. Some had country gifte shoppes, expensive outlets for equipment for the local sports, and cute-menu restaurants; few natives went near any of these establishments except to work in menial jobs. There were even a few bucolic retreats where residents had to lock their doors.[49]

The Decline of Small-Scale Agriculture

The best land for development was level, well-drained countryside near transportation—agricultural land. The new development could outbid agriculture, and it quickly absorbed large amounts of land that had previously been used for farming, ranching, logging, and, to a lesser extent, commercial fishing. One U.S. Agriculture Department study of forty-eight fast-growing western counties found that, over an eleven-year span, urbanization consumed approximately 725 square miles, three quarters of which had previously grown high-value crops. About 610 square miles went for residential uses, 40 for industry, 25 each for government and commerce, 15 for parks, and 6 for airports.[50] A study by the Environment Information Center, a private group, concluded, perhaps with some exaggeration, that between 1967 and 1975 "non-agricultural uses consumed more than 23 million acres of farmland—about one-third of it prime—an area equal to West Virginia, New Jersey, Rhode Island, and Delaware combined."[51]

The country as a whole was in no danger of running out of food, timber, or other agricultural products.[52] The nation's cities took up only about 2 percent of its land. Even if they doubled in area, they would not really disturb the 25 percent of the land now used for farming or the amount, perhaps almost as large, that could become farmland if needed.[53] But rapid urbanization often had severe localized impacts on agriculture. It eliminated truck farms that had survived economically because they were located near cities and therefore had low transportation costs. It also eliminated specialty croplands that were not easily duplicated. For example, a 1972 California study found that in many areas of the state, irreplaceable artichoke fields or prune orchards had nearly disappeared.[54]

Some farming communities, especially those in the path of suburban growth, but those in leisure home areas as well, were entirely wiped out. Bostonians or Chicagoans would buy Vermont or Illinois farmhouses, use them as second homes, and let the land go out of productivity.[55] Or highrolling developers would buy some farming or ranch land, subdivide it, move some earth around to make a few miles of roads, and sell off individual "home sites" that would not really support houses but could never again be put together for agriculture. In 1971, New Mexico's Environmental Improvement Agency estimated that well over 1 million acres (more than 1600 square miles) of the state's land had undergone such bogus development. These sites, if fully occupied, could house about 8 million people—six times the number that the agency expected to live in the whole state in the year 2000. But the sites never would be occupied. In effect, they were lost for any use.[56] And as postembargo energy development swung into high gear, it too seemed likely to remove huge tracts of land, millions upon millions of acres in the West and elsewhere, from agricultural use.[57]

Land close to new, rapid, intense growth rarely remained agricultural for long. A community that, for example, mixed old farms and new suburbs usually got difficult farming conditions and unpleasant suburban life. The sources of friction were endless. The suburbanites objected to the pesticides and fertilizers the farmers used, their escaped livestock trampling the grass, or noisy tractors that also slowed up traffic. The farmers objected to the rise in prices at local stores, the increase in property taxes, the air pollution or congestion caused by the cars the suburbanites brought in, or the mores of their teenage children.

In addition, such mongrelized communities generally looked terrible, much worse than the farm areas they had been or the suburbs they would become.[58] The tensions between agricultural land use and leisure home development were equally bad, and those between agriculture and strip mines or power plants were worse.[59] But usually this transition period of conflicting land uses did not last long. The economic forces behind the new growth were so overwhelming, and those behind the agricultural uses so frail, that the farmers inevitably had to yield to the newcomers. They sold their farms.

In many parts of the country, as the 1978 and 1979 tractorcade demonstrations later indicated, small family farming no longer paid. And because of climbing land prices, property taxes, interest rates, and equipment and fertilizer costs (which depend heavily on energy prices), such farming had become prohibitively costly to enter. Between 1949 and 1969, the number of farmers who owned their land declined from 3.9 million to 2.4 million.[60] Between 1930 and 1970, the number of farms smaller than 100 acres declined from almost 4 million to fewer than 1.2 million, and the number of farms between 100 and 260 acres fell from 2 million to barely 0.8 million. During the same period, the number of farms of over 1000 acres went from fewer than 100,000 to more than 200,000.[61]

Farming and related pursuits were adapting to the industrial requirements of agribusiness. Or they were becoming tenant enterprises vulnerable to rapid displacement by urban growth, energy development, leisure homes, speculation, or downturns in their market. Their future was bleak. Many rural areas suffered from poverty, high unemployment, extreme sensitivity to national recessions, and heavy out-migration by the young.[62] Train service to rural areas declined; many stops were eliminated. Many small farmers had to have additional jobs in town to get by.[63]

The Deficiencies of Local Planning and Zoning

American cities had been expanding since colonial times. And the decline of agriculture, at least in the sense of large numbers of people reluctantly leaving small-scale farming for economic reasons, had been considered a national problem since the early nineteenth century.[64] But never, it seemed to much of the public in the late 1960s and early 1970s, had urban areas grown so much, so fast, and so badly. Moreover, this growth seemed likely to continue, perhaps even to accelerate.[65]

It was easy to blame these problems of growth on the avarice and social heedlessness of developers, but the land-use tangle was clearly more complicated than that. All developers, including public agencies, build to make money, and their ranks contain any number of ecological robber barons who are intoxicated with wheeling and dealing. But they also include plenty of decent people who want to build the best communities or structures they can. Some have almost an artist's sense of what can be done with land and buildings. Most, certainly, have a craftsman's sense. As journalist Martin Mayer wrote of the development business:

What's hard to grasp (because the minds of writers and scholars and book publishers and indeed book readers don't run that way) is that this has been mostly a *pleasurable* occupation. Homebuilders get addicted to it. "I make my living," says Kenneth Hofmann of Walnut Creek, "not by telling people how to do it but by building the house. I'm second generation born in California, I was a very poor guy when I started, and now I'm a very wealthy man. But I'm here every day, I don't play golf, and I don't take European vacations. And there are a thousand of us."[66]

Developers of this cast of mind are not easily restrained. Nor should they necessarily always be restrained. A competent developer is almost by definition building or providing something—whether housing or energy or commercial construction or jobs—that large numbers of people want and need.

Nor are the nation's land-use problems mainly the result of any bad taste or selfishness on the part of the public. In buying housing, for example, most people must function within tight financial and locational constraints. In addition, because housing buyers are diverse and unorganized, their bargaining power is limited. But both developers and buyers have to operate in a context—a market. And by the early 1970s, much of the public had come to believe that government ought to intervene effectively in the land market to prevent publicly undesirable consequences.

Local government, of course, had been active in this area for many years. Individual cities have been planning since they were founded and doing the equivalent of zoning for about 110 years.[67] But the origin of these activities in their contemporary form was a pair of model state enabling acts published by the Commerce Department in the 1920s, when the secretary of commerce was Herbert Hoover. Under these acts, the states delegated planning, zoning, and subdivision powers to localities. By the late 1930s, nearly all the states had adopted versions of these acts, and localities—more specifically, the local planning commissions and zoning boards suggested by the acts—had become the main regulators of land use.

For their day, the state enabling acts were effective reforms. They gave cities and counties specific authority to guide their own development. The localities knew their land far better than the state ever would, and under the enabling acts, some local accomplishments have been substantial. For most of the population, housing standards are now at their highest point in history.[68] In residential areas, local and secondary streets are generally protected from commercial, industrial, and traffic intrusions. Generous requirements for private yards and public open space are conducive to privacy, unobstructed movement, and outdoor living; these amenities in turn provide some guarantee against future deterioration. In commercial areas, local efforts have reduced traffic congestion, especially from heavy trucking. The location, appearance, and operation of many factories are often closely regulated, as are those of many billboards and business signs.

Nonetheless, by the late 1960s the reforms of the 1920s had long since run their course, and were proving inadequate to handle modern rates and scales of development. Local planning and zoning bodies were able to decide where gas stations should be allowed, how large front yards should be, and what occupations could be conducted in the home without disturbing neighbors. They could nearly always deal with small projects in established, affluent suburbs. They could usually handle large projects in established large cities, and smaller ones in slow-growing small towns. They were effective in stabilizing existing communities, but useless in guiding the often explosive development of new ones. The local bodies, geared to the problems characteristic of a simpler era, could not deal with huge residential projects or shopping centers that might affect dozens of rapidly growing communities. They could not deal with power plants or strip mines that might have regional, statewide, or even national consequences. They could not deal with big public works projects. They were overwhelmed in many fast-growing, strip-development cities—for example, by large numbers of applications for gas stations.

One of the reasons why local planning and zoning did not work well was that in most of the country, particularly the rural communities now in the path of urban expansion, they had never really existed in the first place. Such communities had espoused the American ideal of rugged individualism; many of their residents thought that zoning verged on socialism.[69] Few rural localities took advantage of the opportunities the state enabling acts offered. In 1971, the director of the National Park Service became concerned about the proliferation of commercial development on the edge of Mammoth Cave National Park in Kentucky. "I talked to those people down there about zoning," he told writer John McPhee. " 'Zoning?' they said. 'Zoning?' I had the impression that I was in a foreign land."[70] In 1971 only 30 percent of Kentucky's cities and 20 percent of its counties had zoning. Only 25 percent of Wyoming's cities and 10 percent of its counties had it. Even in more urban New York State, only 40 percent of the cities had zoning, and the counties had no zoning powers at all.[71] Many communities that planned and zoned considered those activities a mark of distinction; some had the official town stationery and city limits signs proclaim that theirs was a zoned community. But few local efforts to regulate land use were more than modest.

Even comparatively strong local planning and zoning had serious limitations. Most localities in metropolitan areas had arbitrary boundaries that were the results of historical accidents or physical barriers that, with the coming of the automobile, had long since lost their force. Superimposed over these boundaries was a confusing maze of single-purpose special districts, such as school districts, housing authorities, and water commissions. The Nader study group on California land use found that Santa Clara County south of San Francisco contained, in addition to the county government itself, 15 municipalities, 37 school districts, and 19 other special districts. All 71 governments had their own elected officials, separate financing, and idiosyncratic procedures. Their boundaries were consistently artificial, overlapping, and uncoordinated. The more urban Los Angeles County had 342 special districts.[72]

The splintering of jurisdiction and responsibility obviously constrained the land-use powers of individual local governments, especially in suburban areas where large numbers of relatively small communities crowded in on one another. If all its neighbors were growing rapidly, no single suburban government, no matter how strong its planning or zoning, could resist the economic and political pressures to grow. A community that chose not to grow would in any case bear the burdens of its neighbors' growth, such as pollution or traffic. So, it was argued, the community might as well get the presumed benefits of its own expansion. Even a large rural community in the midst of a suburbanizing region could not realistically hope to insulate itself from the adjoining growth.

But the problem was not just suburban. Almost everywhere, individual communities were dealing with land-use questions of more than local impact and making their decisions without consideration for and often to the detriment of surrounding communities. Without consulting its neighbors, a city or suburb would agree to a proposal for a big new shopping center or power plant. It would get all the tax revenues, but its neighbors would get much of the pollution and traffic.

Alternatively, the cities in a given region might agree that it needed more low-income housing projects, a larger sewage-treatment plant, or a new landfill site. But such developments were inconvenient and unpromising as sources of revenue. Each city took a passive position on burdensome projects to meet regional needs. So the needed facilities were never built; or they were built late or badly or on an inadequate scale or were imposed on the region's poorest cities, and the entire region suffered. No community was so large or self-sufficient that it could not be hurt by the land-use decisions of its neighbors.

Local planning commissions and zoning boards had many other weaknesses as well. Their commissioners were part time. Those commissions that had professional planning staffs underpaid them badly, even by the standards of local government. As late as 1967, the top annual salary for planners in four-fifths of the local governments in the country was under $6,000. Even in big cities, average annual pay was well under $10,000.[73] Governments in metropolitan areas spent only $2.16 yearly for each resident on planning activities. Governments in smaller communities spent $.70.[74]

In the absence of funds, administration was inadequate or nonexistent. Local planning bodies often did not have current copies of their own plans, ordinances, amendments, or maps; they did not keep records of their own decisions that, in any case, they failed to enforce.[75] Many planning commissions excluded the public from their meetings. Few had any environmental or economic expertise. Many were therefore unable to evaluate the complex technical problems a big development might create. They had to rely on the developer's hired planners, who naturally tended to favor the project in question. And they could not influence or control local, state, and federal public works or tax policies, which typically had much more effect on local growth than their own decisions did. For the purposes of guiding a community's development, local planning and zoning had little to offer.

The people who sat on planning bodies and otherwise ran local government generally came from the local economic elite—developers of all kinds, contractors, realtors, other businessmen, bankers, and lawyers.[76] None of them wanted to destroy their city, and many could get as misty-eyed as any conservationist about an endangered forest or lake. But most of them venerated the entrepreneur's right to speculate and profit. They recognized that they could make profits themselves from other people's developments, and they thought that nearly any development paid for itself. They realized that the city's land was its main economic asset—in poor or undeveloped communities, often its only one. They had made their own money from land. Through the property tax, the local government they ran made much of *its* money from the land.

To such people, planning and zoning were not primarily means of guiding land use, protecting the environment, preserving local character, or even maintaining property values; they were, rather, ways to make money. Traditionally, many small-town and suburban chambers of commerce had their offices in city hall or were otherwise subsidized by local government. The most frequent users of the services of planning commissions and zoning boards were developers. Constance Perin, a planner and cultural anthropologist who is a member of the National Architectural Accrediting Board, wrote of

zoning's historically consistent split from the rationalistic ideas of comprehensive, long-range planning. . . . zoning has never been a reliable mechanism for deliberately limiting and channeling growth. In fact, just the opposite is true: it is a major piece of industrial equipment, quickly tooled . . . to produce the latest models favored by the capital market, national and regional. . . . Planning and zoning have certainly accomplished many good deeds for the general welfare and they have often been powerful in braking licentious practices, but all the same, zoning has been legislated widely due to the support primarily of real estate interests and secondarily of municipal reformers.[77]

On paper, city plans often had strong conservationist goals. But these goals were not binding and could be interpreted as the local governments wished. Planning commissions and zoning boards were usually hospitable to applications for zoning variances, rezonings, or exemptions that would aid businessmen or development firms. In small cities and towns, many applicants were friends, neighbors, relatives, customers, or clients of zoning board members, and zoning boards were particularly accommodating. But specific changes in zoning, whether large and sudden (a big leisure home development) or small and gradual (a lot of small gas stations and fast-food franchises) tended to undermine the plan.

In fast-growing communities, huge sums of money rode on particular zoning decisions. The value of land depended largely on what the zoning board would allow to be built on it. Changing the classification of a medium-sized parcel—say, 300 acres, less than half a square mile—from agricultural to industrial, or changing a residential designation to permit more housing units could easily make several development partners and their associates millionaires.

The potential millionaires knew it. Moreover, they operated in a highly competitive, decentralized, volatile market that has notoriously erratic sources of capital. They were dealing with underpaid local bureaucrats or with part-time local elected officials who were, in many cases, businessmen who would profit indirectly from the proposed project or party leaders whose treasuries always needed filling. Developers could help these officials in return for some help at the zoning board. The predictable result was a large number of under-the-table payments and conflict-of-interest abuses.[78]

Zoning and subdivision regulation have traditionally been the greatest single source of corruption in local government. Zoning personnel rarely constitute even 2 percent of a city government's work force, but zoning scandals seem to account for nearly half the convictions of local officials. A few years ago in Chicago, a nasty series of scandals resulted in the imprisonment of some of Mayor Daley's closest associates. At the same time, another scandal in a Chicago suburb showed that the public could get hurt as well. Edmund McCahill, editor of *Planning*, wrote of one of the nation's largest home-building firms:

> For about $90,000 in bribes, Kaufman and Broad nearly were able to plop an entire town of 25,000 residents right in the middle of a community which had no hospital or industry to speak of, an inadequate transportation system, and schools filled to capacity. The rezoning proposal allowed 33 housing units per acre when Hoffman Estates had no zoning specifications other than "residential." . . . One of the incidents that tipped off Hoffman Estates homeowners that something was amiss was when their showers went dry in 1970, as 2,500 new neighbors started tapping into the inadequate water system.[79]

The problem of zoning corruption was not peculiar to the Chicago area. All fast-growing areas had it; during the same period, there were comparable payoff scandals in New Jersey, California, and New York.[80]

In addition, local zoning suffered from other economic deformations. It could not do anything about speculation. Since localities depended on the property tax for the bulk of their financing, they constantly competed for industrial, commercial, and high-income residential developments because these would pay the highest taxes. They would offer developers zoning and tax concessions, which astute developers could increase by playing localities off against each other. Developers often persuaded localities to zone their major thoroughfares for strip development, although the inevitable result was sprawl.[81]

Developers also persuaded communities ringed by unincorporated areas to annex heavily. Such a community might repeatedly snake its boundaries down miles of country road to pick off a piece of land that was the object of a seemingly attractive development proposal. The locality would zone the land in accordance with the proposal, provide it with the services the developer wanted, and avoid the off-road areas with no development prospects. The result was a scattered, inefficient jumble of inadequate services, deformed boundaries, and environmental deterioration. People often could drive in and out of the same city many times while going in one direction.[82]

Frederick Bair, Jr., a Florida planning consultant, has written a *reductio ad absurdum* of such "fiscal zoning":

One conclusion which is general is that vacant land in suburban areas is most "profitable" in terms of municipal cost-revenue ratio. Planners and governing bodies alike have almost completely ignored the magnificent implications of this fact in creating urban development policy. The ideal city consists of vacant, taxable land. Some compromise would need to be made with legal necessity here. The *almost* ideal city consists of luxury high-rise apartments containing the minimum number of tenants necessary to meet requirements for municipal incorporation (but no children), having the city hall in a room in the basement, and surrounded by vast areas of vacant taxable land owned by wealthy outsiders, who, for federal tax reasons, desire neither to use it nor to sell it.

At the other extreme, industrial development, considered as an isolated item, is usually highly profitable judged by the local cost-revenue ratio. Housing for employees of industry is not, since it normally involves relatively high governmental costs for schools and municipal facilities and services and does not, by itself, provide equivalent revenues. . . . sound development policy for a community should encourage industry but discourage housing for the employees who make industrial production possible, since they don't pay their own way. Thus industry without employee housing might be added to the high-revenue high-rise and vacant land in the ideal city.[83]

Blair exaggerates, but not by much. Many communities did roughly what he suggests, in extreme cases virtually zoning out people. Near New York City, for example, Teterboro, New Jersey, essentially consists of an airport, some factories, and their warehouses. A few years ago, it had one public school student, supported by $75 million in assessed valuation. So the tax rate for its several dozen residents was one of the lowest in the country.[84] Similarly zoned municipalities can be found among the industrial suburbs of most large cities.[85]

Perhaps the most notorious feature of local planning and zoning was that they were used to preserve the affluent white suburb composed of single-family detached homes on large lots. In many suburban communities, zoning regulations prohibited the introduction of apartments, town houses, trailers, and rental housing of all kinds. The regulations allowed new building only if it increased overall property values. Densities were to remain low.

A favorite device of exclusionary zoning was to set high minimum lot sizes to raise house prices; in the late 1960s, about half the vacant land zoned as residential within fifty miles of New York City's Times Square had a minimum one-acre requirement.[86] Other devices were establishing large minimum house sizes, excluding multiple dwellings, and administratively harassing anyone who threatened to build something unusual.[87] Such zoning also made the communities look more alike and, by restricting the supply of land and the way it could be developed, raised overall housing costs, both in zoned suburban communities and elsewhere. Exclusionary zoning harmed not only the particular persons whom it was intended to keep out, but also the public at large.[88]

The basic purpose of suburban zoning was to keep Them where They belonged—Out. If They had already gotten In, then its purpose was to confine Them to limited areas. The exact identity of Them varied a bit around the country. Blacks, Latinos, and poor people always qualified. Catholics, Jews, and Orientals were targets in many places. The elderly also qualified, if they were candidates for public housing. Suburbanites feared that one subsidized development might lead to another and concluded that the most effective way to maintain the existing social and design homogenization was to keep all public housing out.

Constance Perin quoted a Philadelphia developer who tried to build suburban housing that was not of the single-family detached sort:

See, you have to understand the fundamental feeling in suburbia is fear.
. . . Fear of blacks, fear of physical bodily harm, fear of their kids being
subjected to drugs, which are identified as a black problem, fear of all the
urban ills. They feel like they've isolated the effect, by moving to the
suburbs. . . . In fact, they haven't, . . . but in their own mind's eye
they've moved away from that problem. They see us—they see non-large lot
developers—as bringing the problems back to them, and this scares the hell
out of them.[89]

The advocates of exclusionary zoning justified it with euphemisms
and technical jargon that sometimes even invoked protection of the
environment.[90] The experiences of those communities in which development had been destructive strengthened the case for the status
quo. But the fundamental purpose of zoning remained what it always
had been. "The immigrant," legal historian Seymour Toll has written, "is in the fiber of zoning."[91] In the 1880s, San Francisco used
zoning to prevent the spread of Chinese laundries.[92] A 1916 New
York ordinance, one of the earliest big-city adoptions of zoning,
appears to have been pushed by Protestant and German Jewish mer-
chants on Fifth Avenue to protect the fashionable shopping district
from the spread of garment factories owned by Russian and Polish
Jews.[93]

It was racism with a progressive, technocratic veneer. Despite the
efforts of higher-level government, open-housing organizations,
inner-city groups, and some suburbanites, zoning gave every promise of continuing to keep many suburbs closed to all but affluent
acceptable whites. It would help deprive minorities and the poor not
just of the chance to move to the suburbs but of the other benefits—
capital appreciation, protection against inflation, improved borrow-
ing power, relative safety, enhanced social standing, and better education for one's children—that typically went along with suburban
homeownership.[94]

By the early 1970s, much of the public had found out what land-
use professionals had known for years: local planning and zoning
were hopelessly inadequate to guide urbanization, to manage
growth, or to achieve environmental objectives. Something else was
needed.

CHAPTER **4**

The Land-Use Reform Movement

In 1966, Richard Babcock called for the creation of state agencies to review local land-use decisions and, if necessary, to override them. He also proposed revising the state enabling acts of the 1920s to compel local governments to consider the regional and statewide implications of their decisions. And he proposed that states enact procedural standards for local land-use regulation.[1]

Similar recommendations appeared subsequently in the reports of public bodies, such as the National Commission on Urban Problems,[2] in the reports of quasi-public bodies, such as the Rockefeller Brothers Fund Task Force on Land Use and Urban Growth,[3] and in those of private bodies, such as Ralph Nader's Study Group on Land Use in California.[4] Professional associations, such as the American Society of Planning Officials (now the American Planning Association) and the American Bar Association,[5] endorsed state land-use regulation, and the American Law Institute issued a Model Land Development Code, with which states wishing to modernize their land-use enabling acts could acquire new powers to regulate land use.[6]

The Spread of the Movement

Since the late 1960s, land use has been one of the most active, innovative fields of state legislation. For the first time, states are drawing up legally binding statewide land-use plans and are requiring state permits for large projects with regional or state implications. They are designating environmentally fragile areas, such as coasts, mountain areas, wildernesses, or marshes, as places where development is to be controlled or slowed by the state. They are setting standards for local planning and regulation and are otherwise intervening in heretofore local land-use decisions.

In recent years, most of the states have undertaken new land-use programs. By October 1975, twenty-seven states had programs involving statewide planning or statewide review of local decisions. Under the auspices of the 1972 federal Coastal Zone Management Act, all thirty seacoast and Great Lakes states had undertaken programs specifically for their coasts. As of October 1975, thirty-four states had programs controlling the siting, design, and operation of power plants. Thirty-eight states regulated strip mines (even before passage of the 1977 federal strip-mining legislation). The states also developed programs regulating wetlands, shorelands, floodplains, industrial siting, land sales, farmland preservation, and pollution; and they engaged in nonregulatory activities, such as devising growth-control policies and providing tax relief for owners of agricultural land.[7]

A few states have emerged as the leaders in land-use reform. Most of these states are richly endowed with areas of natural beauty that are plainly showing environmental strain as a result of development pressures. In other states, the public is less concerned about land-use problems. For example, in 1976 Kent State University political scientists James Coke and Steven Brown wrote: "Public learning-through-events, the most effective form of adult education, is not occurring in Ohio as it is in states with more fragile environments. Ohio eco-systems take many environmental insults in stride and spring back for more. Therefore, the highly visible negative externalities that educated the citizens of Florida, Vermont, and California are hidden from public view in Ohio."[8]

Land-use reform is also relatively popular in states where cities and towns are growing rapidly and in states with histories of at least moderately progressive state governments. It is no accident that comparatively strong land-use reform legislation has been passed in New York, Wisconsin, Oregon, and the states mentioned by Coke and Brown, and not in Idaho, Nebraska, Texas, Mississippi, or New Hampshire. The movement is stronger in the Northeast, the Upper

Midwest, and the Far West than in the Lower Midwest, the Great Plains, the South, and the Southwest.[9]

Oregon is a leader in land-use reform.[10] By 1970, the state faced serious growth problems. In its western portion, the fifty-mile-wide Willamette Valley had doubled in population since 1940; its 1970 population was 1.5 million people, three quarters of the population of the state, and the valley's population was expected to reach 2.5 million by the end of the century. The region's superb and beautiful agricultural land, which produced nearly half of the state's agricultural income, was being rapidly and often badly developed. Parts of the valley were studded with cheap, boxlike houses; paper mills and food-processing plants had made the Willamette River one of the most polluted in the country, certainly the most polluted large river in the Northwest.

The entire valley, stretching 120 miles from Portland south through Salem to Eugene, was threatening to turn into a California-style suburban conurbation. Some mountainside developments in the foothills of the Cascade and Coast ranges, which formed the valley's eastern and western boundaries respectively, resembled those around Los Angeles. These prospects horrified many Oregonians, who had no desire to emulate their neighbor to the south. Indeed, the term "Californication," meaning California-style destruction of the environment, seems to have been coined in Oregon.

In addition, along Oregon's spectacular four-hundred-mile shoreline, several small towns were under heavy environmental stress. Lincoln City, for example, had sprawled out along the coastal highway to become a shambles of condominiums, high-rises, amusement parks, and highly polluting industry—"twenty miserable miles," as former Governor (now Senator) Mark Hatfield called it.[11] In 1972, the Oregon Health Division found thirty-four places in Lincoln City where untreated sewage was flowing onto ocean beaches.

Across the Cascades, the arid rangelands, deserts, and plains of central and eastern Oregon had become sites for low-quality leisure home developments. In 1972, Oregon's Revenue Department estimated that 160,000 acres—250 square miles—had been subdivided; many of the companies involved had violated the law by not registering with the state. The land had been sold to speculating but credulous Easterners, older people with limited incomes looking for a retirement haven, and a surprising number of Willamette Valley outdoors enthusiasts who perhaps should have known better. These buyers often got for their money little more than a trailer site without water, electricity, or heat and with difficult roads to the nearest town, which in many cases was as much as twenty miles away.

Oregon's local governments were plainly unable or unwilling to deal with these problems. So in early 1973, Governor Tom McCall, his allies in the legislature, and environmental groups around the state began to push for state land-use laws. McCall proclaimed:

> There is a shameless threat to our environment and to the whole quality of life—the unfettered despoiling of the land. Sagebrush subdivisions, coastal "condomania," and the ravenous rampage of suburbia in the Willamette Valley all threaten to mock Oregon's status as the environmental model for the nation. We are in dire need of a state land-use policy, new subdivision laws, and new standards for planning and zoning by cities and counties. The interests of Oregon for today and in the future must be protected from the grasping wastrels of the land.[12]

Later in 1973, after a complicated struggle, Oregon's legislature passed a series of land-use bills, of which the most significant was SB (Senate Bill) 100. This law created the Oregon Land Conservation and Development Commission, which regulates development "activities of state-wide significance" and designates (with the approval of the legislature) "areas of critical state concern," where building is to be more strictly regulated by the state. In addition, the commission sets statewide planning goals; requires all cities, counties, and regions to establish plans and regulations; and publishes guidelines to keep these plans and regulations consistent with statewide goals.

The activities of statewide significance regulated by the commission consist of both private and public projects, including those of state agencies. In developing its statewide planning goals and guidelines, the commission was to "give priority consideration to" public construction projects, estuaries, wetlands, lakes, wilderness and recreation areas, beaches and dunes, wild rivers, floodplains, unique wildlife habitats, and agricultural land. These goals and guidelines went into effect in January 1975; the law called for all proposed activities of statewide significance to conform to them immediately and for substate plans and regulations to conform within a year. In June 1975 the state appropriated nearly $6 million to help cities, counties, and regions produce the required plans and regulations.[13]

In 1972, the United States Congress passed the Coastal Zone Management Act, which, as amended in 1976 and 1979, gives the thirty coastal states Commerce Department grants totaling about $16 million annually to plan and regulate coastal development.[14] In 1977, Congress passed the Surface Mining Control and Reclamation Act, which gives the states $110 million annually in Interior Department grants to regulate strip mining.[15] The 1970 and 1977 amendments to the 1967 Air Quality Act, the 1972 and 1977 amendments to the 1948 Water Pollution Control Act, the 1972 Noise Control Act, and the 1974 Safe Drinking Water Act collectively offer states perhaps $3 billion annually in Environmental Protection Agency grants to carry out regulatory programs and construction with complex but definite land-use implications, including controls on the siting of new projects.[16]

If the National Land Use Policy Act had passed, it would have given states federal funds ($100 million annually in the 1975 bill, probably coming from the Department of the Interior) to draw up land-use plans, and to devise procedures to define and protect critical environmental areas, control big private developments and growth produced by large public works projects, and override local government opposition to development needed by a region or metropolitan area.[17] Other proposed federal land-use legislation that now seems close to passage would give states money to regulate power plant siting.[18]

The federal government also has enacted a great deal of nonregulatory legislation affecting state and local regulation of land use. The 1969 National Environmental Policy Act required federal agencies to write extensive statements describing the environmental impacts of their actions.[19] (As of April 1976, twenty-six states had similar requirements for their own agencies, and in some states the requirements also applied to local governments and private projects.[20]) The 1973 Flood Disaster Protection Act requires that a state's or locality's laws regarding floodplain development be approved by the Federal Insurance Administration (FIA) before its residents can buy flood insurance from the FIA.[21] The 1974 Housing and Community Development Act requires all plans funded by HUD's Section 701 program, which supports many of the current local and state planning efforts in the country, to provide specific information on land use.

Federal legislation dealing with specific aspects of land use has largely eliminated the need for a National Land Use Policy Act. As Fred Bosselman, a Chicago lawyer (and partner of Richard Babcock), who was a key draftsman of the Florida land-use law, the American Law Institute Model Code, and some versions of the National Land Use Policy Act, wrote in 1975: "Congress has passed so many federal land-use regulations that in a few years only a rare development project of any size will get by without two and probably more federal approvals."[22]

In addition, several states have created strong agencies to regulate development in particular environmentally critical regions. Most of these regions lie within one state; thus, California has created its San Francisco Bay Conservation and Development Commission, New Jersey its Hackensack Meadowlands Development Commission, Minnesota its Twin Cities Metropolitan Council, and Massachusetts its Martha's Vineyard Commission.[23] In some regions that cross state lines, the states involved have joined forces to produce, for example, the California-Nevada Lake Tahoe Regional Planning Agency.[24]

Many localities, too, have become more active in regulating land use. Some communities have voted down new development proposals; for example, a number of Maine, New Hampshire, and South Carolina towns and counties have rejected oil refinery projects.[25] Others have applied commonsense, nuts-and-bolts planning techniques. Columbus, Ohio, plagued by strip development and fast-food restaurants on its main thoroughfare, reduced the number of curb cuts permitted between intersections. This measure forced new restaurants to group themselves into clusters, reduced congestion, increased safety, improved aesthetics, and in no way harmed business.[26] Several hundred communities have enacted building, sewer, or road construction moratoriums; set population caps or restrictions on the number of housing units that can be built annually; established urban limit lines beyond which they would offer no services; or otherwise exercised newly rigorous judgment in dealing with development proposals.[27]

The Battles over Land-Use Reform: Their Political Participants

Most developers, many landowners, and some homeowners have regarded the regulatory aspects of land-use reform as infringements of their property rights—more specifically, as a violation of the Fifth and Fourteenth Amendments, which bar federal and state governments from taking private property for public use without just compensation.[28] Some developers also argue that their industry can, through trade associations and more informal mechanisms, regulate itself better than government can; certainly, members of the industry know more about their own markets and concerns than any public body.

Developers also view land-use reform as hampering their efforts to provide housing and other construction at reasonable prices. Chamber of Commerce members believe land-use reform costs them business; unionists, especially in the building trades, believe it can cost them their jobs. Utility interests argue that land-use reform crimps their operations and increases the price of energy, and agribusiness regards it as an obstacle to providing consumers with food at a reasonable cost.

Many small farmers dislike land-use reform because the possibility of selling their land to a developer forms the basis of their retirement, estates, or opportunities to escape from a life whose hardships few city dwellers appreciate. Many farmers also dislike it because they are accustomed to speculating in land. As Hector Macpherson, the Oregon state legislator (and farmer) who has been called "the father of land use in Oregon," put it: "Scratch a farmer, and you'll find a subdivider."[29] Local government officials regard land-use reform as a constriction of their tax base and their ability to undertake public works projects.

Many developers, business people, taxpayers, and some government officials object to the centralizing aspects of land-use reform because they oppose either the creation of any new bureaucracy or the power shifts that would be caused by new nonlocal land-use bureaucracies. Local government officials consider land-use reform a usurpation of their home-rule powers and often denounce it as "state zoning." The swing votes that defeated the National Land Use Policy Act in the House in 1974 came from Chicago Democrats controlled by the late Mayor Richard Daley. They did not want to give substantial land-use reform powers to the state government then headed by Governor Daniel Walker, Daley's rival for control of the Illinois Democratic party.[30] Robert Healy of the Conservation Foundation, an environmental research and education organization, has quoted an unidentified state legislator who supported a land-use reform bill as saying of the local officials who opposed it: "These guys want to keep their own ball game. There are a lot of political contributions available from people in the development business. The local officials don't want it all going to [the governor]."[31]

Many officials of existing state agencies object to the creation of new state agencies not under their control or with the power to regulate their public works projects. Like local officials who object to state regulation, some state officials object to federal land-use reform legislation because they fear it will diminish their powers or constrain their activities. Many farmers keep up the rural tradition of distrust of any government beyond their own township. Many local residents believe that they and their local government know their land and its possibilities better than any more distant government ever could.

Objections to centralization are, in theory, distinct from objections to regulation, but land-use reform measures typically combine centralization and regulation. Hence, in practice, opponents of such measures unite in simple bitter opposition that is largely conservative and sometimes libertarian. This Friedmanite opposition sees land-use reform as an unwarranted intrusion by distant, obtuse, uniformity-loving bureaucracies. It regards the movement as a statist attack on private activities, the diversity of local life, and the ultimately benevolent operation of the market. This opposition construes the movement as an assault on an enormous range of cherished American values and institutions—competitive individualism, private property, commercial freedom, the corporation, the entrepreneur, home rule, and the desire for limited and unbureaucratic government. Those who share these values are numerous, various, and powerful. They include many politicians of both major parties.

Although the movement's main opposition has come from the right—that is, from the large number of people who are more conservative than most liberal Democrats—a smaller, weaker opposition has arisen from the left. Many radicals of the left dismiss the environmental and land-use reform movements as devices by which middle-class liberal energies are diverted from more basic economic, class, and racial issues. Those radicals—mainly agrarian populists and a few urban socialists—who have thought seriously about land-use issues consider the proposed land-use reform measures purely procedural alterations that are not remotely sufficient to deal with the country's fundamental land problem—concentrated landownership, particularly by large corporations.

These radicals, motivated by some of the same impulses that animate Theodore Lowi's attacks on centralized regulation, have sought on occasion to break up large landholdings, an agrarian approach that has proved surprisingly popular in the recent controversy in the West, particularly in California's San Joaquin and Imperial valleys, over whether farms larger than 160 acres should continue to receive water from federal irrigation projects.[32] More typically, leftists concerned with land use try to limit the growth of large corporate holdings, especially in rural areas.[33] They usually seek government action to mitigate the social effects of concentrated ownership.[34] Their concern is not environmental or economic planning but social equity. Their objective is land reform rather than land-use reform. They maintain that regulation does not go far enough and too easily becomes a tool of the rich, and that centralization can quickly take away what control local people have and give it to large absentee corporations. To these leftists, land-use reform is at best a complacent irrelevancy; more likely, a self-serving creation of the liberal wing of big business, as conveniently exemplified by the Rockefeller family; and at worst, a ruse devised by conservatives against liberals.

A leftist review of the Rockefeller Brothers Fund Task Force report, *The Use of Land*, described it as

a report by a corporate elite to its willing supporters. . . . If this report is implemented—and it may be, judging by its wide acclaim in the media—it would do nothing to redistribute land to the poor and dispossessed. . . .

Given [their] reasonable and "responsible" but not very fundamental criticisms of the present scene, the authors predictably make "responsible" and palatable suggestions which mesh neatly with their corporate interests. . . . the report asks local citizens to help implement environmental guidelines which will effectively cut their own throats by taking away local prerogatives. I know it is considered neanderthal in the age of the global village to question master planning, but one cannot be too scrupulous about what and whose interests such plans serve. . . . [The report has] legitimate concerns, but they do not adequately address such economic and social realities as who has power, who makes profits and who gets exploited by whom.[35]

Political, economic, or occupational position does not, however, invariably determine an individual's or organization's stand on the movement. Some environmentalists who cannot otherwise be classified as radicals nonetheless view land-use reform as a praiseworthy but minor procedural change that is unlikely to make much difference.[36] Landowners and homeowners have on occasion supported the movement when it gave promise of improving their property values or preserving areas they wanted left undeveloped. Some local government officials, too, have supported the movement as a way to accommodate a strongly environmentalist constituency, to control their city's growth, to improve property values, or to cut property taxes. At times, local officials have wished to avoid political responsibility for particular land-use decisions (or for land-use regulation altogether) and have therefore favored an upward shift in regulatory powers. Particularly in some western states where the federal government owns the bulk of the land, many local and state officials have supported state land-use programs as both a lesser evil than federal regulation and a means of enhancing state (and local) influence on federal policies.[37]

Even development interests sometimes favor land-use reform. Some may believe that centralized regulation will improve the image of their company or industry. Others may expect land-use regulation to hinder their competitors—particularly these that are small or from other industries paying higher wages—by imposing difficult new procedures on them. Development interests also may believe that centralized regulation will neutralize local regulation, overcome local controlled-growth sentiment, or have no real effect at all.

In addition, development interests, especially firms involved in supplying energy, may feel that centralized regulation will rationalize and stabilize the development process by reducing the confusing, costly, messy variations in regulation among different localities. Thus, journalist Peter Meyer wrote that the supporters of the 1975 version of the National Land Use Policy Act were

generally divided between two types of conservationists: those of the environment and those dominating the economic status quo. Favorable testimony came from the National Wildlife Federation as well as from Exxon; from the Izaak Walton League as well as the Bank of America. . . . Just as the environmentalists were concerned with finding the most consistent way of preserving *all* of America's natural heritage, so national and multinational corporations and special-interest groups preferred a system that would minimize the risks inherent in an uncoordinated and decentralized approach to land-use planning and natural-resource allocation. In the words of an Exxon executive, testifying before the Senate Committee on Interior and Insular Affairs, "We believe the time has come for a more orderly, disciplined way of planning for and managing the future growth of the nation."[38]

Development interests may legitimately differ as to the effects of untried land-use reform legislation. Discussing the struggle over the National Land Use Policy Act, William Reilly, president of the Conservation Foundation, cited

the case of two major forest products corporations, both large landholders with substantially similar interests in the legislation. Officials of one strongly favored the bill, while executives of the other vehemently opposed it. One corporation believed the bill's provisions for states to overrule local governments in favor of "development of regional benefit" would overcome antigrowth localities on behalf of large corporate landholders. The other firm feared the bill's provision for states to overrule localities in favor of "areas of critical environmental concern" would lock up the best land and reduce its value.[39]

The tendencies of liberals to support reform and conservatives to oppose it suggest that Democrats should be for state land-use regulation and Republicans against. In general they are, but with important exceptions. Some Democrats with union (especially building-trade union) ties support most liberal causes but feel that they cannot afford land-use reform. On the other hand, some Republicans, often those whose fortunes are based on the land-development practices of a bygone era, feel that they can. In 1977, Reilly wrote: "Prior to the last congressional vote on land use planning assistance, the Democratic National Committee asked an advisor to assess the bill politically. He looked at the bewildering lineup of opponents and supporters, studied the confusing and contradictory claims and criticisms, and pronounced it politically neutral—no gain, no loss in being for or against it. So the bill went down.''[40] Most of the time, environmentalists and Democrats favor reform, and business interests, Republicans, local officials, and officials of competing state agencies fight it. Usually, these two sides are more or less equally matched.

The Battles over Land-Use Reform: Their Social Roots

With some justice, opponents of land-use reform point out that the movement's social center of gravity falls somewhere in the upper middle class, if not higher. This observation should not come as news: the conservation movement, the historical predecessor of the land-use reform and environmental movements, always had a somewhat elitist, almost patrician tone. Its creators, for example, were such figures as Theodore Roosevelt, Gifford Pinchot, Frederick Law Olmsted, and John Wesley Powell—tribunes of the people perhaps, but hardly plebeians themselves.[41]

Today, most of the political support for land-use reform comes from relatively affluent urbanites and suburbanites, most of the opposition from poorer suburbanites and dwellers in rural areas. Similarly, the main editorial support for the movement comes from large metropolitan newspapers, its main opposition from smaller suburban or rural dailies and weeklies. In 1970, journalist Jon Margolis noted that land-use reformers and environmentalists generally

are not steelworkers or assemblyline workers or small farmers or hotel clerks. They are Wall Street lawyers and junior faculty and editors and writers and corporate vice-presidents. . . . Searching for their hundred-fifty-year old Vermont farmhouses, conservationists wonder how people can actually want to live in a new $25,000 split-level in the suburbs, apparently never thinking that for most people the alternative is a three-room walk-up in the downtown smog.[42]

Most of the major individual land-use battles of the past decade have concerned entirely rural areas or the partially rural edges of metropolitan areas. In these battles, the opponents of reform usually were conservative, rural local inhabitants who knew the land in dispute better than did the supporters of reform, most of whom were more liberal, urban outsiders. Many of the opponents of reform depend for their livelihood, directly or indirectly, on the activity of the local land market; most supporters do not.

As a matter of political strategy, the opposition from the right therefore emphasizes the reformers' lack of roots in the land in question (or in any other land) and their ignorance and idealization of the economic realities of rural life. From a different perspective but for the same reasons, the opposition from the left emphasizes the reformers' wealth and corporate affiliations. Both left and right characterize the movement as a campaign to keep rural areas in picturesque poverty for the aesthetic benefit of comparatively rich city people who visit them only occasionally. In addition, the opposition sees the movement as hindering development, urban or rural, that helps or employs the poor—for example, low-income housing, commercial and industrial establishments, or tourist facilities offering jobs for unskilled labor or construction opportunities for minority contractors.

The urban and suburban upper middle classes can effectively publicize the movement, but they cannot by themselves guarantee public acceptance of it. Lower-middle-class people are likely to oppose it, particularly through unions, because they fear it will reduce their job opportunities. City slum-dwellers, who live under the worst environmental conditions of any Americans,[43] are nonetheless indifferent to the movement. No doubt, day-to-day survival takes precedence over abstractions like land-use regulation and long-term environmental planning. As a Chicago ghetto activist said, "Open space does not draw a great deal of attention down at the pool hall."[44] Those urban minority-group members who are somewhat better off, along with civil rights activists, are ambivalent about land-use reform because, although it has the virtue of attacking exclusionary zoning, its concern for the environment may provide a new pretext for exclusion.[45]

Rural people—especially those in the vast portions of the American hinterland where national recessions arrive early, hit hard, and linger long—usually oppose the land-use reform and environmental movements, regarding them as obstacles to badly needed economic development. The rural Adirondack Park region of upstate New York is for the most part a poverty-stricken region of this sort. In recent decades, some of its towns, notably the formerly tranquil and romantic Lake George, have been growing comparatively rapidly; in the opinion of many environmentalists, much of the new development is shoddy and garish. In the late 1960s, Harold Hochschild, a wealthy part-time resident, gave a collection of photographs of the modern Lake George to the Adirondack Museum. The photographs showed what might be in prospect for the rest of the Adirondacks. Although to Hochschild and some of the museum staff the pictures seemed to show the ugliness of rapid development, "most of the people who came from Lake George to see the exhibition were pleased by the attention lavished on their hometown, while those from other towns in the park expressed the hope that similar manifestations of progress would be visited on them."[46] Robert Healy has written, "For every city or town that feels its growth is too rapid to accommodate, there are a dozen that wish growth could be accelerated."[47] Some farmers or ranchers may see land-use reform as a means of defending their way of life against encroaching construction. Large landowners also may want the holdings surrounding theirs preserved rather than developed. But given the chronic poverty of most rural areas, most of these people are in a minority in their own communities.

Along the California coast, the accepted definition of an environmentalist is a San Francisco doctor who bought a beach house last year.[48] In the hills of Vermont, the definition invokes Boston lawyers and their ski chalets. Certainly, newcomers to such desirable places have an interest in discouraging further newcomers, demanding that the gangplank to the pleasure boat be lifted as soon as they have gotten aboard.[49] As journalist William Tucker, an opponent of much environmentalism, put it:

The environmentalists in any given area seemed very easy to identify. They were, quite simply, members of the local aristocracy, often living at the end of long, winding country roads. They had learned the lessons of conspicuous consumption and had allowed a certain amount of genteel rusticity to enter their lives. . . . environmentalism . . . offered the extraordinary opportunity to combine the qualities of virtue and selfishness. . . . If tweedy people living at the end of country roads with fireplaces in their living rooms could protect their "environments," why couldn't tacky people living in pink-and-gray houses at the end of cul-de-sacs do so as well? "Environmentalism" always seemed to work in favor of people who were already well established in "the environment." I didn't realize how true this was until I learned that a group of middle-class whites in Newark had been able to block a highly controversial low-income housing project by bringing a long series of challenges to the project's environmental impact statements.[50]

The critics of the movement suggest that its supporters have, however innocently, found in ecological interdependence and the darker, more risky aspects of rapid growth a convenient pretext for prohibiting activity that affects the environment and encourages growth. In this view, the supporters favor intervention by distant regulatory bureaucracies that will have the effect of repressing the aspirations of the have-nots of American society.

These attacks, which may be valid to the extent that poor people benefit from unregulated development, are certainly embarrassing to those liberals who pride themselves on their egalitarianism. Equally distasteful is the charge that the land-use reform movement is primarily interested in preserving land for recreation—which often consists of little more than passive viewing from a car—by a few people and has a somewhat neurotic, touch-it-not attitude toward the environment. The movement springs, according to some critics, from an overbred, snobbish, and somewhat escapist disgust at the products of a mass-consumer democratic society and tends to disregard legitimate human needs, as though humanity and its needs were not themselves part of nature. Thus, in the view of its opponents, the movement distorts and prettifies nature, metaphorically putting it in a terrarium—at a distance, under glass, and with nobody in it.[51]

The Battles over Land-Use Reform: Their Course

Despite its opponents, the land-use reform movement has become steadily more influential, particularly at the state level. But most of the major, best-known pieces of land-use reform legislation were passed in the early 1970s. Since then, they have been only cautiously extended. The main reason is clear enough: the laws were intended to deal with rapid growth, but after the early 1970s, growth leveled off markedly. The 1969–71 recession and especially the 1973–75 recession and fuel crisis drastically slowed building and in some places nearly wiped out the leisure home industry. Increased construction and housing costs, tight money, and inflation constrained development as well. The oil embargo (and later the severe 1977–79 eastern and midwestern winters) stimulated energy development but crimped other forms of growth. Hard-pressed treasuries made governments reluctant to build, to undertake new programs, or to expand existing ones. Quite apart from land use, conservatism enjoyed a revival, and public confidence in government, particularly large-scale centralized government and its regulatory activities, fell to its lowest level in at least a generation.

The environmental movement reached its peak of public support between 1968 and 1973.[52] But by late 1972 the economy was beginning to weaken again. President Nixon, never really an environmental advocate despite the legislation passed during his administration,[53] vetoed that year's Water Pollution Control Act amendments on the grounds that their cost made them inflationary. Congress overrode his veto, but for the next two years he impounded funds for the act. The Coastal Zone Management Act also passed in 1972, but Nixon impounded its funding for two years, arguing again that the act might cause inflation and perhaps unemployment. Presidents Nixon and Ford generally opposed federal land-use planning, power plant siting, and strip-mining legislation on inflation and unemployment grounds throughout their administrations, and for energy reasons after the oil embargo. In late 1974, when Kenneth Cole, director of President Ford's Domestic Council, held a closed-door meeting with House Republican leaders to inform them of the contents of Ford's upcoming 1975 State of the Union speech, the *Washington Post* wrote:

According to participants in the meeting, Rep. Barber B. Conable, Jr. of New York [from an economically depressed district centering on Rochester], head of the GOP Research Committee, forcefully interrupted Cole when the Domestic Council director started to tell about administration plans for a revised land-use proposal.

Conable said that Congress didn't want to hear about land use at a time when everyone was worried about the state of the economy and the prospect of new energy shortages. Instead, he said that Mr. Ford should clearly tell both the country and the Congress what he intended to do to revive the lagging U.S. economy.[54]

Ford followed the advice of his former colleagues and gave a speech about how the nation would need 640 new power plants within ten years. He did not mention land use at all. And in general by 1975, and certainly into President Carter's term, energy arguments alone were often enough to blunt environmental and land-use reform efforts.

In response to these changes in the political climate, the land-use reform movement shifted its efforts away from the comprehensive state programs envisioned in the National Land Use Policy Act; the movement no longer attempts to achieve legislation regulating all large developments or all of a state's land. Instead, it emphasizes state programs regulating particular kinds of big projects—for instance, power plants or strip mines. The movement has also worked increasingly for state programs that would regulate development in particular natural areas—for instance, coasts or wildernesses. It has shown more interest in state programs with a large role for local government.[55] It has sought to expand the many federal programs that affect state and local land-use regulation, while trying to simplify and lighten some of the regulatory demands of existing state land-use programs.

These modifications of the movement's original intentions have in fact worked. State programs regulating specific types of projects or natural areas still pass state legislatures, indeed more readily than comprehensive, multipurpose ones ever did.[56] The National Land Use Policy Act may be dead, but other pieces of legislation with land-use implications for state government keep being introduced, and Congress frequently passes them. Moreover, federal agencies keep undertaking administrative land-use programs that do not need congressional approval. In 1979, Lance Marston, former head of the Interior Department's now-defunct Office of Land Use and Water Management (which might have administered the National Land Use Policy Act if it had passed), said that within the federal government there had been "at least—*at least*—a 20 percent growth in land-use programs in the past three years."[57]

Thus the land-use reform movement, although not so ambitious as it used to be, is nonetheless alive and well, particularly at the state level. Robert Healy wrote in 1976 that against a "gloomy background" state land-use programs "have shown little erosion.

There has been almost no weakening or repeal of such programs in states that have enacted them. In some places, most notably California, significant progress has been made in completing previously mandated plans and programs. Legislatures have filled loopholes in laws while resisting temptations to create new ones, and a few states have enacted new laws or extended the coverage of old ones.''[58] The movement has remained alive not merely because of its adaptability. A more important reason is that although the nation's urban and economic growth rates have abated since the early 1970s, the effects of that growth remain with us and increasingly impinge on the public consciousness.

Many of the effects of the intense development that took place, say, ten or fifteen years ago were essentially unknowable at the time the projects in question were proposed and approved. The few technical or academic specialists who might have been able to guess disinterestedly at what these effects would be did not, in that period, play any large part in land-use decisions. Many rural communities that agreed to big leisure-home or energy developments and many exurban communities that welcomed suburbanization may not have grasped in any politically useful manner what they were doing to their air quality, traffic, property taxes, or farmers until long after the damage was irreversible.

Only after a number of developments were built did the magnitude of the undesirable effects become widely apparent. Even now, the communities most interested in managing their growth are not those for which intensive growth is imminent but those that have recently undergone such growth or are still undergoing it. For example, in most of the cities that have taken the strictest measures to limit growth, the land is already 80 or 90 percent developed.[59] The belated struggle to rescue a little land from poor development is still more common than the timely struggle that may yield extensive preservation and improved development.

But increasingly, communities experiencing intensive growth are making serious efforts to contain its worst effects, and they see many of their neighbors doing likewise. Growth that for the most part was uncritically accepted by the public fifteen years ago must now justify itself. The public does not necessarily dislike growth or oppose it, but it has become suspicious of unchecked—that is, unregulated—

growth. The result is that devices to manage growth, whether land-use regulations, environmental controls, or other measures, have suddenly acquired a wider constituency and legitimacy than their long-time supporters ever expected.

In 1973 *The Use of Land* found "a new mood" among Americans, a mounting skepticism about the presumed benefits of urban growth.[60] In a 1977 paper titled "Environmentalists and Developers: Can They Agree on Anything?" Robert Healy described the new public acceptability of growth management:

since the first Earth Day in 1970, critics of growth have enjoyed an unprecedented success. This is partly because it has become widely accepted that the critics had a case. Too often were suburban homes built with inadequate sewers or faulty septic systems. Too often were wetlands and wildlife habitats destroyed to accommodate development. Too often were local agricultural economies broken up by the sprawl of large house lots or the random scattering of dense, urban-like concentrations. As scientists and the average citizen alike became more sophisticated about the working of natural systems, they came to understand the damage that insensitive construction could do. The energy crisis, with its implied indictment of urban sprawl, served to reinforce the environmentalists' point. . . . Developers found their freedom of action much more limited than it had been in the past. . . . Many of them now concede that the critics of growth had a point.[61]

Colorado provides an instructive example of this transformation. In 1974, Democrat Richard Lamm was elected governor on a controlled-growth platform, but then the state land-use law he had successfully sponsored as a member of the Colorado House quickly, according to the *Wall Street Journal*, "ran afoul of a hostile Republican legislature." In 1978, when Lamm was campaigning for reelection, he and his Republican opponent, conservative state senator Ted Strickland, sounded surprisingly like each other. "Both men now claim to be pollution-fighters. . . . Governor Lamm, although an environmentalist, takes pains to argue he isn't 'anti-growth'; Senator Strickland, although more of a growth advocate, takes pains to argue that he isn't against the environment." Indeed, early in the campaign, Strickland accused Lamm of favoring "unparalleled, uncontrolled growth."[62]

In achieving this acceptance, the land-use reform movement has undergone a subtle change. It no longer stresses the biological consequences of poor land use—air and water pollution, destruction of ecosystems, and the like. Comparatively few people have responded to those issues. Instead, the movement emphasizes the adverse economic, social, and quality-of-life effects of faulty land-use decisions. The movement has thus expanded its base, moving from a small constituency interested in comparatively narrow environmental issues to a much larger following interested in broad growth-management ones.

CHAPTER 5

The Six State Programs

California, Florida, Maryland, New York, Pennsylvania, and Vermont have land-use reform programs that are among the strongest in the country. If land-use reform works, these programs should be showing how. Each is a single, self-contained program of centralized regulation. Some states—for example, Maine, Michigan, Minnesota, Washington, and Wisconsin—have undertaken several different specialized land-use reform programs that, taken together, perhaps have more impact than the six single programs.[1] But the specific effects of a particular program in a state with more than one program might be difficult to trace.

Florida and Vermont have comprehensive programs that regulate all large projects. California, Maryland, New York, and Pennsylvania have single-purpose programs that regulate specific types of big projects or fragile natural areas. All six programs meet particular criteria for the purposes of this study:

1. They have genuine regulatory functions rather than mere advisory ones. These functions include powers to issue and deny permits for development proposals.

2. They had been in full operation for at least two years as of late 1975, when research for this book began. This criterion eliminated, among others, the 1973 Oregon land-use program, which did not get completely under way until 1975.

3. They are widely regarded as environmentally rigorous, model programs for other states to consider.

4. They take approaches that other states may reasonably be expected to follow. This criterion eliminated, for example, Hawaii's pioneering 1961 law providing for statewide zoning because most of the state's most important land-use conditions—eight islands; heavy state and federal, particularly military, ownership; private ownership tightly concentrated among big fruit-and-sugar companies; only four local governments, counties that are consolidated with their cities, in the whole state; and a centralized regulatory law predating the contemporary environmental movement—are not duplicated elsewhere.[2]

5. They are administered and financed primarily by the state rather than the federal government.

6. They are similar to enacted or proposed federal legislation giving grants to states.

7. They collectively represent both large and small states, as well as urban and rural issues within them.

The programs in these states also contain other features that promise to have strong effects on land use, urban growth, and the environment.[3]

The Florida Environmental Land and Water Management Act (1972)

By the early 1970s, immigration of out-of-staters had made Florida the fastest-growing large state in the country.[4] From 1950 to 1970, its population had increased from 2.7 million to 6.7 million. After 1970, the state's growth slowed only slightly; in 1979 Florida had a population of nearly 9 million. Since the 1960s, nearly 5,000 people have moved to Florida every week.

A severe drought in 1971 made the Florida public aware that overbuilding had depleted the state's water supply and had injected saltwater into the supply that remained. Dredging for new developments had seriously damaged Tampa Bay and Biscayne Bay off Miami, particularly by means of "finger" canals cut into the shoreline to create more waterfront land. Over substantial environmental objections, a 2400-megawatt nuclear power plant was being built at Turkey Point, south of Miami. Planning was in progress for construction of an Everglades Jetport and a Cross Florida Barge Canal.

The state's big new developments were getting bigger. Its physical beauty was being destroyed, its distinctive ambience deteriorating. Especially in its southern half—the only tropical portion of the United States except for Hawaii—Florida was beginning to look and feel like a cross between southern California and the New Jersey Turnpike. Its local governments were generally unable or unwilling to deal with these problems. In 1967, Florida had become the last state in the union to delegate zoning powers to its localities; most states had passed this legislation in the 1920s and 1930s. But even five years later, more than half the state's land still had no local land-use controls. So in 1972 the state enacted a land-use legislation package, in which the most important bill was the Environmental Land and Water Management Act.

The legislation required the Department of Administration's Division of State Planning (which in late 1979 became the Bureau of Land and Water Management in the Department of Community Affairs) to prepare a statewide land development plan. It also required the division to set up regulatory standards and guidelines for "developments of regional impact"—that is, developments that affect more than one county. A proposed development large enough to qualify would become the subject of a report by the appropriate regional planning council (the state now has eleven such councils). The report must cover the development's environmental impacts, its effects on local and regional public services, its effects on the local and regional economy, and (since 1976) its effects on energy use. The locality then considers the report and decides on the development application. The developer, the regional planning council, or the Division of State Planning (now the Bureau of Land and Water Management) may appeal the decision to the governor and his cabinet, a six-member body of independently elected officials. Their decision is binding on all parties.

The act also empowered the Division of State Planning to make recommendations for the designation of "areas of critical state concern"—that is, places where development is to be regulated by the state for environmental reasons. These recommendations go to the governor and cabinet, which may approve, modify, or reject them. Within designated areas, all local governments are required to adopt land-use regulations acceptable to the division. If they do not do so within six months, the division (now the bureau) can devise its own regulations for the area, subject to approval by the cabinet, and require the local government to enforce them. If the division (or bureau) believes that the local governments are not adequately enforcing its regulations, it can take them to court.

The Vermont Environmental Control Act (1970)

In 1970, the Vermont legislature passed a bill commonly known as Act 250, that represented a response to growth strains that, although modest by Florida or California standards, nonetheless far surpassed anything in Vermont's history.[5] The completion of the Interstate Highway System had dramatically reduced driving time from New York City and Boston. Large leisure home developments and ski resorts, particularly in southern Vermont, had drastically altered the character of several small towns. Towns such as Wilmington and Dover reportedly had one developer for every twenty-five residents (children included), and developments planned for the towns threatened to increase their populations tenfold. More such developments were on the way all over the state. Land prices and property taxes were shooting up, dispossessing or forcing into trailers many poorer residents.

The state's population grew more in the 1960s than it had in the previous sixty years; much of the growth was concentrated in northern Vermont around Burlington, the state's largest city (1970 population, 38,600), where IBM had a plant. For the first time, sprawl appeared: on several roads outside Burlington; on the road between Montpelier, the capital, and Barre; on the outskirts of Rutland; and on the roads north and south of Brattleboro. The part-time small local governments that still proudly held town meetings every spring could not handle the effects of this growth. They could not handle the traffic the new developments produced, particularly along Route 100, a north-south state highway through skiing country that skirted the Green Mountain National Forest for about 130 miles. Vermont had no county governments, and the town governments could not supply the public services that the new developments and their residents needed. The romantic conception of old Vermont—a misty melange of farm villages, barn-studded vistas, deep forests, maple sugar, noncommercial skiing, and flinty Yankee independence—actually had considerable reality. But much of the state seemed about to become a characterless Boston exurb. Act 250 was intended to prevent it from doing so.

The act created a nine-member Environmental Board, appointed by the governor, to draw up three state land-use plans, which, upon approval by the governor and legislature, would have the force of law. The first plan, essentially an inventory of the state's land resources, was easily passed in 1972. The second plan, which set forth a number of "planning principles" to guide future development in accordance with the capacity of Vermont's land, passed with somewhat more difficulty in 1973.

The third plan divided the state's land into categories (urban, rural, conservation, and so forth), set guidelines for the density of development in each category, and required local governments to draw up land-use plans. The secretary of the Department of Development and Community Affairs, which contains the Environmental Board, was to review each local plan for consistency with the state plan. If a local plan did not get state approval, the state could eventually step in with its own local plan. The state also would control development in unincorporated areas. This third plan, to be administered by the Environmental Board, called for most of Vermont's new growth to take place in cities and towns rather than in the countryside, and at roughly current densities. Leisure homes were to be confined to limited areas, clustered within them, and subject to all the restrictions placed on permanent residences. Versions of the third plan were badly defeated in the legislature in 1974, 1975, and 1976; since then, the Environmental Board has not submitted new versions for legislative consideration.

Act 250 also created a regulatory structure. Nine district environmental commissions, each with three members appointed by the governor, rule on proposals for subdivision of more than ten lots; residential building involving more than ten housing units; all construction above 2500 feet; and commercial, industrial, or public development of more than one acre. However, projects located inside a town with zoning and subdivision laws need state approval only if they cover ten acres or more. The purpose of this provision is to encourage localities to establish their own land-use controls; by enacting such controls, a town can markedly reduce district and state intervention in decisions concerning its land. The act stipulates that a development proposal is to be judged on the basis of its probable effects on water and air pollution, water supplies, soil erosion, traffic, school facilities, and other public services; its aesthetic quality; and its conformity with state, local, and regional plans. The 1973 plan added such criteria as the development's likely effects on agricultural soils, forests, mineral lands, energy conservation, and public-utility services. The developer, the local selectmen, the local planning commission, the regional planning commission, state agencies, and adjoining property owners all may participate in district environmental commission hearings and may appeal district-level decisions to the state Environmental Board.

The New York State Adirondack Park Agency Act (1971)

Across Lake Champlain from Vermont lies Adirondack Park, 6 million acres of spectacular, often mountainous forests and lakes.[6] The park, whose boundaries were established in 1892, is the size of Vermont, but has less than 1/4 of Vermont's population and only 1/165 New York State's. It is the largest wilderness in the East. About two-fifths of the park, mainly forests, is owned by New York State through its Department of Environmental Conservation. The forests are protected by the "forever wild" provision of the state's 1895 constitution and cannot be sold by the state. On this public land, unlike national park or forest land, it is illegal to cut trees or mine for commercial purposes.

The other three-fifths of the park is owned mainly by wealthy nonresidents (predominantly from the New York City area), timber companies, and mining concerns. No town wholly within the park has a population over 10,000. Park residents are generally poor; their average per capita income is less than two-thirds that of other New York State residents. A fifth of the park population lacks indoor plumbing. Prospects for new economic development within the park are slim. Much of its population is unskilled and poorly educated. Its winters are long and severe. Its vastness and remoteness from population centers make it inconvenient for most commercial and industrial enterprises. New York State's tax laws also are comparatively discouraging. The park has some of the poorest agricultural soils and the shortest growing season in the state. Of the park's 2300 lakes, 700 can only be reached by seaplane. The park is a fine vacation spot for people from New York City, Syracuse, or Buffalo, but between September and June its unemployment rate often goes well over 20 percent.

In the late 1960s, the completion of Interstate 87, the Northway, made the Adirondacks easily accessible to much of the Northeast. Several of the larger towns, notably Glens Falls, Lake Placid, and Saranac Lake, began to acquire the garish and shoddy construction that often accompanies an influx of tourists. Some large leisure home developments were on the way, and many small ones were already there. It was possible (and by the early 1970s became probable) that the 1980 Winter Olympics would be held in Lake Placid; preparation for the Olympics was bound to involve a good deal of building. The towns and counties within the park generally did not have lane-use controls and did not think they were needed.

Laurance Rockefeller, the conservationist brother of New York's late Governor Nelson Rockefeller and chairman of the state's Council of Parks, had suggested turning the Adirondacks into a national park. But most Adirondackers opposed this idea. Instead, over opposition that was still substantial, the state in 1971 created the Adirondack Park Agency to regulate land use in the park. The agency has eleven members appointed by the governor, five of whom must be park residents.

The Adirondack Park Agency Act provided for the agency to draw up a state land-use plan for the park's public holdings. The plan, completed in 1972, zoned this land for varying uses (wilderness, canoe recreation, travel corridors, intensive use, and the like). The plan is now being carried out by the Department of Environmental Conservation in consultation with the agency, and has produced relatively little controversy.

But the act also called for the agency to draw up a land-use plan for the park's private lands.[7] Completed in 1973, it may be the most stringent and is certainly the most complex state-sponsored land-use plan in the country. It defines six land-use categories, sets density standards for each category, and categorizes all the park's private land; rural, resource-management, and low-density classifications account for 95 percent of the land.

For each classification, the plan lists primary compatible uses of the land, which are suitable anywhere in the classified area as long as they meet the density restrictions, and secondary compatible uses, which are suitable only if they are also acceptably located. Within each of the six classifications, a pair of size thresholds defines governmental jurisdiction. Developments below the lower threshold—in the moderate-intensity classification, for instance, any subdivision of fourteen or fewer lots—do not require agency approval. Developments between the two thresholds—in the case of the moderate-intensity classification, any subdivision of fifteen to seventy-four lots—do not require agency approval if the locality has land-use controls that have been approved by the agency; the purpose of this provision, much like Vermont's, is to encourage the localities to enact controls. All developments above the higher threshold—in the moderate-intensity classification, any subdivision of seventy-five or more lots—require agency approval.[8]

The plan goes on to list thirty-seven "development considerations" that the agency must take into account before it can approve any project. These resemble the Vermont criteria but are more elaborate. The plan also includes special restrictions on shoreline, riverbank, and (as of 1977) wetlands development. The plan is an extremely intricate document. Local people, who might be hostile to any plan, have been especially hostile to this one because they could not understand it.

The act also calls for the agency to rule, in accordance with the public and private land-use plans, on all public and private development proposals that fall within its jurisdiction. And the act requires the agency to work with the 107 local governments in the park to devise local land-use controls it can approve. These controls—land-use plans, zoning ordinances, subdivision regulations, sanitary codes, and building codes—must be consistent with the overall park plans. The agency can provide the localities with funds to devise and administer controls. Once the controls are approved, the locality gets sole jurisdiction over the middle-sized projects, mentioned above, on which it previously shared jurisdiction with the agency.

The California Coastal Zone Conservation Act (1972)

About four-fifths of California's 22 million people live within thirty miles of its magnificent coast.[9] In the early 1970s, the beaches of Los Angeles and San Diego, which were among the fastest-growing big cities in the nation, were sprouting high-rise condominiums. Small coastal or near-coastal cities—for example, San Jose, Santa Barbara, Santa Rosa, Ventura, and much of Orange County—were undergoing similar growth. Large beach home projects had appeared near Los Angeles and San Francisco. Offshore drilling from Santa Barbara south and logging from San Francisco north were generating public protests. Near most California coastal cities, beach access, loss of farmland, power plants, sprawl, and sheer ugliness had become controversial issues. West of Los Angeles, for instance, a wall of houses shut off both the Malibu beach and the view of it from the nearest road for twenty miles. Commercial and sport fishing were in decline because of deteriorating water quality. Many bays, lagoons, and wetlands, including San Francisco Bay, were being altered and in some cases destroyed by intense, rapid development, especially dredging and filling. The zoning activities of local governments did little to prevent these problems and much to aggravate them.

In the 1970, 1971, and 1972 sessions of the state legislature, California environmentalists tried to pass bills protecting the coast and failed by narrow margins. In 1972, led by an umbrella group, the California Coastal Alliance, they succeeded in having a law regulating coastal development placed on the ballot. In the subsequent campaign the proponents of the law were, by a more than 4-to-1 margin, outspent by developers, oil companies, utilities, logging companies, and most unions and local governments. But the Coastal Alliance mounted a huge grassroots volunteer campaign, and the measure passed with 55 percent of the vote.

The law was modeled on the San Francisco Bay Conservation and Development Commission (BCDC), which had operated since 1965; the BCDC was considered a success, and in fact contributed its chairman, several commissioners, executive director, and chief planner to similar positions in the new coastal operation. The law called for the establishment of six regional commissions covering all of the coast not already regulated by BCDC. Half of the twelve to sixteen members of each commission were to come from specified local governments. The other half were to be appointed by the governor, the rules committee of the state senate, and the speaker of the state assembly.

The six commissions ruled on all development on land within 1000 yards of the water's edge or at sea within three miles of it, except for maintenance dredging of existing navigational channels and minor (less than $7,500) improvements to existing single-family homes. The law permitted the commissions to reach decisions on some projects by majority vote. But it required approval by two-thirds of the commissioners for projects involving dredging, filling, agricultural land, beach access, fisheries, water quality, or the view of the sea from the state highway nearest the coast—that is, most large or waterfront projects. The law required commission decisions to reflect specific environmental policies—for example, maintaining public access to beaches and recreation areas, minimizing alterations to existing land forms and vegetation, and preserving views. Regional decisions could be appealed to a state coastal commission. Six of its members were publicly appointed in the same way as the members of the regional coastal commissions, and six were delegates from the regional commissions themselves.

The law also required the state and regional commissions to prepare a plan for the coast before the end of 1975. The planning zone was to be broader than the regulatory one; it went from three miles out to sea to the highest point of the nearest inland coastal mountain range (except in southern California, where it was to go five miles inland or to the crest of the mountain range, whichever distance is shorter). The law provided that if the legislature failed to approve the plan, or some revision of it, by the end of its 1976 session the commissions would go out of existence.

In December 1975, the commissions produced a plan with 206 policy recommendations.[10] For a time, its passage was in doubt—union opposition was especially strong—but in August 1976, Governor Brown brokered the passage of the Coastal Act, which went into effect in January 1977. Although this law, which replaces the 1972 one, is too new to be extensively covered in these pages, it does represent a major modification of the earlier legislation. And by the time it was passed, the California coastal commissions were also receiving the funds and meeting the requirements of the federal coastal zone management program.

Under the 1976 legislation, the state coastal commission became a permanent body, but the regional commissions were to function for only two and a half years, until mid-1979; a 1978 amendment extended their life to mid-1981. Although they continue to regulate development, their primary task is to work with coastal communities to produce local planning and zoning programs consistent with the coastal plan and acceptable to the regional and state coastal commissions. These programs had to be produced by the beginning of 1980, a deadline another 1978 amendment extended to mid-1981. The commissions may give local governments grants to devise the programs.

Once the programs are approved, the local governments are to take over the work of the regional commissions, except that specified projects—for example, large public-works or energy projects, and developments within 300 feet of a beach or coastal bluff or 100 feet of a wetland—will continue to be regulated by both the local government and the regional or state commission. If the local governments fail to produce acceptable controls, then the state commission can eventually impose its own controls. The state commission is to review all local controls at least every five years. The decisions of regional commissions can be appealed to the state commission.

The law empowers the state commission to designate ''sensitive coastal resource areas'' of regional or statewide concern where both the regional commission (or, if it has expired, the state commission) and the locality continue to rule on development proposals. The designation must be approved by the legislature within two years after it is first proposed. The law raises the maximum cost of a ''minor improvement'' to a single-family home from $7,500 to $25,000. In November 1976, California's voters approved a companion bond issue, advocated by the plan, providing $120 million for the public purchase of coastal land for beaches, parks, and open spaces.[11]

The Maryland Power Plant Siting Act (1971)

Maryland contains two areas that are both beautiful and, from a technical standpoint, perfectly suited for power plant construction—the banks of the Potomac and the convoluted shores of Chesapeake

Bay.[12] The power plants are needed. Baltimore's suburbs, if not the city itself, have been growing rapidly. Maryland's suburbs around Washington, D.C., have been growing extremely rapidly. The growth of the federal government and the private organizations that want to be near it has made Washington the only large northeastern city with a metropolitan growth rate comparable to that of the high-growth southern and western cities.[13]

In 1967, Baltimore Gas and Electric Company (BG&E) announced plans to build a 1600-megawatt nuclear power plant. The company had chosen a site at Calvert Cliffs, sixty miles south of Baltimore, on the western shore of Chesapeake Bay at one of the bay's narrowest points, an eight-mile-wide strait at its midsection. If these waters became heavily polluted, the bay's sluggish estuarine currents would not be strong enough to flush them. The plant as proposed could create a sizable zone of polluted water in the middle of the 195-mile-long bay.

Citizens objected and fought a protracted legal battle with BG&E, the Atomic Energy Commission (AEC; now the Nuclear Regulatory Commission), and the Maryland Public Service Commission, which regulates power companies. The environmentalists proved that the AEC had violated the National Environmental Policy Act by not adequately considering environmental factors in its decisions on the plant, and the plant's design was substantially modified. The first 800-megawatt unit of the plant did not begin operations until 1975, and then only under environmental restrictions more stringent than those contemplated in 1967. (The other 800-megawatt unit did not begin even partial operations until 1979.) But the fight revealed that Maryland, by itself, had no reliable mechanisms for getting the power plants it needed or for minimizing their environmental damage. The result was the Power Plant Siting Act of 1971.[14]

The legislation establishes a Power Plant Siting Program in the state's Department of Natural Resources. The program is financed by a surcharge on electric bills. In the case of an apartment, the surcharge may be ten to thirty cents a month. In the case of a large single-family home that uses more electricity, it may be somewhat higher; in a big factory, higher still. The legislation sets a range of rates at which the surcharge may be computed, but every year the program sets the exact rate within the range. It thus can establish its budget and plan its activities without concerning itself with annual appropriations from the legislature. In recent years, the program's budget has approached $10 million.

The law requires each of Maryland's seventeen power companies to submit annually to the Public Service Commission a plan identifying possible sites for plants over the following ten years. The commission then draws up a ten-year state plan and submits it annually to the Power Plant Siting Program. The program investigates the sites and, after consulting with other state agencies, local governments, and a committee of outside experts, determines their environmental suitability for large power plants. It buys the best sites at fair-market prices (rather than lower eminent-domain prices) and holds them for sale or lease to the power companies. The program can supersede zoning and other local ordinances. The program may hold four to eight sites at any one time. The power companies are not obligated to use the sites; they can, if they wish, buy their own.

The program's operations are unparalleled in other states, although New York has a program of buying potential sites for nuclear power plants. The program ensures the availability of economically feasible, environmentally sound sites on comparatively short notice. The state need not risk power shortages or be compelled to buy expensive out-of-state power. The elimination of these problems justifies the program's independent financing and freedom from annual legislative review of its budget, although a committee of the legislature provides some oversight.

The program also advises the Public Service Commission on the environmental effects of all proposed power plants and transmission lines larger than 69 kilovolts (that is, lines substantially larger than telephone poles). Again, it consults with other state agencies, local governments, and its outside committee of experts. The commission holds hearings on each application, and the program, the other state agencies, the power companies, local governments, local residents, and other interested parties can present their cases. The commission makes the decision on each project and may supersede local ordinances.

The Pennsylvania Surface Mining Conservation and Reclamation Act (1971)

Coal has been strip-mined in Pennsylvania for well over a century, and the state has paid the price.[15] The excavations have reduced several hundred thousand acres of forest, farmland, and hill country to rubble. They have polluted hundreds of square miles of streams and lakes with acid water flowing out of the mines. The damage is worst in the anthracite (hard) coal region of northeastern Pennsylvania near Wilkes-Barre, Scranton, and Hazleton. Here piles of overburden—refuse from mining—sometimes reach higher than the natural hills. Huge pits, thousands of yards across and hundreds of feet deep, extend for miles. The landscape, if that is the word, is lunar. In the bituminous (soft) coal area of western Pennsylvania near Pittsburgh, Johnstown, Butler, and Uniontown, the damage is not quite so devastating. (Because bituminous coal seams, unlike anthracite seams, are level, a coal operator mining a single seam need not dig progressively deeper into the earth.) But in bituminous country, one can still find plenty of scarred, eroded land disfiguring an otherwise lush mountain and farming countryside.

In the late nineteenth and early twentieth centuries, the state's coal powered much of the nation's industrialization, and King Coal (with help from King Steel and King Oil) ruled Pennsylvania. But for the Pennsylvania coal industry, the depression that began in 1929 did not really end until 1973. During the middle third of the century, oil and natural gas captured coal's traditional home-heating and industrial markets and much of its utility market. The railroads abandoned coal-fired engines in favor of diesel and electric ones. The Pennsylvania coal industry's share of national coal production fell to about 10 percent (dropping behind that of Kentucky and West Virginia), its anthracite portion was continually plagued by strikes, and its historic grip on state politics loosened.[16] In 1971, the contemporary environmental movement achieved passage of the Pennsylvania Surface Mining Conservation and Reclamation Act. The law replaces a weaker law that had not covered anthracite mining at all. It also applies to the mining of limestone, gravel, and iron ore, but it is mainly aimed at stripping for coal. The victory was timely too; by 1974, the oil embargo had made it profitable for coal operators to go back and cut into deeper seams.

The law is administered by the Bureau of Surface Mine Reclamation in the Department of Environmental Resources. Before stripping any site, an operator must submit to the bureau plans for mining the land, repairing (reclaiming) the damage done, and preventing acid drainage into water supplies. The law prohibits stripping near roads, streams, parks, cemeteries, and extremely steep slopes (over 40°). It also requires operators to obtain specific permission from landowners to enter onto their property and to strip near an occupied dwelling. The law restricts the locations on which operators can put overburden, specifies the degree of water quality that must be maintained, and defines permissible mining procedures. No cut in the earth can exceed 1500 feet at any one time.

Before stripping, an operator must post with the bureau a performance bond that will be returned if the land is restored to its approximate original contour. If the bureau is not satisfied with the reclamation, the operator forfeits the bond, and the department uses the money to reclaim the land. If the operator is stripping previously mined land, the bureau may require that he undo damage done by his predecessors. The state program to regulate strip-mining supersedes all relevant local programs except zoning ordinances.[17] Any appeals from the program's decisions go first to the Pennsylvania Environmental Hearing Board, a state body independent of the Department of Environmental Resources, and then if necessary to the courts.

In recent years, the state program has overseen the reclamation of 10,000 to 20,000 acres annually. Since 1963, the department has also conducted a program—Operation Scarlift, financed by a $200 million bond issue—to reclaim abandoned strip mines. Working on sites that are generally quite refractory—that, plus the weakness of the earlier laws, is why they were abandoned in the first place—it reclaims approximately 1000 acres a year. Some of this land has become part of the state park system.

The Analysis of the Programs

We have, then, six highly inventive state land-use programs with important elements in common. Each was passed in the early 1970s. Each represents a response to mounting environmental stresses. Each has typically been supported by liberals and opposed by conservatives. Each has provoked especially strong resistance from development interests and local governments. Most significant, each employs centralized regulation as its primary method.

On the other hand, the programs obviously differ substantially. The states in which they are applied vary in their development patterns, populations, economies, politics, government, demography, and topography. The programs themselves vary in the kinds of development they cover, the ways in which they use centralized regulations, the roles they assign to planning and citizen participation, and the relations they produce between state and local government.

Yet the differences between the programs can be useful for analytic purposes. They suggest the implications and results of the different possibilities available under the broad rubric of centralized regulation. The next five chapters examine the adoption, implementation, and effects of the programs.

CHAPTER 6

The Politics of the State Land-Use Laws

Although formulated at the instigation of environmentalists or in response to constituent concern for the environment, the state land-use laws are clearly the products of compromises with such forces as developers, local governments, industry, utilities, farmers, labor unions, homeowners, and existing state agencies. Even at the height of their strength in the late 1960s and early 1970s, the land-use reformers had to make concessions to get the laws passed and put into effect.

It is not necessarily objectionable for the laws to exempt some types of development, to exempt from regulation development below defined size thresholds, to have grandfather clauses, or to provide for some representation of opposed interests on regulatory bodies. But some of the concessions bit quite deep. The reformers often had to agree not to minor or technical exemptions of some projects but to wholesale exemptions of some of the biggest land-based industries. The legitimate purpose of size thresholds was to keep the state from involvement in projects too trivial to regulate, but developers and local governments fought to raise the thresholds so as to keep the state out of as many projects as possible. Reformers sometimes had to agree not only that projects already started should continue unregulated, but also that some projects not yet in progress might avoid regulation completely. They typically had to accept heavy representation of the opposed interests on the regulatory bodies. To be sure, the laws maintained an environmental intent. But because of the concessions, their character was not wholly environmental; in some cases, it was only barely so.

The Entrenchment of the Opposition

Land-use laws, like other laws, derive from the political and economic forces at work in each state—forces that only occasionally favor land-use reform. The main proponents of land-use laws— planners, environmentalists, citizen activists, and land-use lawyers—typically do not have much strength or organization to bring to bear on state politics. Their immediate constituency consists mainly of those who share their professional, good-government, or aesthetic objectives. The reformers have no large-scale economic influence. Their lobbying efforts are weak, ephemeral, and often absent. Few stable environmental interest groups at either the state or the federal level have devoted themselves primarily to land use.[1]

The opponents of land-use laws, particularly development and business interests, are usually strong and well organized. They are numerous and watchful, and they have a long history of influencing state government, especially state legislatures.[2] Many state legislators are developers, businessmen, realtors, lawyers, bankers, insurance people, or labor union members.[3] Development and business interests always account for an impressive proportion of a state's jobs, tax revenues, and campaign contributions. Moreover, they are responsible for most of its urban and economic growth and much of its public construction. They own much of the land in the state.[4] Their lobbying is expert, massive, and well funded. In California, for example, during the 1970–72 legislative sessions that several times rejected coastal legislation, development and business interests had 235 full-time lobbyists in Sacramento. Environmentalists had at most three and were outspent by more than 50 to 1.[5]

As opponents of land-use reform, developers and businessmen have other, more subtle advantages as well. Typically, they are tough-minded people who actually make their living from land. They have specific knowledge of the territory (in the literal sense) under discussion and the self-confident grip on popular attitudes that exponents of private property and free enterprise always have in American society. They are in the main united; they know exactly what they want: the status quo, which has benefited them for years, or something as close to it as possible. The liberal advocates of land-use reform, on the other hand, must invent laws that are essentially experiments. Many of the innovations they propose seem unrealistic or unnatural to disinterested people. And the reformers may be divided among themselves.

Reformers face structural difficulties as well. Even if most of the people in a state favor land-use reform—as they probably did in Vermont and Florida in the early 1970s[6] and certainly did in California, to judge from the 1972 coastal initiative—this sentiment is likely to be relatively lightly held and weakly expressed; that is, diffused. But opposition to land-use reform is strongly felt and cogently articulated; that is, concentrated. Opponents of land-use bills have more to lose, both economically and politically, than supporters have to gain. Opponents turn out in large numbers at public hearings, while supporters often do not.[7] Politicians and bureaucrats, who hold the hearings in part to ascertain the state of public opinion, cannot help being aware of the disparity.

In addition, many land-use issues are complex and abstract, and most have a strong technical component as well. Reformers often do not agree on what better land use is. The benefits of specific laws—particularly the broad social benefits—are typically hard to grasp, long range, and distributed in comparatively small amounts approximately equally throughout the population. The total benefits may heavily outweigh the costs. But the costs are likely to be concrete, short-run, and borne mostly by politically powerful groups. The costs are at hand and so evoke strong objections; the benefits are distant and thus have difficulty arousing strong support. As Michigan State University economist Lawrence Libby has noted:

Unlike the case with food stamps or school buses where public expenditure produces immediate, tangible, and very obvious outputs, returns to comprehensive planning are difficult to pinpoint. The benefits usually are reduced future costs. . . . The costs of a particular plan or implementing law, on the other hand, may be vivid to those affected. The frequent result is that political support for specific control proposals is more illusive than the objections.[8]

The success of the supporters of land-use reform is due not so much to their efforts as to the conditions of the time. Many land-use laws now on the books could not be passed today.[9] But the late 1960s and early 1970s were—compared to the present—a time of environmental crisis and economic prosperity. The public seems to have perceived preservation of the environment as a luxury that its prosperity enabled it to afford. Land-use and environmental laws of all kinds were widely seen as progressive. Many politicians who had been uninterested in land-use reform (for example, Florida Governor Reubin Askew[10]) or opposed to it (Vermont Governor Thomas Salmon[11]) were suddenly eager to support it. In some cases, they did not understand the legislation for which they voted.[12] A former Vermont legislator from a conservative area who voted for the state's land-use law, despite misgivings that he feels have since been justified, commented:

In 1970 there was no way to avoid voting for Act 250. Anybody in politics had to be against those terrible big out-of-state builders, even if they didn't really exist or turned out to be small guys from Vermont. So I made my reservations known, did what I could to damp down the excesses, and then held my nose and said yes. The vote came out unanimous. Then I—and I'm sure a lot of my colleagues—went out looking for a speaking date with the Rotary Club or some other respectable businessmen's group to explain why I'd done it. (AI,* Kirby, Vermont, September 1975)

Thus, some opponents of land-use reform reluctantly accepted the legislation in order to retain credibility in the prevailing political climate. They adapted, shifting their resistance from the goals of the laws to the means by which these goals were to be achieved. They concentrated on securing concessions buried in the fine print.

All the laws ended up with concessions, but some laws had more concessions than others. The magnitude of the concessions in general did not depend on the strength of the supporters of the laws but on the strength of their opponents. It is no accident that Florida has both the weakest law of the six states examined in the pages that follow, and the highest growth rate.

*The abbreviation AI is used throughout the text to indicate anonymous interview. Such interviews were conducted in person, except for those by telephone, which are indicated by the abbreviation ATI.

Some Legislative Comparisons:
Florida versus California, 1972

The legislative battles and resulting concessions attending the passage of two of the laws it supported—the relatively weak Florida land-use law and the relatively strong California coastal law, both passed in 1972—highlight the political barriers facing the land-use reform movement. These cases generally confirm Theodore Lowi's view of interest-group liberalism; the legislative battles are essentially struggles between interest groups contending for control, whether overt or covert, of the machinery of state government. State legislators show surprisingly little personal volition or autonomy. Lobbyists, especially moneyed ones, obviously draft a great deal of legislation.[13] Legislators apparently believe that their main task is to respond to the demands of organized interest groups—primarily by achieving compromises among them. This practice naturally favors the stronger, more organized interests, and harms causes, such as land-use reform, that lack money, organization, and experienced lobbyists. It also is relatively unresponsive to grass-roots sentiment. Florida offers a well-documented example of these tendencies at work.[14]

FLORIDA. In the early 1970s, and particularly after the 1971 south Florida drought, public revulsion at the environmental results of the state's development boom was widespread. But no more than two full-time environmental lobbyists were operating in Tallahassee at any time. The main political impetus for the passage of the 1972 law came from Governor Askew, who personally introduced the bill as his top priority for the year, and from state legislators from large urban areas such as Miami, who were heavily lobbied by local environmental groups and some local governments concerned about excessively rapid growth. The state's major newspapers, led by the *Miami Herald*, supported the bill. Development interests in Florida seem to have been caught off guard and to have organized themselves tardily.[15] Luther Carter reported that the Arvida Corporation, a large Florida builder, "saw an advantage in more orderly and controlled development and strongly supported the bill all the way."[16] Several of the state's biggest developers—for example, the

Deltona Corporation and the GAC Corporation—chose, given the public mood, not to involve themselves in efforts against the bill.

The legislative battle was nonetheless quite close. The bill was several times nearly killed before it finally passed on the last day of the 1972 legislative session. Its most important portion, dealing with developments of regional impact (DRIs), on several occasions came close to being removed altogether; twice, once in the House Natural Resources Committee and once on the House floor, motions to eliminate the DRI provisions were defeated by a single vote. Governor Askew expended a great deal of his personal influence to secure the bill's passage. Just before the key vote in the Florida House, he called in two dozen legislators, including a number of opponents, for an informal question-and-answer session about the bill. As he said good-bye to them, he shook hands with each, saying, ''I'll see you at the roll call.''[17]

But he and his land-use reformer allies still had to make important concessions. Construction for farming, hotels, and highways, as well as for utilities on existing rights-of-way, was exempted from the law. The exemption of hotels and highways was a response to pressures from both builders and Florida's powerful tourist industry. The farming exemption represented a triumph for agribusiness lobbyists and a serious setback for environmentalists. As Carter wrote: ''The drainage of wetlands for agriculture has, beyond question, done more damage to the Florida environment than any other kind of development.''[18] In 1970, according to the Census Bureau, Florida's farms employed over 80,000 people, making agriculture one of the largest industries in the state.[19]

The building industry also succeeded in obtaining exemption for any construction for which even preliminary planning had begun as of the July 1973 effective date of the law, nearly a year after the law was passed. This generous grandfather provision gave builders an incentive to start preliminary planning on a vast scale immediately. Its effects are being felt even now because of the huge scale and long buildout periods of much Florida development. Development interests also managed to delay for a year the implementation of the law's provisions on developments of regional impact, while a study committee examined how they might be put into effect. According to Wade Hopping, a lobbyist for several big corporate developers, it was this concession that "allowed the entire DRI process to go through."[20] It also gave his clients more time to start projects without regulation. In 1970, according to the Census Bureau, nearly 200,000 people were employed by Florida's construction industry.[21]

The law stipulated that in "areas of critical state concern"—that is, environmentally fragile areas—local land-use controls must be approved by the Division of State Planning. The law also provided that no more than 5 percent of Florida could be designated as such areas. But more than half of Florida lies on top of the Floridan Aquifer, a gigantic water-bearing limestone formation that supplies 90 percent of the state's water. The depletion and salination of the aquifer had been largely responsible for the 1971 drought.[22] Apart from the aquifer, Florida's land includes beach areas, biologically productive wetlands such as the Everglades and other large swamps, and hard-to-replace groves that supply most of the country's citrus production. Hence, more than two-thirds of the state probably should not be subjected to intensive development.[23] Much of this land is nonetheless undergoing heavy building,[24] and the 5 percent maximum makes the law virtually useless to prevent it.

The original version of the bill called for the Division of State Planning on its own initiative to establish interim land-use controls for areas of critical state concern. But under pressure from local governments, this provision was dropped in favor of a procedure that gave the local governments up to a year after an area's designation to arrive at controls acceptable to the division. In 1974, the procedure was amended to allow only six months. But in the words of Phyllis Myers of the Conservation Foundation, "since most developable areas either had weak local controls, or none at all, the state by signaling an area as 'critical' could actually start a development rush in unprotected areas."[25] Developers could (and often did) use the six-month grace period, which did not start until an area was declared critical, to begin as many unregulated projects as possible.

Finally, the law stated that no area could be declared critical until a $240 million bond issue for the state purchase of environmentally endangered lands passed in a referendum. This provision, which, according to Myers, "saved the bill,"[26] had been insisted on by the powerful vice chairman of the Senate Ways and Means Committee, Jim Williams, who represented Ocala, in rural north central Florida.

(At an earlier point in the legislative battle, Williams had been able to kill everything in the bill except for a study committee.) The bond issue passed, half a year later, but it further delayed implementation of the law.

CALIFORNIA.   In 1970, 1971, and 1972, California reformers had secured passage of coastal legislation in the Assembly, only to see it narrowly beaten each time by the traditionally more conservative Senate and the opposition of Governor Ronald Reagan.[27] Lobbyists for development, power, and oil companies were so sure of defeating any coastal bill that they were reportedly unwilling even to discuss the issue with the reformers.[28]

So the reformers, led by the California Coastal Alliance, an umbrella group of environmental organizations, decided to circumvent the legislature entirely by placing the bill on the ballot. They needed the signatures of 5 percent of the California electorate to qualify the bill for the ballot. In a little over a month, they managed to collect 418,000 valid signatures of voters, nearly 100,000 more than they needed. They then mounted a massive door-to-door and telephone canvassing campaign that, for example, called each of Orange County's voters—more than one million of them—twice. They also persuaded the president pro tem of the California Senate to lead a Great Coast Bike Ride from San Francisco to San Diego.

Whitaker and Baxter, a politically experienced San Francisco public relations firm, spent more than $1 million fighting the law for its development-minded clients. But the firm's tactics backfired, and its credibility became an issue in the campaign. The speaker of the California Assembly was moved to denounce one of the firm's advertisements on the theme of "Don't Lock up the Coast" as an "out and out fraud."[29] While the California AFL-CIO and building trades unions opposed the law, a number of important unions, including the United Auto Workers, supported it.[30] The League of California Cities, a local-government interest group, opposed the measure, but the city councils of Los Angeles and San Diego endorsed it, as did the city council of noncoastal Sacramento. In the end, the coastal law obtained 55 percent of the popular vote. Support for it was predictably weakest in the poorest areas of the state—for example, the rural logging counties of the North Coast above San Francisco—and among coastal landowners. Support for the measure was particularly strong in the big cities and among college graduates and affluent people generally.[31]

With this support, and especially because it originated in an initiative procedure that freed reformers of the need to negotiate with their opponents, California's law, unlike Florida's, covered virtually all development in the area it regulated. It included no exemptions for politically influential industries and no limitations on the amount of land that could be protected.

In addition, California's law allowed no delays in implementation and contained only a grudging grandfather provision: to be exempted from California's law, a project had to have obtained a local building permit or similarly advanced approval by the effective date of the law—February 1, 1973, less than three months after the coastal referendum.[32]

Florida's law did not have strong citizen-participation procedures. California's law allowed any interested person to participate in the coastal commissions' deliberations and to appeal regional decisions to the state commission and the courts.

The 1972 California law contained some concessions to the opposition. These were broadened by the 1976 Coastal Act, which was wholly the product of the legislature and passed during a period of economic and energy difficulties.[33] But even now, the California legislation is more effective in protecting the environment than is the Florida law.

The California land-use reformers had a number of political advantages over their Florida counterparts. The California Coastal Alliance, for instance, consisted of over 100 component organizations with 1400 local chapters across the state. It had a mailing list of over 1.5 million, and it worked with more than 600 other statewide organizations and their local chapters.[34] Florida had neither a comparable organization nor a comparable outpouring of citizen sentiment. The Florida law was the product of numerous legislative drafting sessions at which many of the main participants were its opponents. Several of the key sessions seem to have had no citizen representatives at all.[35]

The California reformers had an additional political advantage: their law only applied to a small part of the state. California's land-use problems were apparently perceived by the public as primarily coastal. Consequently, the reformers, who undoubtedly knew that the state had other land-use difficulties as well, decided to concentrate on dramatizing the coast. The Florida reformers made no such decision. Florida's provisions for developments of regional impact and for areas of critical state concern could, in principle, apply to any part of the state. Every Florida developer, landowner, and local government could rightly feel threatened by the law—if not immediately, then at least potentially. In California, however, comparatively few persons held property in the area, only about 200 square miles of the state's 159,000, that was actually to be regulated. For many voters, including those who held property elsewhere, the coastal issue often meant not environmental protection or private property rights but continued public access to beaches and other attractive shore areas. These persons were willing to vote for any measure that promised to preserve that access, which they considered their right.[36]

The opposition of California's local governments also was to some extent defused by the limited area to be regulated. The law did not affect noncoastal governments at all. It affected small, admittedly important portions of the jurisdictions of coastal governments. Both state and local officials also realized that many of their constituents saw the measure primarily as a matter of maintaining public access to the coast and tempered their reactions accordingly.[37]

The Loopholes

Legislators, even those who strongly support the land-use laws, point out that it is politically and physically impossible to regulate all activities that should, in theory, be regulated. The general inclination to limit regulatory activity is particularly strong in land-use reform, where new legislation involves the state government in a field in which local governments have operated undisturbed for decades. The local governments usually and development interests almost invariably oppose the intrusion of state officials on what has previously been a local or private preserve. And without the help of both groups, land-use reform laws may be, for all practical purposes, unenforceable. So it is sensible for the state to move cautiously, to avoid giving unnecessary offense.

The loopholes that result from legislative practicality or timidity are of two kinds: outright exemptions of all instances of specified types of development, and high thresholds of state intervention beneath which a great deal of unregulated development may take place.

EXEMPTIONS. In many states land-use laws have granted exemptions, as in Florida, to precisely those development interests that fought the laws hardest. As a result, these large, powerful industries remain substantially free to continue doing the environmental damage that presumably inspired the introduction of state land-use regulation in the first place. Indirectly and perhaps inadvertently, the exemption of certain industries also gives them an advantage over other, less powerful or less alert industries with which they are competing for land.

In Florida, for example, the state land-use law exempts construction for the politically influential agriculture, highway, and hotel industries. Vermont's law exempts nearly all construction for farming, forestry, power plants, and their many short (under 2200 feet) transmission lines; the only exception to the exemptions is the relatively small amount of building that occurs above 2500 feet. Farming is the largest single industry in the state, and the forestry and utilities industries are not much smaller.[38] California's 1976 coastal law, reflecting its origins in the state legislature, represents a retreat from the initiative-authorized 1972 law; it partially exempts development for agriculture and forestry, which are among the largest industries in the state.[39] Other state land-use laws provide comparable exemptions of politically powerful industries.[40]

In several states, certain industries have received exemptions not just because the industries wanted them but because state agencies already regulating them resisted giving up their powers. All Florida utility construction on existing rights-of-way, as well as most Vermont power-plant construction, is exempt from the state land-use laws largely because the two states' public service commissions have insisted on remaining solely responsible for regulating such construction. These commissions rarely take into account a proposed project's land-use effects.[41] The Vermont and Florida power companies have benefited accordingly.

THRESHOLDS. In Vermont and the Adirondacks, the laws vary the thresholds for state regulatory intervention, ostensibly to encourage the adoption of local land-use controls. But the thresholds in these laws and those elsewhere are often much higher than such encouragement requires. As a result, the states do not regulate many small projects that are individually negligible from the state standpoint, if not from the local one, but whose cumulative effects are massive from both perspectives.

Vermont's law, for instance, exempts developments smaller than one acre in towns that do not have zoning and subdivision laws, and developments smaller than ten acres in towns with such controls. But small gas stations, motels, stores, and restaurants can easily be built on less than an acre. Quite large ones—as well as fair-sized examples of leisure home projects, other housing construction, shopping centers, and industrial development—can be built on less than ten acres. In New York State, in areas designated as hamlets—the small towns that are the Adirondacks' only built-up residential areas—a developer can build subdivisions of up to 99 units without a permit from the Adirondack Park Agency if he does not build on swamps or marshes.

Florida, where the development-of-regional-impact process does not involve encouragement of local controls, has particularly high thresholds for DRIs. The threshold for residential building varies with the population of the county in which the project is to be located. In counties of less than 25,000, the state can intervene only in projects that have more than 250 housing units. In counties of more than 500,000—as of the 1970 census, the counties centered on Miami, Tampa–St. Petersburg, Jacksonville, and Fort Lauderdale—the state can intervene only in projects that have more than 3000 units. The state can intervene in factory and industrial park construction only if it includes parking for at least 2500 cars. Shopping centers smaller than 40 acres and with parking for fewer than 2500 cars, strip mining (in Florida, mainly for phosphates) disturbing less than 100 acres annually, and public and private colleges of fewer than 3000 students also are exempt from state regulation. All elementary and secondary schools, regardless of size, are similarly exempt.

Builders who have a choice are widely acknowledged to be deliberately ducking under the thresholds, often choosing to string out large numbers of small projects.[42] But as Montpelier attorney Jonathan Brownell, one of the authors of the Vermont law, has written:

the aggregate of the small, haphazard and unplanned developments not falling within the state jurisdiction, which may be ignored or granted blanket
variances by the local jurisdiction, can cause as great or greater pollution of
our water and air, cause as severe an impact on our existing roads and
schools, and result in as great a loss of our farm and forest productivity as
those developments our statutes define as large enough to be of "critical state
concern."[43]

In effect, then, the high thresholds encourage exactly the sprawl and
environmental degradation the laws were intended to limit.

A North Florida developer who had difficulties in getting state
approval for his project commented that if he had it to do over again
he would redesign to keep under the thresholds:

We thought we had convinced the locals of the benefits of our condominium
project, but apparently not. They got the regional planning [i.e., state]
people to come and take a close look. The regional people wanted a complete, million-dollar sewage system years before it would be heavily used.
They wanted our buildings to be set back 1000 feet from the beach in some
places and 500 feet everywhere. That would have cut off 180 single-family
lots and eleven holes from the golf course. And if there was pollution in the
bay for any reason, including one that had nothing to do with us, we would
have to stop building immediately. Ridiculous. They stopped us cold. We
should have built up the place in small pieces and stayed under the 250-unit
limit with each chunk. Our mistake. Just up the coast, there's a fellow
building a place with exactly 248 units. That number is no accident. The DRI
people know what he's doing, but they can't do a thing about it. That's the
way to go. (AI, Tallahassee, Florida, January 1976)

No reliable figures are available on the acreage, dollar value, or
volume of development under regulation. But the officials in charge
of the six state programs examined here supplied estimates of the
percentage of their state's total relevant development they regulated.
In California, where until 1977 the coastal law covered all coastal
development above the level of home repairs, the estimate was 95
percent or higher. In the Adirondacks, where the stringency of the
law has been the subject of local complaints, estimates clustered
around 50 percent. In Vermont, where the complaints have not
been quite so loud, they were around 30 percent.[44] In Florida, which
plainly has the least demanding program of the six, they were around
10 or 15 percent.

The Pennsylvania strip-mining and Maryland power plant siting programs, like similar efforts to regulate energy development in other states, cover all significant construction in their fields. For the most part, such programs lack thresholds because the power and strip-mining companies—the interests regulated—do not want them or need them. They consider it impossibly expensive and inefficient to try to operate large numbers of separate small power plants and, to a lesser extent, strip mines. The economies of scale favor large projects. So the regulation of energy development need not try to prevent the equivalent of sprawl—many small projects with impacts that are individually small but collectively massive. Energy developers, unlike other developers, do not bother to fight for high thresholds.

The energy-development laws also lack thresholds in part because the land-use reform movement has taken the position that no power plant or strip mine is too small to need regulation. To many environmentalists and land-use reformers, all strip mining is inherently offensive. In many states, there have been attempts, none successful, to ban it entirely. (Occasionally, such campaigning leads to grand but empty gestures; in 1971, West Virginia prohibited strip mining in the twenty-two counties where it had never been practiced.[45]) Land-use reform advocates generally consider the environmental effects of all fossil-fuel and nuclear power plants equally objectionable and take great interest in alternatives, such as solar energy. Environmentalists and land-use reformers may consider such details as the size, location, or technology of particular strip mines or power plants in certain cases, but they do not regard these matters as the central issue. The land use is considered objectionable in itself, and all instances of it have to be regulated.

But not even the most ardent land-use reformer argues for state regulation of all residential development or even all commercial or public works developments—not if he or she wants to have any political effectiveness. The movement has generally sought to regulate only developments that seem likely to cause significant environmental damage, and it has usually equated potential damage with large developments. Thus, the state laws include thresholds, the heights of which vary with the strength of the opposition toward reform. However reluctantly, the movement has conceded to local government the regulation of projects below the threshold.

Constrained Powers

In addition to loopholes, the land-use laws contain: (1) procedural restrictions on the application of regulatory powers; (2) provisions for substantial representation of development interests and local governments in the regulatory agencies; (3) gaps between state and local jurisdiction through which regulated interests can slip to avoid regulation; (4) insufficient financing and staffing for the agencies; and (5) inadequate citizen-participation provisions.

RESTRICTIONS ON APPLICATION OF POWERS.   The Adirondack Park Agency cannot directly regulate the two-fifths of the park that is owned by New York's Department of Environmental Conservation. The agency can only offer advice to the department on what to do with its lands. The law requires the agency to include these areas in its plan, but the plan is in no way binding on the department.[46] This restriction has meant that the agency, which was supposed to control the large amount of development needed for the 1980 Lake Placid Winter Olympics, was frequently unable to regulate this construction since much of it occurred on state land (and a good deal of the remainder fell beneath the threshold for APA intervention applicable in the town of Lake Placid).[47]

Similarly, Maryland's Power Plan Siting Program can only advise the state's Public Service Commission, which makes the final decision on power plant proposals. What is called the commission's ten-year state plan for plant siting consists of the collected individual plans submitted by the state's power companies.[48] The law requires the commission to accept without question or comment the company estimates. Both the commission and the Power Plant Siting Program must confine their environmental reviews of proposals to land-use, pollution, and public health issues. In neither the plan nor the reviews can they, for example, examine the state's actual need for a proposed plant or the effect a proposed plant may have on the state's energy consumption.

REPRESENTATION OF DEVELOPMENT INTERESTS AND LOCAL GOVERNMENT.   All of the commissioners of the Florida regional planning councils that evaluate DRI proposals are locally elected officials. Under both the 1972 and 1976 California coastal laws, half the members of the regional commissions must come from local government. Beginning in mid-1981, half the members of the state commission must come from local government.[49] Similarly, five of the eleven members of New York's Adirondack Park Agency must be residents of the park. Given the park's chronic poverty, these members generally can be expected to favor development proposals, as can the state secretary of commerce, who is an ex officio member of the agency.[50] The legislation that created the agency also created an Adirondack Park Local Government Review Board, an official watchdog organization consisting of twelve park residents, each appointed by one of the twelve park counties. The board has consistently opposed the agency, has held a series of public hearings critical of it, and has issued recommendations that would in effect abolish it.[51]

Pennsylvania's Bureau of Surface Mine Reclamation, which does not have a board of commissioners, has not experienced this kind of penetration, but other states, such as Texas, Kansas, Alabama, and West Virginia, have. The strip-mining laws of these states specify that such persons as coal operators, residents of heavy coal-producing counties, and mining engineers be assigned seats on the boards.[52]

GAPS IN JURISDICTION. The laws frequently create relationships between state and local regulatory bodies that permit and sometimes encourage local governments and developers to escape the laws. These constraints do not appear in power plant and strip-mine laws because local government typically does little to regulate these developments. But they appear in most other land-use laws. For example, the 1976 California coastal law, as amended in 1978, gives localities until July 1981 to produce land-use controls acceptable to the regional commissions but forces the commissions to go out of existence at that date. A recalcitrant city may benefit from stalling until the regional commissions are defunct. It could then submit its controls to the state commission, which, being far from the local scene and preoccupied with other tasks, might be able to give them only cursory attention.

Moreover, controls that are strong on paper and have been approved by the regional or state commission do not by themselves guarantee adequate local land-use regulation. If a city is too free about giving out zoning variances, this abuse may not come to light until its effects are irreversible. The requirement that a state land-use commission review local controls at least every five years after approval may have little deterrent effect on a city eager for development.

The Vermont law, like the Adirondack and 1976 California legislation, allows a locality to reduce the state's jurisdiction over its land by enacting land-use controls. But unlike the others, Vermont's law does not require that the controls be approved at the state or regional level. At a 1975 land-use conference Governor Thomas Salmon accurately described local controls in the state as consisting mostly of "one-acre zoning and one-page plans."[53] The controls are deficient because the localities want them that way and have made sure that the state land-use law is compatible with their wishes.

In Florida, the provisions concerning developments of regional impact offer localities a whole series of escapes. If a development big enough to be a DRI is proposed for a city or county with no land-use controls and the locality does not adopt them within ninety days, then the DRI process never comes into play at all. The development is not regulated by either the state or the locality. This provision gives developers incentives to build in localities without controls. It also gives these areas, most of which are rural and may constitute nearly half the state, incentives *not* to introduce controls. In effect, then, the law drives development toward those parts of the state least willing to regulate it.

Once activated, the DRI process consists of the preparation of a report by the regional planning council concerning the development's probable environmental and economic effects. The regional council merely advises the locality, which in most cases makes the final regulatory decision. In principle, the regional planning council, the Division of State Planning, or the developer may appeal the local decision to the governor and cabinet, but in practice such appeals have been relatively rare.[54]

INSUFFICIENT FINANCING AND STAFFING. The state land-use laws often do not provide enough money or staff to enable the agencies to perform their tasks effectively. Vermont's Act 250, for example, has a budget of about $250,000 and a professional staff of about ten. The seven district environmental coordinators have to double up to cover the nine district environmental commissions. And they have to administer approximately thirty other state permit programs—for instance, sewage disposal, water supply, and pollution efforts—in addition to Act 250.[55] The executive secretary of the program has estimated that eleven additional professionals—a doubling of the present staff—would be needed to administer the program adequately.[56]

The Florida program is equally hard-pressed. The land-use portions of the Division of State Planning (since 1979 the Bureau of Land and Water Management) usually have a budget and staff about half the size of the Dade County Planning Department in Miami.[57] The division also disburses about $500,000 to the eleven regional planning councils.[58] The regional councils perform many other duties—for instance, planning for economic development, transportation, criminal justice systems, and housing—besides administering the state land-use law.[59] The councils rarely have as much as one full-time staff person assigned to DRIs. In 1973, the director of the Division of State Planning estimated that it would take $3.5 million annually to "fully implement" the law.[60]

Other state land-use agencies also are short on money and staff.[61] The Adirondack Park Agency could, its top officials estimate, use a staff of sixty-five (as of late 1979 it had forty-eight), and it has not been able to give town and county governments more than a few thousand dollars each to produce the local land-use controls it requires. State agencies dealing with energy development are especially understaffed. The Maryland Power Plant Siting Program and Public Service Commission together have at most ten professionals to regulate hundreds of millions of dollars' worth of power plant construction annually and to monitor billions of dollars' worth of power plant operation. Pennsylvania's Bureau of Surface Mine Reclamation has not hired enough inspectors, especially to keep pace with the expansion of bituminous coal mining in the western part of the state. In 1971, the bureau's twenty inspectors were having trouble covering about 800 stripping operations on 16,000 acres.[62] In 1979, according to the bureau, the number of inspectors had increased to thirty-five, but they were responsible for perhaps 5000 operations on about 80,000 acres.

INADEQUATE CITIZEN PARTICIPATION. Few of the laws have strong citizen-participation provisions.[63] California has such provisions, but its coastal law originated in a citizen-sponsored initiative, and is now receiving funds from the federal coastal zone management program, which requires extensive citizen participation. Citizen participation also is strong in Vermont, where the New England town meeting tradition remains alive. In Maryland, too, the Power Plant Siting Program and the Public Service Commission are sensitive to charges that their operations and the power companies' could easily preempt local government and ignore citizen sentiment.

But Florida's law, formulated without citizen participation, virtually excludes citizens from reviews of developments of regional impact. The DRI procedure essentially takes place among existing organized interests—the developer, the local government, the regional council, and, if the decision is appealed, the Bureau of Land and Water Management, the governor, and the cabinet. The law provides no room—and no legal standing—for citizens who want to oppose or modify a project proposal.

In addition, the Florida regional council has only fifty days to prepare its report for the local government, insufficient time for the council to examine the potential consequences of a large and complex project and for citizens to organize to influence the local decision. If the interests of a local environmental group happen to coincide with those of a local government on the council—as they might, say, in the case of a proposed shopping center that would cause high levels of pollution and traffic for surrounding communities but yield them no taxes—then the environmental viewpoint may get a hearing. But under these circumstances environmental arguments may lack credibility with the government in whose jurisdiction the project would be located. And in any case the regional council can only offer advice.

Pennsylvania's citizen-participation provisions are, if anything, even weaker. The law requires the Bureau of Surface Mine Reclamation to give public notice of and hold public hearings regarding proposed stripping operations only if they adjoin a home, a highway, or public land. Notices of pending applications appear in the *Pennsylvania Bulletin*, a monthly journal published by the state. Subscriptions in 1979 cost $35, a high price for an underfinanced citizens' group to pay. A citizen or group wishing to challenge a bureau decision has to go through a complex legal procedure charging the state employee in question—not the bureau itself—with willful failure to uphold the law.[64] This sort of charge is difficult to prove; the individual's failure may well be inadvertent. Ernest Preate, Jr., an assistant district attorney in Scranton who opposes strip mining, has commented that the provision "seems more designed to inhibit citizen suits than to permit them."[65] Other state strip-mining laws raise comparable obstacles to suits.[66]

Similarly, the Adirondack Park Agency does not have to give public notice that it has received a development application, and can decide on a project without public hearings. It does not have to make any of its decisions, regulatory or otherwise, in meetings that are open to the public. It does not grant requests from individuals or groups for notice of all hearings about a proposed project, although it does supply notice of particular hearings to citizens who request it. Citizens and environmental groups do not have full legal standing to participate in agency hearings and so cannot cross-examine witnesses. In contrast, at New York's Department of Environmental Conservation, such groups have full standing, including the right to cross-examine.[67]

The Lack of Standards

The state land-use laws rarely establish clear development standards for the land-use agencies to uphold. Apart from a broad commitment to improving land-use practices by means of centralized regulation, the laws generally lack precise policies or objectives. This lack can be justified on a number of grounds. First, even the experts do not agree on absolute standards for good land use or for good land-use regulatory decisions. Second, in legislative battles, laws that are too specific might be impossible to pass. Moreover, laws that are vague or lacking in standards give the land-use agencies that are to implement them administrative discretion. Detailed standards might inhibit regulatory flexibility in the face of unforeseeable circumstances, special local conditions, information that might emerge only after regulation is actually under way, or the sheer complexity of many regulatory decisions.

Vermont's law states that district environmental commissions are to judge projects on the basis of their likely effects on water and air pollution, water supplies, soil erosion, traffic, aesthetics, the cost of school facilities and other public services, and conformity with state, local, and regional plans.[68] But the law does not define unacceptable levels of pollution, water depletion, erosion, or anything else, nor does it suggest how they might be defined.

Similarly, the Adirondack Plan sets forth thirty-seven "development considerations" that the Adirondack Park Agency is to take into account in every regulatory decision.[69] These factors, in general quite similar to those in Vermont, cover such matters as water quality, topography, air quality, noise levels, unique natural features, wildlife, aesthetics, historic sites, public service costs, and conformity with state and local land-use controls. But nowhere does the plan set any criteria for them or suggest any means of setting criteria.

Some of the other laws are, if anything, even vaguer. The Florida law requires that the regional planning council examine a proposed DRI's environmental, economic, public service, transportation, housing, and (as of 1976) energy impacts. But it never tells how the impacts should be investigated or against what criteria they should be judged.[70] The Maryland Public Service Commission need only find that a proposed power plant will not cause harm; the power plant siting law does not specify what such harm might be or how it might be measured.[71] Other state land-use laws are equally vague.[72]

But the California coastal law, because of its popular origin and limited geographic scope, has relatively precise standards. For example, any development that involves dredging or filling wetlands reduces the size of beaches or public access to them, blocks the view of the ocean from the nearest state highway, or affects water quality, fisheries, or agricultural land must be approved by two-thirds of the commission membership rather than a simple majority.[73]

The Pennsylvania strip-mining law is even more specific. Strip-mining laws—although widely believed to serve the interests of coal operators—tend to be quite specific,[74] in part because the damage caused by strip mining is obvious and strip-mining technology is comparatively simple to understand.[75] Pennsylvania's law requires coal operators to make no cut in the earth that exceeds 1500 feet at any one time. It defines certain areas—roads, streams, parks, cemeteries, and slopes over forty degrees—from which stripping operations must keep specified distances away. It also restricts locations for disposal of debris, defines the level of water quality that must be maintained in mine drainage, and restricts the choice of mining procedures. It requires, too, that after mining, operators restore the land to its approximate original contour.[76]

Pennsylvania's law could be stronger still. It includes no specific requirements for revegetation of mined sites. The approximate-original-contour standard for reclamation does not guarantee that land, especially farmland, will be restored to its original productivity or that streams, forests, wildlife, or aquifers will be preserved. Only a handful of coal counties have even a few slopes over forty degrees, and restoring slopes that exceed twenty-five degrees to their original contour generally is uneconomical.[77] Hence, sharply sloped land is seldom stripped in Pennsylvania, and the forty-degree prohibition is largely meaningless. Nonetheless, Pennsylvania's strip-mining law, like California's coastal one, is stronger, clearer, and more specific than most state land-use laws.

Laws that lack standards create a number of practical problems. They give little guidance to the regulatory agencies on how they should regulate. They are uninformative to development interests as to how they should build. They give environmental groups no benchmarks against which to measure the performance of the regulatory agencies or developers. Thus, such laws deprive the agencies, development interests, and environmental groups of objective physical criteria for their own performance and that of the others. The lack of criteria also deprives courts of a basis for judgment.

The Implications of the Concessions

Compromises have always been the very stuff of American politics. But because of the compromises that they embody, the land-use laws are not really environmental legislation at all, but rather legislation that balances environmental and economic interests. Many public officials view the laws favorably for precisely this reason. An aide to Washington Senator Henry Jackson, one of the chief congressional sponsors of the proposed National Land Use Policy Act, described it as designed

as much to save us from the environmental movement as to encourage the continuation of that movement. . . . The purpose of the bill is to balance economic, social and environmental concerns. . . . The bill is a typical Jackson bill in the sense that it has been attacked from both extremes. It has been attacked by environmentalists; it has been attacked by certain members of the business community and by such ideological groups as the Liberty Lobby. We regard that as a sign that perhaps the balance is in the bill.[78]

The state land-use laws, as their administrators often acknowledge, do exactly the same kind of balancing.[79] "Any day I don't catch it from the builders in the morning and the bird-and-bunny people in the afternoon is a day I'm not doing my job well," a Vermont state land-use official said. "The way I know I'm on the right track is when I get attacked by the extremists on both sides. By their attacks, they clarify the middle for me" (AI, Essex Junction, Vermont, September 1975). The chairman of a California regional commission well known for its environmentalism stated: "Our law, and certainly the 1972 version of it, was put in by zealots. The commission's job is to make sure they don't run away with it. The law is often impossibly, unworkably anti-developer, so we sometimes have to smooth out that bias" (AI, Santa Cruz, California, August 1975).

This emphasis on balancing competing interests helps account for a number of features of the laws. It explains why laws such as Florida's or Vermont's that regulate all kinds of development in all parts of a state tend to be weaker than those regulating only one kind of development (e.g., Pennsylvania) or one part of a state (e.g., California). The single-purpose or single-area laws do not have to balance as many interests as the multipurpose or whole-state laws; it is easier to achieve a consensus for them. They are enacted and implemented in a much simpler political and administrative setting, one that also limits the amount of technical information needed to resolve conflicts.[80]

The practice of having land-use legislation balance opposed interests also helps explain why no large, heavily developed state has enacted, or has even come close to enacting, a comprehensive land-use law that covers all its territory; it would be impossible to balance so many interests. Florida has a comprehensive law, but it is relatively weak because it has to balance so many opposed groups. Arthur Davis, director of the Pennsylvania Land Policy Project, wrote:

The job of balancing uses and benefits of various kinds of land becomes more difficult as the economy of the state or region becomes more complex. It is no slight to such states as Vermont, Maine, or Nebraska to point out that their land use problems are less varied and therefore, on the whole, less complex than those of a major, industrial, urbanized state, such as Pennsylvania. Perhaps this is the reason that none of the so-called "big" states have yet adopted comprehensive land use policies or programs. . . . Whether states such as Pennsylvania, New York, Ohio, Illinois, and Michigan take steps in this direction will depend on the ability of planners to present useful, effective, and realistic answers to the difficult and complex land use problems such states face. This requires going well beyond environmental determinism. It demands that a balance be struck between environmental protection, economic imperatives, and social priorities.[81]

Yet, as the Florida case suggests, striking this balance in large states is a politically difficult task whose results, from the point of view of land-use reformers, may turn out to be disappointing. So the task has rarely been undertaken, much less satisfactorily accomplished.

It is now clear that the state land-use laws exemplify what Lowi calls interest-group liberalism: they are the products of clashing interest groups that institutionalize their own presence within the mechanism of government. These laws therefore embody compromises between the groups and delegate a great deal of discretionary power to their administrators. Yet the laws give the administrators little real guidance about how they should be implemented. They create new centralized regulatory powers but do not try to determine how they will be used. They establish a political process without attempting to influence the decisions it will produce. The contending interests are left to struggle among themselves.

CHAPTER 7

The Public
Implementation Struggle

Once the laws were passed, the political controversy over state land-use regulation changed dramatically. It entered a more open, more public setting, where the actual decisions of operating regulatory programs were at issue and became fiercer. It became more vivid to more people; it directly affected real communities, projects, incomes, and lives.

Skirmishes: Appointments, Budgets, Staffing, and Enforcement

Many of the issues and concerns that emerged as the programs began to be carried out had their origins in the drafting of the land-use laws. For example, all the members of the Florida regional planning councils, half the members of the California regional coastal commissions (and, as of mid-1981, of the state coastal commission), nearly half the members of the Adirondack Park Agency (APA), and a good proportion of the members of many state strip-mining boards are required by law to come from either local government or the relevant branch of the development industry.

Such appointments also occur informally as a result of some combination of political pressure, the desire for balance in the implementation of the laws, and a simple recognition that the regulated inter-

116

ests know a lot about the activities to be regulated and have a serious, entirely legitimate stake in how the laws are carried out. In Vermont, the governor has typically appointed someone with a background in local government or land development (or both) as one of the three members of each district environmental commission and has provided comparable representation of these interests on the state Environmental Board.[1] One of the three members of Maryland's Public Service Commission customarily has a background in corporate utility law—that is, in defending power companies.

In 1977, Judy Rosener of the University of California at Irvine conducted an empirical study of how the appointments affect implementation. At the time, Rosener was a member of the Los Angeles area regional commission; later, she became a member of the state coastal commission. Polling those who had been members of the Los Angeles and San Diego area commissions between 1973 and 1975, she found that 52 percent of the commissioners who came from local government had voted in 1972 against the coastal initiative. Only 21 percent of the commissioners who did not come from local government—the so-called public members—had voted against the initiative. Moreover, the more local the constituency of the local government member, the more likely he or she was to have voted against the initiative. That is, 78 percent of city council members voted against the initiative, while only 25 percent of county supervisors did so.[2]

Rosener also examined the behavior of the commissioners in day-to-day regulatory practice over more than 19,000 individual votes. As a group the public members of the commissions voted against 24 percent of proposed development projects, while local government members voted against only 11 percent. County supervisors voted against 16 percent of proposed projects, while city council members voted against only 10 percent.[3]

Moreover, city council members voted against 10 percent of the projects located outside but only 7 percent of those located inside their own constituencies. (In contrast, the county supervisors voted against 15 percent of the projects outside their constituencies and 17 percent of those inside.) Finally, commissioners without substantial business affiliations (as determined by the questionnaire) voted against 21 percent of the proposed projects, while those with such affiliations voted against only 15 percent.[4]

The failure of the laws to provide adequately for financing and staffing of the state agencies also has come back to haunt implementation. From the beginning, many agencies found themselves overwhelmed by the volume of applications that came before them. And as a result of the financial constraints that have afflicted most state governments in recent years, they have been unable to increase their budgets or staffs.

This debility has been a serious problem in Pennsylvania where in 1977, a state budget crisis at one point threatened to cripple the entire Department of Environmental Resources, which contains the Bureau of Surface Mine Reclamation.[5] It has been less of a problem in Florida, where the collapse of the development market in the mid-1970s substantially reduced the number of applications for developments of regional impact.[6] But most state land-use agencies have been overwhelmed with both applications and complaints from developers and local governments about delays and backlogs in processing.[7] Of course, those who make these complaints do not lobby for increases in funding or staffing for the agencies; their objective is to discredit the agencies and their function.

"Bureaucrats ought to be overworked," said the head of the Maryland Power Plant Siting Program (AI, Annapolis, Maryland, December 1975), and the state land-use ones certainly are. For example, the Los Angeles area regional coastal commission, which usually receives over 3000 applications per year, in 1979 employed only nine staff members to review them.[8] These officials naturally spend most of their time on proposals for large projects. Nearly all proposals for single-family homes and most for other small developments are administratively approved at the staff level and do not go to the commissioners.[9] The only exceptions are especially large homes, projects that seem poorly designed from an environmental point of view, or projects that are located in areas of exceptional environmental sensitivity. Thus, the regional commissioners review fewer than 10 percent of the applications for single-family homes along the Los Angeles area coast.[10] Large numbers of applications for small homes and other small projects get through the commission without any serious examination of their environmental effects, which may be individually negligible but collectively massive. In short, the lack of financing and staffing has the same effects as a high threshold for agency jurisdiction.

This problem shows up along the rest of the California coast[11] and in several other states.[12] In Maryland, where the sole objects of state regulation are small numbers of large power plants, the problem does not arise. But elsewhere an overworked and underfunded staff, knowing that it cannot handle all the applications before it, focuses on the largest projects and lets many of the smaller ones go. Developers, particularly small ones, profit from this practice.

Budget and staff shortages also impair the ability of state land-use agency staffs to inspect development projects for compliance with their rulings. Again, the developers and local governments that consistently opposed increased funding and staffing for the agencies may have done so precisely for the purpose of disabling them. But in any case, few state agencies do much enforcement work. Staff members sometimes visit and investigate the suitability of the sites of proposed developments, especially large ones. But they do not monitor development activities to make sure that they have received applications for all the projects that legally require agency approval. Nor, for the most part, do they systematically check projects in progress or in operation for compliance with the conditions placed on them by the state agency. A few developers—usually those involved in small projects or even isolated single-family homes—have been prosecuted, fined, or even jailed, but even these questionable examples of vigorous enforcement are rare.[13]

In general, the agencies seem to operate on the land-use equivalent of the honor system. Vermont's land-use program went into effect in 1970; in 1975, for the first time, the state assigned three people, two of them part-time, to make spot checks to enforce Act 250 and the thirty or so other state permit programs related to land use.[14] The Florida program has never had any enforcement staff; the regional planning councils are not empowered to check for violations of DRI (development of regional impact) orders, and the local governments, which are, rarely do.[15] California, with its 1100-mile coast, has no staff member assigned to enforcement; as one citizen activist put it, "To the commissions, enforcement is a matter of relying on neighbors running in and tattling" (ATI, Los Angeles, California, May 1978). Eventually, the state will hand enforcement responsibility over to local governments, few of which are likely to discharge them with greater diligence than the state has shown. The Adirondack Park Agency had two people working full-time on enforcement problems until early 1976, when local objections forced the curtailment of their activities.

Lacking the means to do otherwise, a Vermont state land-use official said, "We like to think we can trust our applicants" (AI, Montpelier, Vermont, September 1975). But a Vermont builder stated: "It is easy to cheat on the permit orders. Nobody ever comes by to check up on them. Nobody ever has" (AI, Burlington, Vermont, June 1976).

A *Los Angeles Times* survey of the effects of the 1972 coastal law in the Morro Bay area north of Santa Barbara found that "there has been little enforcement of the act so some projects have been constructed without permits. Others have been granted permits with conditions but the contractors have not complied with the conditions."[16] A developer was quoted as saying: "Who are they going to send out and check up on you? What are they going to do, revoke your permit after the house is up?"[17] In one development approved by the regional commission, nine of the planned twenty-eight homes were not merely built but actually occupied at the time of approval.[18]

The state agencies are not financed or staffed extensively enough to be able to find violators or to undertake strong—that is, deterrent—enforcement, especially against the kind of large developer who can pay for solid legal representation to appeal the enforcement. And, as an observer of the Vermont land-use scene has pointed out, "Without investigators to discover violations, there has been very little to prosecute."[19] The state agencies typically receive their information about violations in the form of citizen complaints; these are often officious, trivial, self-serving, or erroneous. District attorneys' offices usually feel they have more pressing cases to pursue. The state agency, too, may be reluctant to subject any portion of the land-use law or agency procedures to a test in court. In some states, such as Florida and, after the passage of state-approved local coastal controls, California, enforcement of the law is largely the province of local governments that may not have been eager to see the law passed in the first place.[20]

By far the largest, costliest, most technologically complex, hard-to-manage developments the state land-use agencies regulate—and the ones whose environmental consequences are most dangerous if something goes wrong—are power plants. None of Maryland's power companies has ever been found violating the directives of the

Public Service Commission. But neither the commission nor the Power Plant Siting Program inspects for compliance with the regulations. Even with the best of intentions, it seems unlikely that all regulated power companies have always complied perfectly.

Pennsylvania's strip-mining program, like most programs that regulate mining, has put a great deal of effort into inspection. Yet the program has still had difficulties with enforcement. It employs thirty-five inspectors and an equal number of engineers, foresters, and geologists, who continually visit stripping sites, but many of these staff members have been recruited from strip-mining companies. Until it was superseded by the 1971 law, a law enacted in 1945 had required that strip mines be monitored by inspectors with practical experience in strip mining. The Pennsylvania Bureau of Surface Mine Reclamation still employs many inspectors hired before 1971 and has hired others since who qualified for the job because they had experience working for stripping companies.

Each inspector is responsible, on the average, for about one hundred fifty separate stripping operations. The Bureau of Surface Mine Reclamation directs its inspectors to make unannounced visits to each site once a month. But it takes two to four hours to inspect a small site—say, ten acres—and six to eight hours to inspect a large one, say, one hundred acres.[21] Automobile travel between sites also takes time. In a month of twenty-two working days, even a conscientious inspector is unlikely to visit more than forty stripping operations—little more than a quarter of the hundred fifty that are his responsibity.

Inspection itself is difficult, both physically and psychologically. On the many sites that are over 100 acres, some serious but easily detectable violations—such as allowing excessively acidic water to drain from the mining—can be temporarily corrected before the inspector comes by. Coal operators and miners who do not try to deceive the inspectors may prefer, instead, to intimidate them. The inspector, after all, is alone on an isolated site, entirely surrounded by men who may perceive what he is doing as an attempt to diminish or cut off their livelihood. They may be neighbors of the inspector, they may be in a position to offer him a better paying job with the coal company, or they may, at least in the anthracite regions of eastern Pennsylvania, have connections with organized crime or be willing to hint at them.[22] Even if no corrupt transaction occurs, even if no money changes hands, an inspector may for any of several reasons choose to overlook violations. For instance, during 1974, a year of intense activity in the coalfields, the inspectors reported no anthracite violations whatsoever.[23]

Pennsylvania has, however, achieved tougher environmental enforcement than most other state land-use agencies. A Pennsylvania strip-mining official reported:

We've been after the coal operators both directly and through the inspectors. We fired an inspector in 1971. He'd been taking payoffs, which came to light when we noticed that reclamation in his area wasn't up to snuff. More recently, we had an inspector who was sick and wasn't getting around to his sites. We started to hear rumors that the operators were taking advantage of his absence. The head of our program went out to look and sure enough, there were violations all over the place. On the spot, Bill shut down every one of those operations. He got away with it, too; none of the operators had the guts to complain. They cleaned up their operations and went back to work. I think we taught them a lesson they'll never forget. The nerve of them: taking advantage of a sick man and at the same time yelling about how rough the law is on them. We've heard very little yelling from them since. (AI, Harrisburg, Pennsylvania, October 1975)[24]

By 1979, the Bureau of Surface Mine Reclamation's inspectors were using helicopters to spot violations from the air, to make more inspections per day, and to avoid intimidation by operators. They were using computers to identify operators with poor reclamation records and to schedule them for more frequent inspection. They were filing criminal charges against operators who violated state requirements or tried to bribe inspectors. And they were focusing on watersheds with especially prominent environmental damage or evidence of violations by operators.[25]

Skirmishes: Citizen Participation, Standards, and Information

In 1974, the executive director of the California state coastal commission warned an audience at the Conservation Foundation:

Don't think you can pass a law that sets up an agency and then go on to the next battle. It may drive you nuts, but unfortunately you can't. The people being regulated will capture the regulatory agency without exception if the public doesn't stay interested. If the public ever loses interest in any of these regulatory agencies, they're dead as doornails, and you might as well wipe them out.[26]

The public has for the most part taken this warning to heart. Except in Pennsylvania, where the land-use law makes relatively little provision for citizen participation, environmentalists generally approve of the way in which such provisions are administered. Even in the Adirondacks, where the law is not much stronger than Pennsylvania's in provisions for citizen participation, the Adirondack Park Agency has responded to local pressure for such participation. For instance, the law does not obligate the agency to make its decisions in meetings open to the public; but in practice, the agency has made all its recent decisions in open sessions.

The California coastal program, largely because of its origins in a citizen initiative and continuing popular support, but to some extent also because of the requirements of the federal coastal zone management legislation, has extensive citizen-participation features. During the preparation of the state's coastal plan, the commission solicited literally thousands of comments from the public.[27]

Developers, on the other hand, are less than pleased. Not long ago, a Palo Alto developer stalked out of a coastal commission meeting, furious because the commission had referred his proposal for completing an already-started beachfront condominium project to a citizens' committee for comment—the fourth such group, he said, that had passed on his application since its inception, over a year earlier. He raged:

I don't know where these so-called citizens came from, except maybe out of the woodwork. Most of them seem to be bored housewives with nothing to do with their time. You never see or hear from these people except when they cause trouble for a builder or invent some new animal or strange biological process or kook sociological function that the project, bless their little hearts, would disturb. I don't know how much of a constituency these people really have, and I don't think anybody does. They probably don't represent anybody but themselves, but they've got me stymied good, damn them. If my project doesn't go through, two million dollars and ten years of my life disappear. How would you like to spend years of your life writing a book, and then have some nice little group come out of nowhere and tell you you can't publish it because part of it is pornographic? How would you feel? (AI, Santa Cruz, California, August 1975)

Of course, citizen participation cannot please everyone, and it is unlikely to please anyone all the time. It is an inherently untidy, unpredictable process (which in the end allowed the Palo Alto builder to finish his project). It provides an occasion for the emergence of the various parties' latent feelings of misunderstanding and persecution, the sense of all sides that their opponents essentially control the instruments of government. Environmental groups frequently complain of being listened to for the sake of appearances and then mostly disregarded in the final regulatory decisions. "You talk and talk and talk," said a Maryland environmentalist, "and then you don't see a whole lot of evidence that they've heard anything you've said" (ATI, Rockville, Maryland, July 1979). Developers dislike the delays and procedural difficulties citizen participation creates. So, from a different perspective, do the officials of state and local land-use agencies. "Every time we hear from a new environmental group, my heart sinks a little bit," said a Vermont official. "Sure, they can bring up good points, things we ought to consider. But there's always a big chance they'll waste your time or set you off on a wild goose chase or just get the public mad at you. I'm an environmentalist myself, but I have to wonder what good some of these citizen groups are actually doing their cause" (ATI, Montpelier, Vermont, October 1979).

But not all the groups that show up at state land-use agency meetings or otherwise take part in the agencies' deliberations are environmentalist or anti-development. Many are developers' or construction workers' or businessmen's groups who support the projects in question. In relatively poor areas, such as the Adirondacks or California's North Coast, grass-roots citizens' groups attend the meetings to support projects that they feel will give the local economy a badly needed boost. Sometimes, local government officials appear before state land-use agencies to endorse proposals, especially for local public-works projects.

The diversity of groups, some for and some against development, that may take advantage of the state programs' citizen-participation provisions naturally makes the state officials wonder how representative any single group actually is of the population as a whole. In particular, many land-use agency officials believe that the environmental and citizens' groups that purport to speak most directly for the public at large in fact represent a limited, somewhat privileged constituency. As a Pennsylvania strip-mining official put it:

I know all those people out there screaming about how the coal operators are raping the land because they violated some minor order for ten minutes have safe, secure jobs in some line of work that's one hell of a lot less entrepreneurial and risky than the coal business. These people essentially have nothing to lose, and nothing to do with all those little communities that basically depend on the coal industry for livings that are very chancy even in the best of times. (AI, Harrisburg, Pennsylvania, October 1975)

An environmentalist California coastal commissioner said:

In some ways our citizen-participation procedures aren't honest. They're slanted toward smallish groups that want to present themselves as the public when they're really the same people, the same membership, over and over again. I resent it when the Sierra Club lobbyists get up and say they represent thousands of members who are all up in arms about some project. I'm a Sierra Club member, and I know those people don't represent me. (AI, Pacifica, California, August 1975)[28]

Because many of the laws lack explicit standards, the agencies have made some rulings on project proposals that seemed to be based on nothing more than pressure from developer or environmental groups or that could be attacked as such. This lack of standards has impaired the apparent legitimacy or fairness of agency decisions and has hampered agency effectiveness.

The difficulties produced by the lack of standards and the resulting uncertainty have provoked considerable complaint. "Our main task," said a Maryland power plant siting official, "has always been to humanize an impossibly vague law, to give some definition to a piece of legislation that didn't have it. Sometimes the absence of specifics drives us wild" (AI, Annapolis, Maryland, February 1976). The Florida land-use program has been criticized by one of its former officials for lacking any sort of "driving policy."[29] "Whenever you go to a district environmental commission," said a Vermont environmentalist, "you've got to be prepared to be surprised at what you find. The commissioners are groping, and sometimes they grope wrong" (AI, St. Johnsbury, Vermont, June 1976). "One of the main gripes I have with the APA," said an Adirondack builder, "is that it often doesn't seem to know what it wants me to do" (ATI, Saranac Lake, New York, November 1978).

M. Bruce Johnson, an economist at the University of California at Santa Barbara and former member of the Santa Barbara area regional commission, has written:

My fellow commissioners were unwilling to discuss, let alone publish and disseminate, a set of standards, rules or criteria that would have informed all interested parties what the commission wanted and did not want. No member of the public could reasonably infer the outcome of a particular issue until the case had been decided. Cases that came before us were handled on an *ad hoc* basis and, in my opinion, were decided by whim or chance. It was impossible to detect even after the fact any systematic theory or principle underlying the decisions of the commission.[30]

Several state agencies have recently begun efforts to clarify their standards in order to rationalize their operations, to protect themselves from political attack, and to avoid disorienting or alienating developers and environmentalists. In 1977, for instance, the Adirondack Park Agency published a set of guidelines on what building practices it would consider acceptable,[31] and in 1978 the Vermont Environmental Board produced a similar manual.[32]

In 1977 and 1978, the California coastal commissions embarked on the most ambitious and detailed attempt yet to spell out the demands of a state land-use law. Both the 1972 and the 1976 coastal laws included comparatively clear standards. The 1976 law also required each regional commission to issue "interpretive guidelines" as to how it would judge development proposals. These geographically based guidelines were not binding and were to be in effect for a community only until it produced acceptable coastal land-use controls of its own. The commissions produced the guidelines, after extensive consultations with citizens and the local governments; they were then approved by the state commission. Today, they are widely acknowledged to be influencing commission decisions and the direction of local controls.

The guidelines are in fact remarkably specific. The Los Angeles area commission's guidelines for Orange County, for instance, contain twenty-six pages, including charts, diagrams, and equations,[33] of detailed policies that apply throughout the county. Among other requirements, they specify that proposed developments should be set back at least twenty-five feet from the edge of any coastal bluff and that multiple-story commercial and public buildings with ocean views must make those views accessible to the public by such means as glass elevators and roof gardens.[34]

The guidelines also include twenty-one pages on specific communities and areas within them. For example, they state that the city of Seal Beach (population 28,000) should not have an overall density of more than thirty dwelling units per acre (except in specified areas of the city), and that its new buildings should not be taller than three stories or thirty-five feet (again with the exception of specified areas).[35] All the guidelines, both countywide and for communities, are set forth as elaborations of specific policies in the 1976 Coastal Act, most of which are in turn based on specific policies in the 1975 Coastal Plan. Having participated in the formulation of the guidelines, the county and municipal governments have not greatly objected to or (apparently) evaded them. The state and regional commissions have now begun to produce guidelines on functional issues such as geologic hazards, beach access, wetlands, low-income housing, new construction, condominium conversions, and wildlife habitat areas.

But implementation has encountered another law-based problem: information. The agencies make their decisions primarily on the basis of information provided by the applicants, information that naturally presents the applicants in the best possible light. "The builders always make their projects look so rosy in the applications," said a California coastal planner. "They never tell you about the drainage that won't drain or the wildlife they're slaughtering. The package they give you has entirely too much glossy wrapping. It's our job to try to see through it" (ATI, San Francisco, California, March 1977). But the agencies, understaffed and underfunded, rarely have good independent information sources of their own. And alternative sources—for example, citizen groups, other government agencies, perhaps even the applicant's competitors—may for various reasons not be entirely credible. "There is no way," a Pennsylvania strip-mining official maintained, "we will make a decision based solely on what some outsider organization or agency says" (ATI, Harrisburg, Pennsylvania, April 1978).

Yet the reliance of the agencies on developers' information in effect shifts the burden of proof in regulatory proceedings from the

regulated interest, where, according to the law, it belongs, to the
regulatory agency, which is ill-equipped to bear it. A key administrator of Maryland's Power Plant Siting Program commented:

It's true that the burden is nominally on the power companies, but that's too
legalistic, too mechanical a way to look at the situation. In fact, the burden is
at least as much on us. If we make recommendations to the Public Service
Commission about a project or about the conditions we want placed on it, we
have to be able to back them up. The only way to back them up is to use the
information the companies give us, but there are times when it is not all that
we would want it to be. It's a handicap we have to live with. (AI, Annapolis,
Maryland, December 1975)

Similarly, Paul Sabatier of the University of California at Davis
wrote of the California coastal commissions:

While Section 27402 of the [1972] Act explicitly places the burden on the
applicant to prove that the proposed development will not have any substantial adverse environmental effect, both commissions and their staffs have in
effect placed the burden of proof on their respective staffs; thus the presump-
tion is in favor of the applicant unless the staff can provide sufficient justification for denial.[36]

Skirmishes: Lobbying, Lawsuits, and Departures

In no state has the struggle over the implementation of a land-use
program been confined to the details of the program. Developers and
local governments have launched broad-scale political attacks aimed
at weakening or undoing the state agencies altogether. In 1974 the
Vermont Home Builders Association advocated that public hearings
be eliminated, that four of Act 250's ten criteria be dropped, that the
permit-processing period be cut to twenty days with automatic approval granted if the environmental commissions took no action, that
the commissions be elected rather than appointed, and that appeals of
their decisions should go directly to the courts rather than first to the
state Environmental Board.[37]

In its 1976 annual report, the Adirondack Park Local Government
Review Board recommended that all the powers of the Adirondack
Park Agency be transferred to the review board, and that the board be
required to exercise them so as to give more weight to economic than
to environmental factors and more to local than to state consid-

erations.[38] Early in the 1977 session of the New York State Senate, a senator from the Adirondacks with a long history of opposing the APA (he happened to be the husband of the Review Board's executive director) presented these recommendations in a bill.[39] Similar weakening bills have been introduced in other states. In 1979, the California Assembly approved a bill that would exempt from the coastal law 5600 acres in the Topanga Canyon area of the Santa Monica Mountains to permit construction of an 1800-unit subdivision of homes costing from $200,000 to $1 million.[40] None of the states has passed such bills, but they are evidence of continuing opposition to state land-use regulations.

In some states, this opposition has given rise to permanent organizations for the specific purposes of resisting the state agencies, keeping an eye on their operations, and fighting extensions of their powers. These groups typically are grass-roots organizations whose names emphasize their ties to the land, their small businessman's and farmer's conservatism, and their opposition to centralized regulation of any kind; several of them amount to anti-environmentalist citizens' organizations. Vermont has the Green Mountain Boys and the Landowners' Steering Committee; upstate New York has the Adirondack Minutemen and the League for Adirondack Citizens Rights; and the California coast has Straight Arrow and the California Citizens for Property Rights.

A few more politically moderate but financially high-powered operations have been formed by businessmen and labor leaders. The California Council for Environmental and Economic Balance, for example, was chaired until late 1977 by Edmund Brown, Sr., the former governor of California whose son was by then governor. The council publicly opposed most of the provisions of the California Coastal Plan when drafts of it were first published, and has consistently voiced reservations about the work of the coastal commissions.[41]

In state and local elections in Vermont, Florida, California, and the Adirondacks—areas with multiple-purpose programs that therefore affect large numbers of people—the land-use programs have become political issues. But the results of the elections show no clear overall trend; they seem, not surprisingly, to reflect the diversity of the state programs and the political conditions under which they operate rather than any broad-scale national consensus about land use. "Anybody running for public office in the Adirondacks," an opposition politician said, "has to be against the APA, just like anybody running for office in south Boston has to be against Northern Ireland" (AI, Long Lake, New York, June 1976). He was exaggerating, but anyone who seeks political office in the Adirondacks must take a position concerning the APA, and most politicians are critical of the agency. Along the California coast, on the other hand, most local politicians are likely to support the coastal commissions, with reservations.

In Vermont, the situation seems more mixed, at least at the state level. In the 1976 state elections, Republican gubernatorial candidate Richard Snelling pledged to weaken the administration of Act 250, succeeded in defeating a pair of candidates who promised the opposite, and once in office did little to redeem his campaign promise. In the same election Thomas Salmon, a Democrat, then governor and closely identified with Act 250, lost a senatorial campaign to incumbent Republican Robert Stafford, who made Salmon's general stand on environmental issues a major campaign issue. The winner of the 1978 Florida gubernatorial election was Democrat D. Robert Graham, the legislator most responsible for the passage of the state land-use law, but he did not greatly emphasize that particular achievement in his campaign; indeed, in a campaign speech to the Junior Chamber of Commerce in Key West (part of the Keys, which had been designated an "area of critical state concern"), he claimed that the Florida law produced some of "the poorest administered state programs in recent years."[42]

Some land-use laws have specifically come before the electorate in statewide campaigns. The 1972 California coastal initiative is, of course, an example. In 1974, the voters of Utah decisively rejected a state land-use program, which the legislature had just passed, after a citizens' coalition of developers and conservatives collected enough petition signatures to force a popular vote.[43] In 1976 Oregon's land-use program survived a similar challenge, and in 1978 it did so again by a greater margin, with the bulk of the increase coming from new support in the rural areas outside the Willamette Valley.[44]

In addition, the constitutionality of any strong state land-use law may be subject to politically motivated legal challenge. Developers in a number of states have brought suits arguing that the laws represent an unlawful taking of private property, abridge the powers of local governments, or create illegal, inequitable, or otherwise unjustifiable bureaucratic procedures. For example, in mid-1975 the Adirondack Park Agency was involved in seventeen legal actions; ten of the plaintiffs sought damages ranging from $200,000 to $36 million.[45]

Such suits rarely succeed in getting a state land-use law, agency, activity, or decision declared unconstitutional or in collecting any damages. In a typical finding, in 1976 the New York State Supreme Court ruled, against two developer plaintiffs, that the APA had the right to consider aesthetic and scenic values in its regulatory decisions. Later in the year, the New York State Court of Claims dismissed the $36 million suit brought against the APA by the Horizon Corporation of Arizona, which claimed that the agency's rulings had deprived the corporation of almost all economic use of its 24,000-acre property by substantially lowering its value. In later cases, state courts ruled against other builder suits, finding that the APA did not violate the home-rule provisions of the state constitution, was empowered to draw up a master plan for state-owned public lands, and had not attempted to impose a total freeze on all development within the park or to lower land values in one part of the park while raising them in another.[46] In formal legal terms, the findings of such suits upheld the positions and actions of the state land-use agencies.

But in more practical political and administrative terms, the suits harm the agencies. They drain enthusiasm, staff time, money, and credibility from the agencies. Even the threat of a suit inevitably inhibits the agencies somewhat. A Pennsylvania strip-mining official has said: "When I hear the lawyers for a coal company sounding like they're getting even a little bit serious about a court case instead of just flapping their mouths about it, I perk up. I hate the thought of having to gear up to fight another lawsuit, and I try to make sure I don't get gun-shy because of the possibility. It can be an effort. No question, the possibility of a suit makes me think twice" (ATI, Harrisburg, Pennsylvania, November 1977). As a California lawyer told it from the other side: "The trick is to convince those coastal commission bureaucrats that you want to cooperate with them, but at the same time to convey that you'll be a mean bastard in court if you're crossed" (AI, San Francisco, California, August 1975).

In the last few years, the developer opposition may have found a point of legal vulnerability in the laws: the absence of standards. In

1977–78, the American Petroleum Institute (API), the primary trade association of the oil industry, launched separate units in federal courts against the California, Wisconsin, and Massachusetts coastal zone programs. The API essentially charged that federal approval and funding of the programs was based on uncertain and therefore arbitrary procedural standards, in terms of both the programs' relations with the federal government and their operating regulatory powers. The three programs were upheld, but in his decision in the California case, Judge Robert Kelleher criticized Congress for trying to please too many interests when it passed the Coastal Zone Management Act:

> The message is as clear as it is repugnant. . . . Congress is constitutionally empowered to launch programs, the scope, impact, consequences, and workability of which are largely unknown, at least to the Congress, at the time of enactment; the federal bureaucracy is legally permitted to execute the Congressional mandate with a high degree of befuddlement as long as it acts no more befuddled than the Congress must reasonably have anticipated.[47]

The resulting regulations, he added, were "almost wholly unmanageable," but he nonetheless upheld the federal approval of the California program, saying that it was "consistent with the evident Congressional intent."[48]

In November 1978, in a decision on a pair of builder suits, the Florida Supreme Court actually struck down the provision of the state's land-use law allowing designation of "areas of critical state concern" because it lacked standards. The Division of State Planning (as of 1979 the Bureau of Land and Water Management) had used this provision to make subject to its approval the local land-use controls in the Green Swamp between Tampa and Orlando and in the Florida Keys, a chain of ninety-seven low-lying islands stretching from the tip of the Florida peninsula 130 miles west into the Gulf of Mexico. But the court found that the law had not specified environmental criteria for the designation or described how they would relate to other possible criteria. In the words of a Miami lawyer, "the court said the law was unconstitutional because there were no standards to guide administrative choice among competing state interests—nothing to distinguish environmental resources from historical, natural, or archaeological resources of statewide importance."[49]

In response, a special session of the state legislature met in early 1979 and redesignated the two areas as environmentally critical by law rather than by administrative action of the Division of State Planning. This action avoided the strictures of the Supreme Court, which applied to "administrative choice" but not to legislative enactments. The legislature also required that the division obtain the legislature's approval for any future designations of critical areas, which had to be guided by more specific standards. Moreover, to be approved, such an area had to have had in operation for at least six months a resource planning and management program combining state, regional, and local government efforts. This provision is a way of ensuring that no area would be designated as critical unless all the alternatives to designation were exhausted. All future designations are automatically to lapse three years after the Bureau of Land and Water Management approves the local land-use regulations; under some conditions, the designations are to lapse after only one year.[50] These legislative actions, heavily supported by local government and other pro-development forces, plainly weaken the state's land-use program. But the changes were also supported by environmentalists as the only practical way of maintaining the critical-areas provision at all.

As a final form of skirmish, some developers have threatened to stop building at all or to stop building in regulated areas. There is little evidence that state land-use laws—as distinct from financing problems, low market demand, taxes, local land-use controls, or other environmental legislation—have actually dissuaded anyone from trying to build. (One document that constructs such an argument is *The Death of Dover, Vermont*, a novel written by a small entrepreneur and former selectman in Dover, Vermont, and published by a vanity press.)[51] It seems plausible, though, that developers might change the locations of their projects to avoid stringent application of the state land-use laws. Florida developers building DRIs admit that, given a choice, they gravitate toward areas with no land-use controls or weak ones—areas that are unlikely to invoke the DRI regulatory process, or unlikely to invoke it heavily. Vermont's land-use law seems to have helped drive some potential development into neighboring New Hampshire, which has no similar law (plus a more favorable tax climate);[52] Pennsylvania's strip-mining law seems to have pushed a few bituminous coal operators into West Virginia, Maryland, and Ohio, all of which have distinctly weaker stripping laws.[53] Delaware's passage of strong coastal zone legislation in 1971 reportedly forced New Jersey to enact comparable legislation in 1973 to keep builders from siting their more objectionable projects on the nearby New Jersey shore of Delaware Bay.[54]

Confrontations with Local Economic and Political Power

Some parts of a state usually support land-use reform more strongly than others. These differences show up most obviously and importantly in the implementation of the state programs that were designed to include regional mechanisms: California, Florida, and Vermont. In each of these states, some regional regulatory bodies demonstrate—through approval rates, the severity of the conditions they impose, the backgrounds of their members, the instructions they give their applicants and local governments, and their general reputations—greater receptivity to new development than others.

The regional bodies most disposed to favor new development are those in permanently depressed rural areas that generally do not have strong local land-use controls and want all the new construction they can get—for example, the North Coast of California (Del Norte, Humboldt, and Mendocino counties, adjoining the Oregon border), the Northeast Kingdom of Vermont (Essex, Orleans, and Caledonia counties on the border with Canada and New Hampshire), and most of panhandle and inland Florida and some of the state's coastal areas. (The entire Adirondacks would also count as such an area, at least as compared with most of the rest of New York State.) Almost equally development-minded are the regional bodies in high-growth urban areas whose local governments for the most part want continued rapid growth—for example, Los Angeles–Orange County, Orlando, and Jacksonville.

Least disposed to favor new development are the regional bodies in rural or small-town areas with relatively strong economies—for instance, Burlington, Santa Cruz, or much of southern Vermont—and those in large, fast-growing urban areas where environmentalist sentiment is strong and local governments are comparatively willing to question the supposed benefits of new growth—for instance, San Francisco, Tampa, and Miami.

In California, for example, 55 percent of the voters supported the 1972 coastal initiative, but support varied from region to region; 60 percent of the voters in San Francisco area counties supported the initiative, but 60 percent of North Coast voters opposed it. The 1972 per capita income was under $4,000 along the North Coast; it was over $6,500 in the San Francisco area. In 1970, only 42 percent of the North Coast's population lived in towns of 2500 or more; 91 percent of the San Francisco area's population lived in such towns. In 1970, unemployment along the North Coast was nearly 10 percent, while in the San Francisco region it was around 6 percent. A poll of regional commissioners published in 1975 indicated that they faithfully represented their constituencies; eight of the twelve North Coast commissioners had voted against the coastal initiative and would do so again (thus they found themselves in the interesting position of administering a law they opposed), while at least eleven of the fourteen San Francisco area regional commissioners had voted for the measure and would do so again.[55]

Another poll, taken at 130 town meetings in Vermont in 1975, asked, "Should the legislature adopt a state land use plan?" The state as a whole voted 48 percent to 36 percent in favor of such a plan (the remainder were undecided); the Northeast Kingdom voted 50–36 percent against it, while Windham County, in environmentally oriented southeast Vermont, went 52–29 percent in favor of the plan.[56] The same sort of poll would undoubtedly reveal similar regional differences in Florida.

In all three states, the decisions of the regional land-use bodies legitimately reflect regional differences. During fiscal 1974, the South Florida Regional Planning Council, centered on the Miami–Fort Lauderdale–Palm Beach area, recommended unconditional approval for one proposed development of regional impact, conditional approval for twenty, and outright disapproval for fourteen.[57] In the same year, the Tampa Bay Regional Planning Council, centered on the Tampa–St. Petersburg–Sarasota area, recommended unconditional approval for two proposed DRIs, conditional approval for nineteen, and disapproval for fourteen.[58] During the same period, the rural Withlacoochee Regional Planning Council, centered on Ocala (1970 census population 22,500) in the northwest portion of peninsula Florida, processed only three applications for DRIs and recommended conditional approval for all of them.[59]

In 1977–78, California's rural North Coast commission turned down 3 percent of the applications submitted to it, while the San Francisco and Santa Cruz area commissions turned down more than 14 percent.[60] The decisions of the San Francisco area commission have been generally more compatible with the environmental goals of the Coastal Plan than have those of the North Coast commission.[61] A planner at the state coastal commission commented:

The interpretive guidelines the regional commissions have been submitting show the same pattern the commissions have been showing in appointments and decisions all along. The North Coast commission is environmentally lenient, the Los Angeles and San Diego commissions are middling, and the San Francisco and Santa Cruz area ones are strict. You have to know there's a message there: the regions differ and the commissions show it. (ATI, San Francisco, California, March 1979)

No formal information on regulatory variations between regions is available for Vermont, but a district environmental coordinator who has held the post in both the environmentally oriented portion of southern Vermont and the poorer, development-minded Northeast Kingdom said:

In the south we always look closely at relatively fine points of design—lighting, signs, landscaping, the elevation of buildings, the resulting views from the road, whether the project breaks the view of the treeline, things like that. So developers know they have to work this stuff out pretty well before they even come to us. But in the Northeast Kingdom we do a much less detailed job. We work faster, and we place fewer and lighter conditions on a project. We spend a lot of time on parking lots, access to highways, and lots of other fairly crude points. We let the fine points go, and of course we lose a lot environmentally. But that's the way our commissioners want it. They don't want to do anything that would even remotely risk antagonizing the developer or scaring off the project. The commissioners' towns rarely participate in our hearings except to endorse project proposals. I can't really blame them. Economic development has to be the main point in such a poor area. (AI, St. Johnsbury, Vermont, June 1976).

In the states that have both regional and state land-use bodies, the state agencies, comparatively insulated from the developer-oriented pressures of local politics, usually show greater support for environmentalist views than do most of their regional counterparts. The exception has been Florida, where the Division of State

Planning was noticeably diffident in intervening in DRI cases, drawing up a state land-use plan, and designating areas of critical state concern even before the legal challenge to its power to do so. But in California and Vermont, the state-level bodies are widely agreed to be more environmentalist than nearly all the regional bodies.[62]

In California in 1977–78, for instance, the comparatively demanding San Francisco and Santa Cruz area regional commissions turned down more than 14 percent of the applications that came before them. But during the same period, the state commissions denied more than 26 percent of the 205 applications whose appeals it heard. It also refused to hear on appeal 53 percent of the 800 cases where appeals were sought, thus letting the regional commissions' decisions stand.[63] Since the appeals from regional decisions were typically brought by developers,[64] the high refusal rate in effect favors environmentalists. Whether the state commissions will continue this rate of refusal after mid-1981, when half its membership will start coming from local government, is uncertain.

The programs have had little success in fostering local land-use plans and zoning ordinances. The success of such efforts seems to depend on local popular support, the availability of state funds to finance devising the local land-use controls, and the setting of explicit standards for acceptable local controls. The California coastal program has been the most effective. It has offered localities a reduction in state jurisdiction and substantial grants—a total of nearly $350,000, for instance, to the city of Los Angeles and $166,000 to rural Sonoma County north of San Francisco[65] to finance the preparation of coastal zoning regulations and land-use plans for its approval. (Much of the money came originally from the federal coastal zone management program.) By July 1979, the original deadline for completion of the local coastal programs, only San Francisco's controls had actually been approved and put in place, but a number of other heavily environmentalist localities—for example, the cities and counties of Santa Barbara and Santa Cruz—were moving rapidly toward approval, and nearly all California coastal localities appeared to be making satisfactory progress toward the amended deadline of July 1981.[66]

The experience in Vermont, the Adirondacks, and Florida has been much more mixed. Vermont's law gives localities no financial incentives to establish controls, and although it limits state regulatory jurisdiction in cities and towns with controls, it does not require that the controls be acceptable to the state. Although such local controls have proliferated in Vermont in the last ten years, they are generally acknowledged to be the result not of Act 250 but of a growing local environmental consciousness and the requirements of other state and federal programs. Local governments generally seem to resent the additional pressure of Act 250. "If it was just a matter of 250," a town selectman said, "we probably wouldn't lift a finger, and neither might a lot of other places" (ATI, Arlington, Vermont, August 1978). In any case, many of Vermont's local land-use controls seem to be of little significance.[67]

The 1973 Adirondack Park Land Use and Development Plan for private lands allows for a reduction of the Adirondack Park Agency's jurisdiction in localities with controls the APA approves. But the localities have strenuously resisted the APA for much of its life. The funds the APA offers the localities are comparatively meager, at least by California coastal standards. From 1973 to 1978, the APA gave a total of $800,000 to the 62 towns (out of 95 in the park) that were willing to accept the money[68]—that is, about $2,400 per town per year for areas that were typically much larger (although usually less populated and developed) than the coastal portions of California cities and counties.

The 1973 plan had originally established a 1976 deadline for local submission of the controls. In late 1976, the APA agreed to accept partial controls—for instance, a land-use plan rather than a complete package of regulatory controls that included zoning and subdivision regulations, or controls over only a portion of a town's land—because none of the park's towns had submitted controls that the APA was prepared to approve. Even after the APA concessions, the local submissions came in slowly. "Of course we're not doing anything to comply with the APA," a local official said. "As soon as we did that, we'd be under their thumb" (AI, Saranac Lake, New York, June 1976). By late 1978, the APA had approved only nine proposed local land-use programs. Some of these had been submitted by the town planning boards rather than the town governments. Actually, four of them had not been adopted by the town governments.[69] As of August 1979, these figures had not changed.[70]

In Florida, only two "areas of critical state concern" where local controls had to be approved by the Division of State Planning have thus far been designated—the Florida Keys and the Green Swamp. (In 1973, the Big Cypress Swamp northwest of the Everglades also received this designation, but by legislative action separate from the state land-use law.[71]) In each case, even before the legal challenge, the local governments strenuously opposed the designation, delayed it as long as they could, and extracted important concessions as to the size of the designated area and the severity of the controls placed on it.[72] Local government enforcement of the imposed controls may be less than vigorous. In response to a question about compliance, an official in the Division of State Planning stated: "We're not really sure, and I'm not certain we're all that interested in finding out. The areas of critical state concern are almost by definition rural, and some of those swamp places where violations are most likely are still pretty isolated and primitive. A nosy state official could easily get killed by some backwoods property-rights zealot" (AI, Tallahassee, Florida, January 1976).

The two designated areas constitute 1.5 percent of Florida's 58,560 square miles, so in principle the Bureau of Land and Water Management could designate more than 2300 additional square miles of "areas of critical state concern" before it reached the state land-use law's 5 percent limit on such designations. (The areas available for designation will increase further if, as seems likely, the city of Key West, the only large town on the Keys, gets its way and is allowed to be excluded from the designation.) In practice, the political resistance, the legal difficulties, and now the 1979 legislative restrictions make further designations unlikely.

In response, the bureau has for some years been experimenting with other means of protecting environmentally endangered areas. In 1976 it persuaded the local governments, development interests, and environmentalists of the Apalachicola River and Bay, in the central panhandle, to band together to improve local regulatory abilities and to spell out desired future development patterns in the region; the division also gave the local governments technical assistance for their planning.[73] In 1977, the division began a similar effort in the Charlotte Harbor area on the southern Gulf Coast between Sarasota and Fort Myers.[74] Both initiatives distinctly resemble the multigovernmental resource planning and management programs required by the 1979 legislation as a precondition to (but a step short of) state designations as a critical area.

The division, moreover, has been noticeably reluctant to appeal local government decisions on developments of regional impact to the governor and cabinet; Luther Carter has described the division's performance as "generally passive,"[75] and although the division has occasionally filed joint appeals with other public bodies, it has never undertaken one by itself.[76] The appeals that are filed by public bodies acting on their own initiative have come from the regional planning councils, especially those in the environmentally oriented Miami and Tampa areas.[77] In these cases, it is the surrounding governments that are objecting to the decisions made by the locality in which the project is to be placed. But typically, objections are based on *local* environmental considerations (for example, traffic in a particular neighboring city) rather than regional or state environmental considerations (for example, traffic in the region as a whole).[78] The Bureau of Land and Water Management is supposed to represent broad regional and state considerations. If it does not—and it seems not to—then these perspectives are largely lost from the DRI process, and the localities continue to control land-use decisions.

Recalcitrant Florida localities can evade the DRI process in other ways. A number of communities have rezoned parcels of land to accommodate a prospective DRI they very much wanted; adverse reports from the regional council after the project was actually proposed have not induced the zoning board to reject or modify the project.[79] A Florida planner in a pro-development county told Robert Healy: "The county commissioners don't always review the 4000 pages that are presented to them—and even when they read them they have many biases."[80] A Florida local planner said:

Practically speaking, you can't change back the zoning classification. The position of the local government would become untenable. Too much hassling and political bloodletting has already occurred for it to want to deal with the question again. Maybe some money has changed hands. Once the zoning approval has come through, the locals and the developer have a common interest in seeing the project fly. They don't want to see it threatened by the region or the state or environmentalists or anybody else. This is the hidden flaw in the DRI procedure. (AI, Tallahassee, Florida, January 1976)

In any case, Florida's regional planning councils have little desire to threaten reluctant local governments. Indeed, most council members are themselves local elected officials who, in their council work, continue to represent their constituencies. Few strive to identify and serve a vaguer, less organized regional interest. Commissioners generally engage in a great deal of vote-trading and logrolling. "I guarantee you we can get any project approved by our regional planning council," a commissioner from a large central Florida county told Healy. "We wouldn't have to say a word—they know there would be polar bears in the streets of Miami before they got another favor from us."[81]

Other state land-use agencies likewise have only limited influence over the actions of local government.[82] Even the comparatively successful California coastal commissions have suffered political defeats at the hands of local government. For example, in mid-1977 the opposition of the localities persuaded the commissions to abandon the designation, provided for in the 1976 legislation, of parts of the coast as "sensitive coastal resource areas" to be jointly regulated indefinitely by the commissions and the localities.[83] The localities wanted to be certain that once the commissions approved the local coastal land-use programs, the localities would regulate the coast (except for some extremely large or otherwise threatening developments), and the commissions would function, in general, only as a distant point of appeal. The localities got their way.

The clearest indicator of the constraints on state land-use agencies in their dealings with local government is the implementation of the provision in many state land-use laws—including those of California, Florida, and Vermont—that the state agency, if dissatisfied after some specified time with the content or administration of local land-use programs, may step in and carry out its own program. State agencies have frequently been dissatisfied with local performance. But in practice no state agency has ever intervened. It has become obvious that doing so would be administratively impossible and politically disastrous.

The Difficulties of Statewide Land-Use Planning

The provisions of state land-use programs for the states to draw up statewide land-use plans that will guide the actions of builders, local governments, and state agencies have usually fared badly in implementation. This generalization has its exceptions, but for the most part even the exceptions tend to confirm it. For instance, the Maryland Public Service Commission's ten-year plan for siting power plants has never drawn much political opposition because it involves only a small portion of the state's land. The officials responsible for Pennsylvania's strip-mining program, like those doing the same work in other states, have never considered a statewide plan for the siting or regulation of strip mines to be necessary.

Florida's state land-use law required the Division of State Planning to prepare a statewide plan. But the division apparently (and, it would seem, accurately) anticipated opposition and gave low priority to this task. The division moved slowly and cautiously, and eventually made the land-use plan a small, vague, and permissive part of a much larger State Comprehensive Plan.[84] This plan, which the Florida legislature approved in 1978, deals with land development and urban growth as well as education, employment and manpower, social services, agriculture, and utilities.

In the land-development section of the comprehensive plan, the subsection on "wetlands and submerged lands" sets forth a highly general "objective: retain and protect the values and functions of wetlands and submerged lands."[85] In pursuit of this objective, the plan outlines eleven equally benign but vague "policies"—"encourage the development and use of wetlands and submerged lands only for purposes which are compatible with their natural values and functions," "enable wetlands to be reasonably used by individuals for purposes which will not adversely affect the values and functions of these resources," "encourage research aimed at assessing the relative values of various wetlands and submerged lands in the state," and so forth.[86] The section never mentions the dredging for "finger" canals characteristic of a good deal of Florida development, much less the enormous environmental damage such dredging does or how it might be prevented. The plan includes no standards for implementation of its policies and few details on how they might be carried out.[87] The conclusion of the land-development section offers a number of predictable recommendations—for example, "The Legislature should continue to support the preparation of detailed soil surveys for all counties in the state"[88]—but does not relate them to the preceding objectives and policies.

In contrast, California's 1975 Coastal Plan emerged from a law that had exact standards and a limited area to regulate. The plan also had broad popular support that could express itself in extensive citizen participation. It could draw on three years of commission experience in regulating coastal development.[89] As a result, California's plan is a far stronger, more precise document than Florida's.

California's section on "Coastal Waters, Estuaries, and Wetlands"—the counterpart of the wetlands subsection in the Florida plan—begins by describing the biological and economic productivity of such areas, identifying the most productive areas along the coast, and showing how they have been degraded by dredging and mining. The section then sets forth five highly detailed polices. The subsection on dredging lists the purposes for which dredging would be permitted: among others, repair of previously dredged channels, creating or expanding commercial fishing harbors, and building port or energy facilities. It also establishes clear criteria against which any dredging proposal would be judged: water depth, water circulation, siltation patterns, sedimentation, and contamination of bottom materials.[90]

The plan also includes long, specific sections on how state and local government might carry out and finance the plan and its policies and what priorities government should apply in acquiring private land. Summaries and maps describe how the plan would be put into effect and what results it might be expected to have in the regions of each of the six coastal commissions.[91]

The plan greatly influenced the 1976 Coastal Act; large portions of the legislation, including the section on dredging, were lifted almost verbatim from the plan.[92] The plan also seems to have influenced the coastal commissions' regulatory decisions, the interpretive guidelines they have issued, and their examination of proposed local land-use programs.

In Vermont and the Adirondacks, state land-use plans, which were fairly strong and precise but lacked the political and technical advantages of the California coastal plan, have been much less effective. In the Vermont legislature, increasingly weak versions of a state plan, drawn up by the State Planning Office and the Environmental Board, were defeated in 1974, 1975, and 1976 by steadily widening margins.[93] "It probably won't have a chance for the next decade," a Republican legislator sympathetic to the plan commented in 1976

(AI, Montpelier, Vermont, June 1976). The first chairman of the Environmental Board expressed some doubt about whether a plan was even necessary.[94] And in late 1977, the Vermont legislature repealed the Act 250 provision requiring a state plan.[95]

The opposition to state plans springs from more than the usual sources—the economic ambitions of developers, the political misgivings of local governments, and the ideological inclinations of conservatives. It even goes deeper than the traditional American individualist's aversion to centralized government planning of any kind.[96] The problem is simply that much of the public seems to regard land-use planning as worthwhile in the abstract but objectionable as it becomes concrete. Environmental lawyer Victor Yannacone, Jr., who has worked for the Adirondack Park Agency, has written:

> Think of what it means to the people of a small community who walk into a public meeting and for the first time are confronted with walls full of multi-colored maps, beautifully rendered sketches and detailed proposals for the future of their community. Or worse yet, consider the plight of the poor citizen in the darkened Town Hall who watches these maps, sketches, and charts wink by on a dimly lit screen—"The Magic Lantern Show of Progress"—planning. The primary reaction of the homeowner, the citizen-taxpayer, is "My God, my house is in there somewhere. What are they going to do to it?"[97]

A California coastal planner commented: "People come in, look at the plan, get alienated, get glum, and it all happens fast. We worked our tails off to get citizen input on the plan, and somehow the guy walking in here has never heard of us and the plan, is learning about this stuff for the first time. Naturally he's a bit annoyed" (ATI, Long Beach, California, August 1978).

All the strands of resistance to state land-use planning—indeed, to land-use reform generally—came together in extreme form in 1973–77 in the Adirondacks.[98] The vast majority of Adirondackers and their politicians had never tried to conceal their contempt for the Adirondack Park Agency, its mainly out-of-park staff, and the plan it administers. The Adirondackers have always regarded outside attempts to preserve the park as ways of imposing the values of a populous, cosmopolitan, liberal, wealthy urban state on a sparsely populated, isolated, conservative, poor rural area. The stringency and complexity of the land-use plan especially annoyed the local people, who simply did not see why it was necessary.

Walking along the main street of a small Adirondack town, a prominent APA opponent suddenly gestured to the surrounding, quite present, mountains and wilderness and let out the frustration he and his neighbors felt:

Look at it all. It's gorgeous. It may not be pristine enough for those APA purists, but it's basically undeveloped and nearly all of it has no chance of ever being built up. That's fine with me. It shows we've done a good job of protecting the place all these years. Now those arrogant outsiders from the Agency come in, tell us we're ignorant about our own land, and shove these huge complicated documents at us that they don't seem to understand themselves. (AI, Lake Placid, New York, June 1976)

For years the localities had refused to submit their land-use controls for approval by the APA, even though approval would reduce the agency's control over their land. Most of the localities passed resolutions calling for the abolition of the APA. A number of developer groups, unions, farm organizations, school districts, and statewide local-government professional associations did likewise, as did a local group of priests.[99] The Adirondack Park Local Government Review Board continually attacked the agency, called for its abolition, and held a series of "citizen speak-outs" around the park at which 1400 people heard dozens of irate Adirondackers tell of alleged harassment, arrogance, overregulation, and mistakes by the agency.[100] Bumper stickers appeared, bearing such slogans as "Adirondack Park Agency is another word for tyranny" and "Adirondackers are feudal slaves to the APA." Anti-APA groups such as the Adirondack Minutemen and the League for Adirondack Citizens Rights emerged, the latter plainly well financed and claiming 16,000 members out of a total park population of 120,000. The league was the prime force behind several anti-APA demonstrations in Albany that each attracted several hundred Adirondackers. Anti-APA publications appeared; one was the *Adirondack Defender*, a handout with heavy local advertising whose motto proclaimed it "the freedom fighter's news." Seemingly deliberate violations of APA permit orders came to light. Opponents also embarked on a campaign to embarrass the APA: they submitted bogus project applications and then publicized the agency's delays and mistakes in processing them.[101]

Incidents of low-level violence also occurred. The local style was nothing if not blunt. At the scene of a permit dispute, an angry woman slapped the face and broke the glasses of an assistant director of the APA. Someone dumped a pile of horse manure on the APA's lawn with a sign saying: "We've taken yours for three years, now here's ours." Agency staff cars had their tires slashed. An APA staff member whose car needed towing found that the charge doubled when the wrecker learned where he worked. The agency received threats of worse to come.

The agency had been created primarily to regulate large developments, but most such projects had evaporated because of the national economic slowdown that, as usual, hit the Adirondacks with special severity; other projects were enmeshed in negotiations or litigation, sometimes with other state agencies. So the APA found itself embroiled mainly in disputes with small property owners about the development of small, often isolated pieces of land. It easily acquired the image of the enemy of the little man.[102] When it tried to prosecute some of the violators, it happened to pick as its first targets a highly respected state conservation officer and a real estate agent widely known for his Boy Scout work; he was, in fact, on his way to a Scout meeting when the APA summons was served on him. Local juries refused to return indictments.

In another well-publicized episode, a small auto-parts dealer, Joey Hickey, who intended to live above his newly built store in the village of Oswegatchie near the western edge of the park, received a permit from the APA in 1975 telling him he could work in the building or live in it, but not both. Hickey somehow got the impression that the APA intended to tear down the building if he didn't comply. Outraged, he lived and worked in the building anyway, in defiance of the APA. An extended imbroglio followed, during which the slapping incident occurred. The APA finally relented and sent Hickey a second permit, saying he could legally live and work in the building. He sent it back and urged his neighbors to send their permits back. "Go ahead and build wherever you want," he told everyone. Hickey became a folk hero throughout the park.[103] At the same time, a state attempt to establish an APA equivalent to plan and regulate development in the Catskill Mountains in southeastern New York State failed because of local opposition. A good part of the reason for the opposition was the publicity surrounding the APA controversy.[104]

In the face of all this pressure and willful noncompliance, in the 1976 legislative session the APA sought and obtained a number of amendments that diminished its own power. Civil penalties, primarily fines, for violations of its orders replaced criminal ones. The APA could now approve local land-use controls even if they covered a town only partially or did not consist of all the kinds of controls the agency desired. The state agreed to provide free legal assistance to any local government sued because of its APA-approved controls. The Local Government Review Board was empowered to submit a slate of candidates for APA members; from this list the governor had to appoint two of the five members of the agency who were required to be residents of the park.

The APA also gave up jurisdiction over wetlands smaller than one acre, except where they adjoined a body of water. The APA could not now deny a permit to build a single-family house on land its plan had classified as a resource-management area (the most restrictive classification) if the applicant had owned the land when the Adirondack Park Agency Act took effect in 1971; in such cases, the APA could only rule on the type and placement of the sewage system. In addition, the APA diminished its already small enforcement effort, began opening all its meetings to the public, and adopted procedures to expedite processing of applications, especially small ones. The first APA chairman resigned in 1976; his successor, Robert Flacke, a town supervisor of Lake George, was widely considered more conciliatory to local government.

The actual result of all these changes is still somewhat uncertain; the local governments still seem extremely reluctant to submit their land-use controls for APA approval. But the APA's intent is clear. In late 1976, after the amendments had passed, Flacke declared that the APA had in the past been overzealous and misguided. The agency, he said was "finally coming of age. We are more sure of ourselves and of the soundness of our law. Thus we can afford to be more flexible and more humanistic in the way we administer the program. There will be no more Joey Hickey cases, where we interpreted our law too literally."[105]

Asked by the *New York Times* whether the agency was "caving in,'' R. Courtney Jones, chairman of the environmentalist Adirondack Council, replied, ''I think caving in may be too strong, but there's no question that the agency is responding to political pressure. I think that strict preservationist values are not going to be adhered to.''[106] In late 1976, the APA approved resubmitted project applications that were not much different from the versions it had previously turned down.[107]

After 1976, the APA took other steps to improve its local image and acceptability. It began hiring Adirondackers for its staff, opened new offices in Lake George and Old Forge (each about one hundred miles from the original office in Ray Brook), established a toll-free telephone number, and published a short, readable guide to its permit requirements.[108] It established a local advisory committee to report to it on developing the park's towns, took a series of steps to encourage tourism, and appointed a staff economist who was an Adirondack native.[109] It took every opportunity to approve acceptable large projects,[110] to meet with local business leaders,[111] to simplify procedures for applicants,[112] and to tell the world, by means of press releases and annual reports, that it had done so.

By late 1978, local anti-APA feeling had much diminished. The public uproar, the acrimonious disputes with applicants and local governments, the demonstrations, the violence and threats of violence, the bumper stickers—all were things of the past. The APA was not greatly beloved in the Adirondacks, but it was for the most part accepted. The failure of localities to submit land-use programs was still bothersome but seemed remediable over time. In December 1978, the APA's old enemy, the Adirondack Park Local Government Review Board, wrote in its annual report: ''The heated controversy which marked the early years of the Agency has been calmed. Lengthy delays in processing project applications, and the abusive tactics in enforcement activities . . . are now history.'' The board further noted that the new relationship between the APA and the local population was ''long overdue'' and was ''a delicate one that must be given an opportunity to prove itself.''[113] In early 1979, a local magazine observed that while the opposition to the APA ''will be a feature of the local political scene for many years to come,'' it was now a ''loyal opposition''—not one that would try to ''chop down the Agency, root and branch.''[114]

The Regulatory Bargains

In implementation, state land-use agencies have generally proved not to be the powerful regulators that their supporters wanted and their opponents feared. At their worst, the programs suffer from a large number of compromises and weaknesses. At their best, the programs administer a new and complicated process that is typically guided by no precise objectives; they are bound to make mistakes, and in any case, they arouse substantial opposition from influential development and local-government interests. In Florida, Phyllis Myers commented, "the DRI review is evolving as a moderate technique for balancing interests. It is cautious governmental process that is neither go-go growth nor no-growth."[115] The point applies to all the state programs; they all make a virtue of steering a middle course.

But in practice, what does a hard-pressed state agency do when confronted by an application pushed by a tenacious developer or located in a resistant locality? Many developers have lawyers adept at pointing out why this particular project is different from most of the projects the agency handles. And virtually all of the information about the likely effects of the project comes, in any case, from its sponsors. The agency also confronts pro-development political pressures generated by economic slowdowns or energy difficulties. Under such circumstances, the agency bargains and negotiates with its applicants. More precisely, it treats every project on a case-by-case basis. It thereby concedes the lawyer's argument of differentness. Taken together, such ad hoc decisions are inevitably arbitrary and inconsistent with each other. The agency in effect grants all proposed projects a putative right to be built and then confines its examination of them to the details of how they will be built. It offers implicit and explicit concessions to the regulated interests. In short, it bargains from a position that may not be weak but is not overwhelmingly strong.[116]

The regulatory bargains take a specific form: the agency approves the vast majority of proposed developments but then imposes heavy conditions upon them. The approval rate is frequently high. For example, the California coastal commissions approved about 93 percent of the 13,000 applicants they received during 1977 and most of 1978.[117] From 1973 to 1975, the Adirondack Park Agency approved 685 projects and turned down 20, an approval rate of over 97 percent. Sixty other applications were withdrawn, but there is no way to know whether they anticipated trouble at the APA, or ran into trouble with other regulatory bodies or in capital markets.[118] In Vermont, between June 1, 1970, when Act 250 went into effect, and July 1, 1978, the state Environmental Board and the district commissions approved 2997 applications and denied 78—an approval rate of nearly 98 percent.[119] In 1975, Pennsylvania's Bureau of Surface Mine Reclamation issued 1442 permits for strip mining and refused six—an approval rate of 99.6 percent.[120] Other state land-use programs show comparable rates of approval.[121]

Yet the conditions that accompany these approvals—the other side of the regulatory bargain—can be quite demanding. The California coastal commissions have, for instance, required developers to preserve larger amounts of open space, build extra drainage and sewage systems, enlarge parking lots, diminish the size of buildings or otherwise reduce the density of projects, improve aesthetics, add middle-income housing for elderly tenants, allow public access to the beach on project sites, and donate land for parks. Such measures generally reduce the profitability of the project.[122]

In Vermont, where the land-use agencies have insisted on equally stringent conditions,[123] the Environmental Board once looked into the question of whether the abandonment of 258 projects after they received state approval—between June 1970 and April 1976[124]—was related to the conditions placed on them. The board concluded that developers were simply running into money troubles during a generally recessionary period, although the state's builders are understandably not convinced.[125] Similarly, Pennsylvania's coal operators are unhappy with the restrictions state permits place on their excavation, backfilling, regrading, and revegetation activities, and Maryland utility companies do not like the conditions the Public Service Commission puts on the pollution levels, design, smokestack sizes, noise, and water use of their power plants.[126]

Moreover, developers frequently accuse the state agencies of placing impossible conditions on their projects, of in effect rejecting their applications under the guise of approving them. A California developer said:

It's as if they put you on trial for wanting to build, and then it turns into some sadistic kangaroo court. They hassle you endlessly, and then turn around and say with a smile, OK, you can build it. Just one or two little provisos, which turn out to be killers. I'm sure a lot of those commissioners know exactly what they're doing: they're putting you in a hole and telling you to be a giant. And they can sound terribly dedicated about how, after all, they approved the project. Except somehow the builder couldn't build it, and it never went up. Or he had to cut fourteen kinds of corners to do it, and maybe had to take some chances with the construction workers' safety or the residents' money. A wonderful system those public-spirited commissioners have got. (ATI, San Mateo, California, March 1978)[127]

Developer objections to some conditions may be misguided, or exaggerated for political effect. The builders may not find it difficult to keep their end of the regulatory bargains, given the weakness of the state agencies' enforcement efforts. Moreover, implicit in the bargaining itself is an assumption that the proposed project will ultimately be built. Decision-making on a case-by-case basis assumes the existence and necessity of each project and makes no attempt to control individual or collective location, rate, or timing. And without detailed state land-use plans or coherent statements of regulatory standards and policies, decision-making cannot be anything but ad hoc. Phyllis Myers cited a Conservation Law Foundation of New England study of Vermont's land-use law that

saw Act 250's impact as "improving development rather than directly forbidding it, and . . . not a mechanism for directing the rate and location of growth."

But one often hears in Vermont, "We don't care if the development is wrapped in plastic—there are some places we don't want it anyway." As Governor Salmon has observed, "The basic question remains: should a development exist at all, irrespective of its ability to meet environmental and social standards?" The Act 250 permit process does not give a comprehensive, implementable answer.[128]

In more general terms, Daniel Mandelker, a law professor at Washington University, has remarked on the need to

build response and feedback into the [land-use control] system. Inflexible controls can be counter-productive. Examples include permit systems that have become very popular in environmental control programs: permits for power plants, permits in the coastal zone, permits everywhere. The difficulty is that I consider these permit controls to contain very little in the way of feedback possibilities. There is no self-correcting mechanism because permit controls require a one-time yes or no decision. Shall we have a power plant here? Shall this part of the coastline be developed? As a result, and given the pressures on most decision-makers, most permits are granted, but with conditions. . . . Is this result self-defeating? Whether it is or not depends on the purpose of the program. If the aim is simply to mitigate what happens but not to affect the location decision, perhaps this experience is acceptable. Nevertheless, the control of location, timing, and phasing decisions appears very difficult under these permit programs, most of which are not very closely linked to conventional land use control and land use planning techniques. Control of these decisions appears essential in any effective land use management system.[129]

The state land-use agencies' use of bargaining and negotiations has another defect. Bargaining can be an acceptable and perhaps socially useful device when the parties involved are roughly comparable in political and technical strength. In these cases, the agencies and applicants have to deal with each other in good faith; in the process, each acquires a greater appreciation for the other's situation and abilities in dealing with it. They may end up working well together, to produce improved development. "You know," a Vermont developer confided, "if you hang in there with Act 250, it doesn't turn out to be so bad after all. Some of the commissioners turn out to be on your side in their own strange way. You learn something from them, they learn something from you, and you all end up better for it" (AI, Burlington, Vermont, June 1976). Many state officials and environmentalists agree that bargaining ultimately produces better development and better regulation.

Such appears to have been the result where strongly environmentalist agencies with solid local (and local government) popular support have encountered a strong developer presence—notably in the cases of the San Francisco area coastal commissions, the southern Vermont district environmental commissions, the Miami and Tampa regional planning councils, and perhaps some western Pennsylvania strip-mining. In these situations, the compromises tend to benefit both the parties involved and the public.[130]

But problems arise when the negotiating parties are not equal in strength. In some cases, the agencies can actually be too high-powered to bargain easily and productively with development or local government forces. The Adirondack Park Agency, at least until its self-effacement, is a clear example of what happens when a regulatory body can ride roughshod over its applicants. The San Francisco and Santa Cruz area coastal commissions also have sometimes been too powerful for their own good, especially when dealing with proposals for smaller projects. One San Francisco area coastal commissioner has expressed considerable uneasiness about this power:

You hate to say no to these people all the time. It wears at you psychologically. It's not just a matter of politics. You start despising youself for being so negative. Some poor farmer has been slaving away all his life and now he wants to finance his retirement by subdividing his acreage. And you're going to say no because of some obscure sewage problem or something. Well, there's only so many times you can do that and live with yourself. So in the end you approve the project, put as many conditions on it as you can, and hope for the best. (AI, San Rafael, California, August 1975)

This state of mind appears to be fairly common among the members of comparatively powerful land-use agencies.[131] Even in agencies with environmental strength, the human impulse to be nice produces a pro-development bias.

At least as typical, however, is a disparity between negotiating parties in which the developer and local government forces have the upper hand. In the Los Angeles, San Diego, and North Coast commissions; the Northeast Kingdom environmental commissions in Vermont; the regional planning councils of Orlando, Jacksonville, most of panhandle and inland and some of coastal Florida; eastern Pennsylvania strip-mining and some in western Pennsylvania as well; and much of Maryland power-plant siting, the use of negotiations by comparatively weak state land-use bodies inherently favors the regulated interests, who have no inhibitions about using their advantages. In short, the regulatory agencies often concede more to the development forces than they obtain in return.[132]

CHAPTER **8**

The Bureaucratic Implementation Struggle

As time goes by, new agencies tend to become part of the governmental landscape. The state land-use agencies are no longer as publicly visible or controversial today as they were when first introduced. They have lost political volatility and gained bureaucratic stability. Attacks on them will continue, and may make them modify their activities, but will not eliminate them. Most state land-use agencies take about three to five years to become established in this way.

The struggle over implementation does not then cease. The political, economic, environmental, and social stakes remain as high as ever. But the protagonists shift their concern from the existence of the agency, the extent of its powers, and the outcomes of its decisions to the comparatively hidden bureaucratic portions of the agency's operations. The assumption underlying this orientation is that by influencing the administrative mechanisms shaping the agency's decisions, the decisions themselves can be influenced. Thus, although the implementation struggle at this point focuses on bureaucratic matters, it still has important political implications.

Complaints about Bureaucracy

Developers and local governments always complain of the bureaucratic delays, costs, and paperwork imposed by the state land-use agencies. They also object to the arbitrariness and unpredictability of

154

many of the agencies' decisions. Some of the complaints are self-serving; some are valid.

Development interests have accused the land-use agencies and environmentalists of using the complexity of the centralized regulatory process to harass them and prevent them from building. The development interests regularly invoke the image of Big State Government—and looming behind it, Bigger Federal Government—squashing private initiative and local self-reliance with its bureaucratic obstructiveness and officiousness. Even in Vermont's capital of Montpelier (1970 census population 8600, the nation's smallest state capital), where underpaid civil servants, part-time legislators, and the town meeting tradition keep its state government exceedingly unobtrusive, developers complain of a Montpelier bureaucracy that can frustrate almost any application.[1] These conditions confirm the reality of the bureaucracy problem; they also suggest that big government has little to do with it. Probably, the real culprit is small government. The land-use agencies are understaffed and underfinanced. The agencies often find themselves unable to keep up with the applications before them. Delays and application backlogs are the result.

Many development-oriented opponents of the land-use laws maintain that the agencies are holding up applications they could process quickly. But giving a development application a thorough, competent examination takes time. The agencies themselves would prefer to process applications quickly and defuse the complaints of their powerful adversaries. "I'd love to be able to get the projects out of here twice as fast because it would take all kinds of heat off us," a California regional coastal commissioner said. "Still, it would mean giving up on a lot of our environmental review, and we won't do it" (ATI, Los Angeles, California, December 1977). In short, the delays to which developers object are due at least in part to anti-environmentalist efforts to undermine the agencies by keeping them understaffed and underfinanced.[2]

The delays are unquestionably real and especially objectionable in places like Vermont or the Adirondacks that have, because of climate, only a short building season. One large Vermont developer finds that his applications routinely take a year to clear the Act 250 process; they had taken only three months under solely local regulation. A large Adirondack builder reports that the Adirondack Park

Agency's permit reviews also add at least a year to the time it takes to build a substantial project. Before the agency was on the scene, he could count on rapid approval in localities that had land-use controls; most localities had none and cost him no time. Officials of state land-use agencies themselves concede that their operations—and the attendant hearings, citizen-participation procedures, negotiations, and (perhaps) court battles—delay many small projects for months and a few large, disputed ones for years. A 1973–74 Urban Institute study of south Florida DRIs (developments of regional impact) found that the regional planning councils and the Division of State Planning took an average of about three months to decide on applications. If the councils' decisions were appealed, the delays averaged over eleven months.[3]

Whether or not the delays are the fault of the agencies, they place them in the position of holding up needed economic, energy, or housing development, and they imply that the agencies cannot do their job. Many of the statutes that created the agencies call for rapid processing of applications. But of the six agencies closely examined, only Florida's and Maryland's have generally met their statutory schedules. These agencies' powers are largely advisory. If a Florida regional planning council is late in submitting its review to the local government or the Maryland Power Plant Siting Program is late in presenting its comments to the Public Service Commission, then both bodies risk having their advice ignored.

More typical is the 1972 California coastal law, which specifically required regional commissions to hold hearings within ninety days after an application was filed and to decide on it within sixty days after the end of the hearings.[4] This apparently generous schedule, though, strained the more harried commissions. The Los Angeles–Orange County commission often either failed to meet the schedule or artificially extended the hearings. A developer can do little to speed up the processing of his application. "Legislatively specified time limits," wrote Robert Healy, "offer the developer little protection from a permit board bent on securing time. The board need only threaten to reject the application because of 'unresolved problems,' and the developer will almost always grant an extension of time."[5]

Yet even a threatened delay is serious to the regulated interests. In a medium-sized $1 million residential project with money borrowed at 9 percent (an extremely reasonable rate in recent years), an unexpected one-year delay may cost a developer $90,000 in simple interest charges, with no revenue coming in during the lost time. The actual added costs may be far higher than $90,000; they include interest compounded over the life of the loan, as well as a year's property taxes, insurance, overhead, increases in material and labor prices, and inflation. One 1976 study, conducted by a developer group, estimated the overall cost of delay as 1.5 percent per month, which means that a year's delay would raise the price of a $50,000 house to $59,000.[6] In 1978 an environmental economist, using similar data, estimated the delay cost as approximately 0.5 percent a month, which still raises the cost of a $50,000 house to $53,000 in a year.[7] A year's delay in the construction of a 1000-megawatt nuclear power plant was estimated in 1976 as costing $50 million.[8] Today, because of higher interest rates and inflation, all these figures would be much higher.

For this price, the developer acquires the dubious pleasure of embroilment with the state agency. The agency may or may not improve the design of the project. The delay, apart from any conditions that the agency may impose, increases the price of the housing and energy. The locality waits a year to get the construction it probably wants and the property tax revenue and employment it may badly need. And the developer and the locality often end up with less construction than they would like.

Delay may have even more serious consequences. Many large developers are surprisingly lightly capitalized. In 1976 a Chicago apartment complex I lived in was converted from rental units to condominiums by fewer than a hundred tenants, mostly middle-income, who were able to outbid decisively one of the city's biggest developers. Many small developers have to borrow money at above-average interest rates. And individuals who want to build or expand their own homes or small businesses—people like Joey Hickey in the Adirondacks—rarely realize that state agencies, as distinct from local ones, may have a say about their plans.[9] (Many state land-use officials believe that local officials sometimes deliberately neglect to inform applicants that they may also have to apply to the state agency.)

An unexpected delay may make any development project unprofitable, unfeasible, or smaller. Moreover, after lengthy delays, a project may be turned down entirely, making the cost of both start-up and delay a total loss. Delays and rejections understandably infuriate not only developers but also construction unions, businessmen, realtors, banks, and the localities that want their projects or want to build public works projects themselves. These injured parties cannot retaliate effectively to salvage individual projects. But when the volume of such cases reaches a critical mass, the accumulated resentment finds political expression and forces overall changes in agency procedures.

The regulated interests also object to bureaucratic paperwork. Most developers, certainly homeowners but even many large companies, utilities, and public agencies, are seat-of-the-pants operations. They seldom commit to print anything lengthier than a memorandum. Yet the application forms of the agencies generally run more than twenty single-spaced pages. Conscientious answers to the questions sometimes add up to hundreds—or in the case of extremely large projects, thousands—of pages. A developer who wants a project approved has no choice but to provide them.

For example, the 1976 edition of the DRI application for large developments issued by the Florida Division of State Planning runs thirty legal-sized pages.[10] On pages 5–8, the application asks for eight kinds of maps of the project, a drainage plan for the site, and a master development plan for it. It also asks for a "breakdown of the existing and proposed land uses on the site for each phase of development through completion of the project" and for a discussion of how "unique topographical and other features" of the site will be protected. In addition, it asks for estimated average daily emissions in pounds per day for six kinds of air pollution over each phase of the project and for a description of the steps that will be taken to reduce them. Then it requests technical information about each soil type on the site, as well as a statement of what steps will be taken to overcome soil limitations, prevent erosion, and take into account "unique geological features."

Pages 9–30 ask for detailed information about water pollution, wetlands, floodplains, vegetation and wildlife, historic and archaeological sites, employment and economic effects, and impacts on eleven kinds of local public service and on housing. Then come questions directed at specific types of DRIs—shopping centers, office parks, factories, and so forth. The whole application is accompanied by a 100-page guidebook on how to fill it out.[11] Moreover, the more demanding regional planning councils—those centered in Miami and Tampa—also have issued their own complex instructions on what they want in a DRI application,[12] although in 1978 a uniform statewide application was adopted.[13] The developer has to submit at least fifteen copies of his completed application. The agencies reserve the right to ask for more information. The developer is in no position to refuse them, but he has no guarantee that the agencies will read the submitted applications fairly, or in fact read them at all.

The other states are not much different. Maryland power company executives show visitors file drawers of material they have to supply to the Power Plant Siting Program for their admittedly large projects. (Planning and building even a medium-sized nuclear power plant can cost well over $1 billion and take ten years, and nonnuclear plants are only slightly easier to build.[14]) The complexity of the Adirondack Park Agency's applications, and of the plan against which their contents are judged, has been a continual irritant to the local population and its builders.[15] "The applications are page after page of gobbledygook questions that don't really have answers," a town assessor said: "Not honest ones you could be sure of, anyway. So you guess, and then those people at the Agency get arrogant about the guesses they made you make. They never seem to be able to remember the hard information you do give them in the application, and then they get difficult about *that*, and say it's your fault. Wonderful" (AI, Saranac Lake, New York, June 1976).

The intricacy of the applications, and particularly of the speculative, often semifictional information they demand of applicants, evokes widespread resentment. Even the staffs of the land-use agencies find them burdensome. But to planners, architects, lawyers, hydrologists, geologists, soil scientists, and engineers, the applications are a new and lucrative market. These consultants and other intermediaries earn money by providing the specialized information needed to fill out the applications. A survey of the economic impacts of Vermont's land-use law, for instance, estimated that Act 250 increased engineering costs for developments by about 20 percent and legal costs by perhaps as much as 100 percent.[16] The boon is more than financial. The Vermont survey noted that "the architects who were contacted seemed to be uniformly enthusiastic about Act 250. Obviously, from a crass economic point of view, this Act enhances the scope of their clientele. But it also fits with their professional training and standards, and probably enables them to oppose what they might consider 'poor' design more consistently and honestly.''[17]

Yet to their clients, the applications often mean nothing but expenses, difficulties, and genteel blackmail on the part of the land-use agency or environmental groups. For a homeowner or other small developer, getting the application filled out—which often means hiring a lawyer who drafts the application, goes to hearings to answer questions about it, and then revises it accordingly—can unexpectedly add several hundred or thousand dollars to the cost of a project. For larger developers, the costs will be less surprising but much higher. They can easily run into hundreds of thousands of dollars, especially if litigation becomes necessary.

Vermont developers estimate that it costs at least $100,000 to prepare an Act 250 application for a large project.[18] A Vermont developer who wanted to build a 200-unit condominium and spent $78,000 in the early 1970s preparing an unsuccessful application three inches thick told the Conservation Foundation's Phyllis Myers: "Since I began, the rules have changed three times. I could never find out what was needed. Government has got to pull itself together. . . . When our project is complete, we will contribute $3 million to the town [Stowe] and $70,000 to the state room and meals tax. . . . As far as I'm concerned, no one in government speaks for business or developers.''[19] Similarly, a Florida builder spent $500,000 in planning a large residential development before he even broke ground on it. Another Florida builder spent more than $200,000 preparing an application for an entire new community and then got turned down.[20] State land-use officials maintain that filling out the application forces developers to think through their projects and that much of this thinking would eventually have to be done in any case. But the developers resent the applications and the agencies anyway, and their resentment is understandable.

The Coordination Issue

Developers also incur delays and costs when they must file applications with a number of different agencies at various levels of government. They particularly dislike the impediments produced by the lack of coordination—the continual contrary pulling and hauling—

among agencies. In addition to filing with the local zoning board and the state land-use agency, a developer contemplating a project of any size must submit applications to the local departments concerned with building codes, air pollution, water pollution, water supply, solid-waste disposal, sewage, and health; to the state counterparts of these agencies; and to their federal counterparts, including not only the various branches of the Environmental Protection Agency but also the Council on Environmental Quality (if the development necessitates any federal involvement through, for example, a grant or license) and the Army Corps of Engineers (if it affects waterways or wetlands).

More specialized projects, such as power plants and strip mines, also require applications to other state and federal agencies—for example, state public service commissions and strip-mining agencies, the Nuclear Regulatory Commission (if the plant is atomic), the Department of Energy's Federal Energy Regulatory Commission (for plants that transmit electricity across state lines), the Bureau of Mines (for mine safety) and the Occupational Safety and Health Administration (for the general safety of working conditions during construction and operation).[21] A big project located in a large city or straddling a number of suburbs may require the filing of dozens of applications.[22]

The diversity of regulatory agencies and powers most annoys developers at the state level. The local agencies have operated visibly for many years. Although the operations of the federal agencies are in general newer, they are highly publicized. But the states have new operations that are not widely known, and state government generally may be less respected than the local or federal government.[23] The state operations also may be more extensive than the others. One study in California found forty-one state agencies besides the coastal commissions with overlapping regulatory responsibilities for the coastal zone.[24] In Oregon's coastal zone, at least eleven state agencies in addition to the coastal commission administer at least twenty-six land-use programs.[25] Along the Maine coast, eleven additional state agencies administer forty laws.[26] Six Minnesota agencies, according to a staff member of the State Planning Agency, exercise 679 regulatory and nonregulatory land-use powers.[27] Most states have twenty or more programs that in some way involve regulation of land use.[28]

Most projects require applications to only a small proportion of the state programs. But the rulings of different agencies inevitably conflict because the agencies have varying objectives and overlapping jurisdictions. A state land-use agency may try to increase the parking facilities of a project, while a state air-pollution agency or the Environmental Protection Agency (EPA) may try to decrease them. The state strip-mining agency may turn down or heavily restrict a proposed stripping operation that the local zoning board and the rest of the local government want because it will increase the local tax base. Local governments, sanitary districts, and state water-pollution agencies may support new sewage-treatment plants because they will purify the water supply and open new land for urban growth; the state land-use agency may oppose them for the latter reason, and the EPA may support them for the former reason or oppose them for the latter one.[29]

The lack of coordination repeatedly produces difficulties and frustrations for all the groups involved in land-use regulation. To environmentalists, it poses the risk that an adverse ruling from an unexpected source may undo months of uncompensated work. To government officials at all levels, it means spending long hours adjusting interagency differences in permit orders or explaining these differences to annoyed applicants or constituents. ("You never see a happy new face coming in here," said a California coastal planner [AI, Santa Cruz, California, August 1975].) No agency today can issue a permit order, as could local agencies in the days before land-use reform, and be sure that it ends the matter.

The officials of the state land-use agencies constantly have to stretch their overworked staffs to deal with or mollify other regulatory agencies, and are always enmeshed in interagency red tape or jurisdictional disputes that erode their political support. "The state runs, I'd say, about thirty-five other programs that in some way affect lane-use," according to a Vermont district environmental coordinator, "and every time one of them turns down a project, whether we're involved or not, Act 250 gets blamed" (AI, Essex Junction, Vermont, September 1975).

Most unhappy with the lack of coordination are development interests. They argue that a state land-use agency is useless if it cannot overrule or replace other regulatory bodies. They also dislike the costly delays and duplications of effort forced on them by the multiplicity of agencies. They resent applications that ask the same questions over and over again, often with subtle differences in emphasis, requiring variant responses that are expensive to supply. They are puzzled by the uselessness of approval by one agency in gaining approval by another. When a developer inadvertently fails to file a permit with an obscure agency, that agency, some other agencies, or environmentalists may use the oversight as a means of holding up the project. Or his application can be turned down by one after it has been approved by others. Even if all the agencies approve, they may place inconsistent or contradictory conditions on the project. Reconciling the differences leads to further delays, costs, and duplications of effort the developer must bear. He can again do little about them if he wants the project approved.

Developers constantly complain about being "horsed around" and "ping-ponged" from agency to agency, of being told by one agency to go see another, of not being able to get straight answers or predictable behavior from any of them. Developers also object to what they see as the excesses of citizen participation. A Vermont builder said:

> You look at the people on the commissions and you look at the environmental groups bringing up the complaints, and it's obvious they'll both do their best to keep you from building. It's no conspiracy or anything—just like-minded people who know where their friends are and want to put the screws to you. The best way is those little fine-print, nit-pick rules of theirs. Nobody in the state really understands them, so they can twist them any way they want. The builder always loses. (AI, Essex Junction, Vermont, June 1976)

In 1973, Robert Hutchinson of Augusta, Maine, treated a conference on state land-use laws sponsored by the National Association of Home Builders to an account of his dealings with his state's Department of Environmental Protection:

> With the aid of a land planner we drew up a proposed garden complex containing 9 12-plex garden-type apartment units. Upon this land planner's advice, I went over and I checked with the Department of Environmental Protection to see if we came under their jurisdiction. We showed the individual over there our plans, and this was not one of the bottom men on the ladder, and we were told that we didn't have to bother with them, that we didn't come under their jurisdiction. . . .
>
> We then determined that the Augusta area would not support such a large apartment complex. Here again, we've been about a million people [in

Maine] for 10 years. So then we came back with a project consisting only of 7 duplex houses. Each unit in the house was going to rent for $270 a month, so they would be probably the most expensive units in the area. The lots were averaging approximately 15,000 square feet per lot.

At the time two of the neighbors, here again one was retired, became upset with the introduction of rental houses in the area. They hired an attorney who in turn contacted the Department of Environmental Protection and then one of the enforcement personnel of the DEP contacted me. He was very belligerent. . . .

The guy wanted to fight. . . . I told him that I had just been over there the previous November, and had been told that I did not come under their jurisdiction.

He calmed down. I showed him that I was willing to cooperate and went through that routine and I think this kind of surprised him, because I think he hadn't run into this attitude previously. . . .

As it turned out, the fellow from the DEP called me back three days later and said it was now determined that I did come under their jurisdiction. . . . So the individual came over and he had an application form for me which consisted of nine pages, and because we had had all the engineering work done, because the area is flat we actually had had a two-foot contour map made. The city has . . . five foot [contour maps] but we worked this out onto a two foot and my office girl, whom I consider extremely capable, she and I both worked approximately 30 hours for a total of 60 man hours just filling in blanks, gathering soils, maps, and so forth. . . .

We have to show that we have sufficient water and sewage disposal systems. Here again, we were served by municipal sewage and water, so there was no problem there. Local planning board approval, we had already obtained. The chairman of the planning board bent over backwards to help me, partially because I think he thought what I was doing was right and I think partially because of the fact he also was a builder, and they had cost him, through price increases and a delay, over $30,000 on a shopping center he was doing for someone else in Livermore Falls, so he had no love for the state DEP. . . .

We had to send in complete plat plans showing water, sewer, surface drains and finally, that there would be no undue harm to the environment. . . . Now once we sent the application in to the Department of Environmental Protection we had to notify by registered mail all the abutting property owners. If you don't think this stirs up a hornet's nest. . . .

So as it ended up, the neighborhood organized. They hired two attorneys. They all wrote to the DEP requesting a public hearing, which was granted. This public hearing, I knew, was going to delay me a minimum of another 75 working days. In Maine, 75 working days in July and August is 50 per cent of our good earth-moving season.

Anyway, we had the public hearing and it was in August. In September we had a decision of a go-ahead. For seven lots, we put Watergate off the front page of the paper for two days in a row.

All for seven lots. When we got our approval it made the fine print.[30]

The Procedural Simplifications

Small developers, such as Hutchinson in Maine, and small businessmen-homeowners, such as Joey Hickey in the Adirondacks, can do little about bureaucratic mistreatment in individual cases. But eventually it becomes clear that many developers, businessmen, and homeowners of all sizes are having these problems. Local government officials are unhappy about them, too. Construction badly needed or wanted is being held up—in some cases, prevented—by the intricate demands of the state regulatory process. And the process seems to produce few compensating environmental or other benefits. So, typically, a few years after the state land-use programs originate, developers and local governments begin to lobby for some loosening or relaxation of the regulatory process. On these grounds, for example, the Vermont Home Builders' Association suggested (unsuccessfully) that Act 250 be amended to eliminate four of the ten criteria for regulatory decisions, to do away with public hearings, to give automatic approval after twenty days to any application on which the district environmental commission had not acted, to make the commissions elective rather than appointive, and to abolish the state Environmental Board.[31]

The pro-development forces have plausible arguments, and the state land-use agencies are hard put not to accede to at least some of them. The impulse that created the agencies has inevitably waned somewhat by now. The land-use reformers and environmentalists who may have been heroes to much of the public now seem on their way to becoming just another self-serving interest group. And the pro-development groups do not want large, politically visible changes in the regulatory process; they want smaller, subtler, less obvious changes.

Moreover, bureaucratic horror stories like Hutchinson's or Hickey's have become common knowledge.[32] It is difficult to defend procedures with such results, although a certain amount of absurdity may be inevitable in any new agency that operates in a relatively new and complex field and owes its existence to reformist zeal. The recent economic and energy difficulties, as well as the rise in construction costs and housing prices, make the hardships that result from agency decisions or procedures seem particularly indefensible. These hardships have figured prominently in the recent rise in conservative popular opposition to bureaucratic government in general and centralized regulation in particular. Under these conditions, citizen groups and public officials, including those of the land-use agencies themselves, also support procedural simplifications for their own reasons. Local governments, under comparable political and economic pressures, are simplifying their own land-use procedures.[33] It seems sensible to streamline the state regulatory process as well.

So the simplification efforts get under way. Throughout, the agencies talk about smoothing out the kinks in the regulatory process while protecting all the interests taking part in it. They sometimes imply that simplification will help comparatively unsophisticated environmental groups. But instead of clarifying or specifying physical standards for development and administrative rules for decision-making, the agencies turn out to be interested only in procedural mechanisms to hasten their deliberations. The general lack of standards and rules in the programs facilitates the adoption of such mechanisms. However justifiable they are in particular instances, the new measures amount to partial deregulation.

Within a year after the Adirondack Park Agency amended its procedures, average processing time for applications went from over forty days to under fifteen. By 1977, the APA reportedly was issuing permits faster than many Adirondack local governments that had previously objected to its tardiness.[34] Similarly, in 1973–74 the Vermont district environmental commissions deliberately speeded up their processing, and the proportion of applications handled within ten days of receipt went from under 10 percent to over 40 percent. By 1977, about 90 percent of all applications were approved or denied within a month.[35] Most other states with land-use programs have recently made comparable efforts to expedite applications.

Faster processing of applications would not necessarily favor developers (apart from eliminating the financial and other costs of delay) if it were the result of enhanced efficiency rather than less intensive scrutiny. But agency reviews were often not particularly intensive in the first place because of understaffing or underfinancing. No evidence suggests that the agencies have developed new approaches to reviewing applications to compensate for the loss of time in which to examine proposed developments. Environmental groups and neighboring governments also have lost time that they formerly used to analyze proposed projects and to mobilize against those they judged unsound. Development interests and the local governments allied with them seem to be the primary, if not the sole, beneficiaries of faster processing.

Other simplification devices have had similar effects. The Vermont, Florida, Pennsylvania, and Adirondack programs have shortened their applications and combined them with those of other state programs. But these measures also seem likely to weaken the environmental thrust of the land-use agencies' reviews and to put environmental groups and opposed local governments at a disadvantage. The Vermont, Maryland, Florida, California, and Adirondack programs have begun to hold joint hearings with other state, local, and federal agencies, but these hearings will probably have similar effects.

In addition, all the programs have started holding prehearing conferences to iron out problems in proposals and to keep the various participants from having to take positions in public from which later retreat would be difficult and time-consuming.[36] Such hearings seem likely to facilitate negotiations and bargains that favor developers. Moreover, the programs have in different ways created a "conceptual approval" stage of the regulatory procedure in which proposals, particularly for large projects, are to be examined in outline, with their details subject to a later regulatory decision. The purpose of this two-stage procedure is to keep large and small issues from becoming mixed, to simplify project design, and, above all, to prevent the developer and the agency from becoming involved in long, complex, expensive proceedings on projects unlikely to be approved. But conceptual approval in effect commits the land-use agency to the project in question and again promotes, this time at a later point in the procedure, bargaining and negotiating that favor the developer.

The Vermont, Florida, Pennsylvania, and Adirondack programs also have begun to restrict public participation at their hearings.

They now require a citizen who wishes to participate to demonstrate that he or she will be directly affected by the proposed project. "Being directly affected" means having an economic interest at stake, usually through ownership of adjacent land. This restriction, intended to eliminate "frivolous" interventions, cuts off most environmental groups, speeds hearings, and favors development.[37]

Many other states have experimented with comparable expediting devices.[38] National and state interest groups of developers have supported the experiments.[39] Some states have devised expediting mechanisms in response to pressure not so much from developers and local governments as from other state agencies. For example, the 1976 California coastal law, in contrast to the 1972 law, reduces the extent of the coastal commissions' operations in relation to the state's Energy Commission, Forestry Board, Water Resources Control Board, and State Lands Commission.[40] In 1977, the state's Liquefied Natural Gas Terminal Act reduced the coastal commissions' operations in relation to the Public Utilities Commission. All these other agencies had been involved in lengthy, permit-delaying jurisdictional disputes with the coastal commissions.[41]

In some cases, state land-use agencies have simplified their procedures by deliberately attempting to narrow the scope of their operations. In early 1979 members of the California legislature were promoting a bill to reduce the California coastal commissions' authority over development in the rapidly urbanizing Santa Monica Mountains in the Los Angeles area; the commissions responded by proposing legislation that would eliminate their control over the construction of homes on coastal lots that have adequate water, sewers, and roads. The commissions would continue to regulate construction that affected public access to beaches or scenic views, but the reduction of jurisdiction would apply not just in the Santa Monica Mountains but throughout the coastal zone. The proposed bill would, said the state commission's executive director, "substantially change the commission's authority" by "streamlining" permit procedures and "getting rid of unnecessary regulation," instead of taking the "drastic measures advocated by the commission's opponents."[42] Similarly, in late 1979 the commissions successfully supported an amendment that will allow them to designate environmentally resilient areas, where they will relinquish jurisdiction over the construction of individual single-family homes.

In no case has simplification dismantled the programs or otherwise gone as far as developers and their allies would like. Nowhere have they obtained "one-stop shopping," the ability to file only one application for a given project. Nor are they likely to attain this goal, which in most cases would tilt regulation overwhelmingly in their favor. The environmental groups are strong enough to veto one-stop shopping and do not want to see further weakening of the state land-use agencies. The agencies themselves are no more willing than other state and local regulatory bodies to give up their powers.

All parties, including many developers, concede that the present fragmented, disjointed process of regulation, so frequently attacked, in fact allows more consideration of different private perspectives and government objectives than would be possible in a more unified system.[43] A California planner-developer commented:

Sure, the process is a mess, but somewhere along the line every little birdwatcher group, every obscure sub-department of agencies you never heard of, gets a say if they want it. I might not always think they have anything to contribute, and they might drive me crazy if I let them, but it would be worse if they were shut out entirely. It's worth the aggravation. Getting them into the process makes it harder for them to say later that they weren't consulted. And if they really do have something to say, it makes it less necessary for them to say later they told you so. It's a good thing. (ATI, Redwood City, California, May 1978)

In addition, all parties, again including developers, agree that fragmented regulation allows one level or agency of government to activate the regulatory process throughout government in a way that may not be possible otherwise. In Vermont, the district environmental commissions have used Act 250 as an "administrative checkpoint" to make certain that developers apply for *other* required state and local permits and that the other agencies in fact issue them. As a result, local building codes in the state are being enforced, apparently for the first time in many cases.[44]

Similarly, the Florida land-use law invigorated the state's regional planning councils by giving them responsibility for DRI reviews. Before passage, less than half of Florida's counties belonged to such councils; three of the eleven regions had no council at all. Now all the regions have councils, and nearly all eligible counties and cities participate in them. As a planner at the active South Florida council in Miami told Robert Healy, "The agency came alive because of the DRI process."[45] Finally, all the state land-use agencies have, whether directly (by law) or indirectly (by education or example), encouraged localities to enact land-use controls and pay more attention to the effects of growth.[46] One-stop shopping and other extreme forms of procedural simplification would eliminate this beneficial stimulation.

CHAPTER **9**

The Economic Effects
of the Programs

It is impossible to examine the economic effects of the land-use laws in isolation from those of such other factors as growth in the entire economy, urban growth, interest rates, housing demand, and zoning and other environmental laws. Putting dollar amounts on or otherwise quantifying the environmental costs and benefits of the programs is also a very difficult exercise. Moreover, assigning an exact economic value to preserving, improving, or destroying unmarketed intangibles such as scenic views, wildlife, air quality, or seclusion cannot, in many cases, be done.

Property values are quantifiable, but the effects of the land-use programs on property values are difficult to measure because of what economists call "the floating value problem." State land-use regulation may induce a developer to alter the design of a proposed project substantially or to move it to an unregulated area. These changes alter the value of the project as well as the value of the land on which the project is located or from which it has been removed, and also the value of nearby land. But it may be difficult to determine which nearby lands are changing in value, in which direction, and to what extent these changes are due to state regulation.

Because of these difficulties and because of simple lack of interest, few economists have done rigorous quantitative studies of the effects of any kind of land-use regulation, centralized or not, anywhere in

171

the country.[1] Economist Robert Healy has commented: "The best minds of our profession have tended either to ignore the economic problems of environmental regulation or to airily impose unworkable theoretical solutions."[2]

Many of the more sophisticated economic treatments of state land-use programs suggest their possible effects but do not seriously attempt to measure them.[3] Consequently, these studies do not yield much evidence. Moreover, most of the available data on the economic effects of land-use programs come from the California coastal program, primarily because the struggle over the passage of the 1976 law provoked political and academic interest in the results of the 1972 law. But large gaps, especially for nonresidential land uses, remain even in the California data.[4]

Effects on Economic Growth

At their inception, the programs had opponents who predicted that the programs would bankrupt developers, put construction workers out of jobs, stifle real-estate and mortgage-lending activity, or harm local economies. Events suggest that these fears were not justified, for two reasons. First, the programs have never been stringent enough to prevent a determined developer from building altogether. If, for instance, the state land-use agency allows him to build only three-quarters of the number of houses he had proposed for a given site, he can recoup his apparent loss, and perhaps even increase his profits, by charging more for each home on the now less dense, more desirable site. The California coastal commissions often require builders to offer two parking places for each apartment. But households that have two or more cars can, in general, afford to spend more on their apartments than households with only one car; builders can charge accordingly. If a builder's proposal is rejected completely, he can usually build in an unregulated area (for instance, away from the coast), duck below the state agency's size threshold, or avoid state regulation by some other means. In very few cases have builders been unable to resort to adaptation or avoidance to keep a project alive or profitable. So state regulation has not caused widespread and substantial economic losses at either the statewide or the local level.

Yet pro-development groups have produced several studies that apparently demonstrate large dollar and job losses resulting from the programs. In 1976, the Construction Industry Research Board (CIRB), an organization of large southern California builders, estimated that between 1973 and 1975 the coastal commissions denied $440 million worth of residential, commercial, and industrial building. It also estimated that the total market value of projects that were denied, withdrawn, or deterred during the three-year period was—not counting land costs, since they were presumably paid or committed before the developers filed their applications—between $1.1 and $1.5 billion. These decisions eliminated some 20,000 to 28,000 full-time construction jobs, which would have generated wages of between $700 million and $1 billion over the three years.[5] These figures suggest that the commissions have inflicted a staggering blow to California's economy.

These figures do not, however, show that the commissions approved $4 billion of construction in 1973 (largely a recession year) alone.[6] The figures suggest that a permit denial along the coast leaves entrepreneurial, labor, and financial resources totally idle; in fact, the permit zone extends only 1000 yards inland, and scores of building possibilities off the coast remain available for every one building possibility on it. The CIRB figures also suggest that the commission decisions apply to projects in progress, not to prospective developments. In truth, the dollar "losses" do not represent money taken away from anyone, and the job "losses" do not represent anyone thrown out of work. In economists' terms, the opportunity costs created by the programs are low, especially since noncoastal California has enjoyed a building boom in recent years.[7] The purpose of the program was to prevent objectionable building on the coast. The measures necessary for this purpose may have resulted in some losses, but nothing on the scale implied by the CIRB figures.

The other reason why the state land-use programs have not been substantial deterrents to economic growth is that they are not among the larger forces affecting the land development market or the economy generally. Recessions, inflation, high interest rates, energy problems, rising costs of labor and materials, tax rates, housing demand—all are widely acknowledged to be more influential in shaping land markets and the overall economy than the state land-use programs. When local unemployment rates in the building trades climbed to well over 20 percent—as they did, for instance, in urban portions of Florida during the 1973–75 recession because of overbuilding[8]—the state land-use laws received little of the blame. "The most you could say," an official of the Florida Home Builders Association conceded, "is that the law is a contributing factor. There's no way to tell how much it contributes. The basic problem is that we just built too much, maybe three or four years' worth of excess residential capacity in the areas around Miami and Fort Lauderdale, and then got caught in the downturn, that's all. We could do without the law, but we've got plenty of worse problems" (AI, Tallahassee, Florida, January 1976).

In 1976, the Adirondack Park Agency conducted a study comparing residential real estate activities within the park during 1973–75 with those in the Catskill Mountains region in the southeastern part of New York State and the portions of Adirondack counties that were not in the park; these other regions are not subject to state land-use regulation. The study found "the same relative decline" in all three areas during this recession period: "No difference in relative changes was noted between the Adirondack Park and similar rural areas not regulated by a regional land use and development plan."[9] Real estate transfers—that is, sales—dropped off by about the same amount (21–23 percent) in all three areas.[10] Construction starts—that is, new houses built—declined by roughly the same amount (53–59 percent) in all these areas and in New York State as a whole.[11] The causes of the Adirondack Park decline, according to the study, were the recession and other national factors—increasing costs of land, construction, capital, and therefore homeownership—combined with a statewide decline in population.[12] These factors affected even projects that had received APA approval:

Most of the construction in the Adirondack Park prior to and following the adoption of the APA Land Use and Development Plan has been residential, especially seasonal homes. Between August 1, 1973 and December 31, 1975, the Adirondack Park Agency approved 1,142 residential building lots. In a survey of project sponsors who received APA permits for subdivision of five or more building lots, the results indicated that only 23 percent of the lots approved by the Agency between August 1, 1973 and July 31, 1975 had been sold as of late 1975. This too is exemplary of the decline in the residential construction market within the Adirondack Park. It appears that the important seasonal home construction business in the Adirondacks, Catskills and other areas of upstate New York is suffering the same general downturn found in the state and national construction industry.[13]

Stiffening of Development Markets

Although the state land-use programs may not prevent economic growth, they make development markets less responsive to wider economic and technological changes, less able to adjust to or take advantage of new consumer needs or desires. The programs tie up land or capital in inefficient, unnecessary, or out-of-date uses that may diminish the choices available to consumers or producers and so create serious losses for society as a whole.

This problem arises in four ways. First, the regulatory process delays or prevents the completion of projects, depriving developers of the entrepreneurial opportunities that inspired the projects in the first place. After several such experiences, developers react defensively. "I've got some options on a couple of big tracts," a Vermont resort developer who had just finished a large project reported, "and obviously I ought to build something on them fairly soon. But the idea of facing all those Act 250 hassles again—well, it doesn't exactly make me want to get to work. Sometimes it just makes me want to go to sleep" (AI, Bolton, Vermont, September, 1975).

A prominent Tallahassee corporate lawyer commented that, in part because of Florida's land-use law, he now advises his developer clients not to start any large or long-term project "if they can't get in and out of it inside of one economic cycle. That's a new kind of thinking for Florida, but the law just makes me hesitate. You need a margin to deal with it. It's just so easy to get hurt bad if the DRI people hang you up on anything at all" (AI, Tallahassee, Florida, January 1976).

The programs also have stiffened development markets by publicly committing developers to long-term site plans. Most developers feel locked in by the necessity of having to make such commitments. The state land-use agencies demand more detail in the plans than the local zoning boards, and are less receptive to requests for alterations in the plans when conditions change. Many builders make long-term site plans for their own internal corporate use, but most have reservations about making the plans public or legally binding. They bitterly resent having to return to the state land-use agency if they want to alter the plans in any way, and they feel that the whole arrangement ties their hands.

The loudest objections come, not surprisingly, from the builders of the largest, longest-term projects—for example, Maryland utility companies and Florida DRI (development of regional impact) builders. The vice-president for environmental affairs of a Maryland power company said:

> It really annoys us when we have to specify, maybe five years or more before the plant actually gets built, exactly how we're going to handle air pollution or keep from overheating the water we use. Say we promise to use a certain kind of scrubber to clean the air coming out of our smokestack. How do we know some cheaper or better scrubber won't come out in the meantime? Or that our distinguished regulatory brethren won't come up with some new pollutant the scrubbers can't handle? We don't, and we have to fly blind. (AI, Washington, D.C., February 1976)

A developer who tried to build an entire Florida community and was turned down has urged "flexibility . . . to allow for technological advances in planning, designing, and engineering concepts which will no doubt occur during the course of development. For example, to demand a firm commitment to the type of waste treatment facility which will be employed for a project to be completed 25 years from now deprives a New Town concept of one of its most important advantages."[14] In response to such complaints, a 1977 amendment to Florida's law allowed an approved DRI to be altered without reapproval, providing that the changes were small or reduced the project's environmental impact. For example, a project could increase the number of its housing units by 5 percent or 200 units (whichever was less), or it could decrease the number, all without reapproval.

The programs have stiffened development markets inadvertently by affecting the availability of financing. Because they fear that stringent state regulation might make their loans to developers turn bad, banks in some states, particularly California and Florida, have become reluctant to lend money for projects subject to state control. They will commit funds only if the project has been approved or the developer can convince them that the state agency will approve it.

"We cop out," a California banker said. "We say we'll make a commitment once all the necessary government approvals are secured. So some builders go off to the coastal commissions and never come back" (AI, San Francisco, California, August 1975).

This posture on the part of lending institutions not only forces builders to bear the early costs of their projects themselves but in effect turns the banks into regulatory bodies. Given their well-known conservatism, financial and otherwise, some banks regulate more stringently than the state land-use agencies whose creation they originally opposed. "Some of our banks," a Florida builder said, "are so frightened about the DRI process that they'll do a tighter environmental review on a proposal than the regional planning council would ever dream of doing" (AI, Tampa, Florida, January 1976).

In addition, state regulation has, more or less inadvertently, led to an unaesthetic standardization of project design. Developers and their planners, architects, engineers, and other technical personnel all admit to watching the decisions of the state land-use agencies closely to see which kinds of projects have regulatory difficulties and which do not. They then, quite understandably, try to design projects that will easily obtain approval. As in other regulated areas, requirements intended as minimums become maximums in industry practice, and past approvals come to define and delimit future proposals, constricting the free play of imagination that leads to good and innovative projects.

Some opponents of the programs profess to see ideological intent in this homogenization of design. A conservative Vermont state legislator said: "Those Act 250 people are all statists. They like to push people around. They want to see developers groveling before them. They don't want you to build a purple hut" (AI, Kirby, Vermont, September 1975). More pragmatically, a Florida developer said:

You can see it in the plans. All the large waterfront projects are starting to look like Hilton Head [a well-known coastal development in South Carolina]. Most of the big operators in the state have always talked to each other, built all over the state, read the same magazines, and used a lot of the same methods and consultants, but I still think the look-alike problems have gotten worse since the state got into the act. All the site densities and layouts are the same. The open spaces have the same shapes or numbers of trees.

The distances houses are set back from the ocean or lake or swamp are the same. (ATI, Miami, Florida, July 1977)

Some land-use agency officials are aware of this problem. A member of the Vermont Environmental Board stated:

As I think back on what we've done, there's no question we've come up with some arbitrary design criteria you'd never know about from reading Act 250. If you try to do something really different your application will at least get delayed, especially if it raises subjective or aesthetic questions. You can't break the treeline. If you're going to paint exposed wood, it's got to be Vermont barn red or Vermont barn gray. You've got to use a particular kind of sewage system if you don't already use a particular kind of septic tank. You'll run into trouble if you try to put in any kind of solar energy system, even though we're on record as in principle preferring renewable energy. It's as if we're setting builders a puzzle that basically has only one answer—do what's been done before. In our defense, I'd say we're only contributing to existing trends. But we're making them worse. We're certainly preventing new kinds of architecture and planning that might be perfectly well suited to Vermont. I get uncomfortable with the thought that in some ways we're just trying to keep the state looking the way we think it did in 1910. After all, how did Vermont get to look so distinctive? By allowing diversity to bloom, not by trying to reconstruct some mythical past. (AI, South Burlington, Vermont, September 1975)

Some state agencies actively encourage some development methods at the expense of others. The Pennsylvania strip-mining program, for instance, has an unwritten policy of preferring bituminous coal operators to use the "modified block-cut" method of mining rather than alternative, often plausible techniques.[15] Such policies clearly limit the adaptiveness of the development market.

Increasing the Costs of Development

State land use regulation raises the costs of development. By prohibiting development of some land, it raises the price of land that is being developed or has been developed. Bureaucratic red tape introduces new costs for developers—the costs of delays, consultants, application completion, and uncertainty. Finally, the satisfaction of regulatory conditions can be expensive. All land-use regulation, whether state or local, produces these three types of costs, but their existence and extent have been more fully documented for local regulation than for state regulation.[16]

The state programs' effects on land prices are hard to measure in part because other factors—most notably increased demand, especially for housing—have been dramatically raising land values across the country in the years since the programs were introduced. Both economic theory and common sense suggest that the programs would tend to lower the demand for, and hence the price of, undeveloped land subject to state control—that is, land that has not (yet) gone through the regulatory process. At the same time, the programs would tend to raise the value of property that is either already developed or not subject to state regulation. Owners whose property had already passed through, or received exemption from, state regulation would benefit. Those whose property had not done so would suffer. Regulatory approval or exemption would add to the value of property.

In Maryland and Pennsylvania, regulation is too limited and specialized to affect significantly the land market as a whole. But in the Adirondack Park, a town zoning administrator said: "I could take you to a hundred places within five miles of here where the APA has raised or lowered land values by 20 percent or more" (AI, Ray Brook, New York, June 1976).

In southern California, an examination of assessors' records between 1971 and 1975 showed that in the city of Ventura the value of undeveloped land parcels in the coastal permit zone rose 8 percent while those further inland rose 26 percent. In Oxnard, the values of undeveloped land parcels rose by 28 percent along the coast and by 41 percent inland.[17] A study by Los Angeles's Security Pacific Bank found that in the five southern California coastal counties (San Diego, Orange, Los Angeles, Ventura, and Santa Barbara) prices for single-family homes in the coastal planning zone rose 41 percent in 1972–75, while prices for inland homes rose only 27 percent.[18] In other words, when one combines the results of the two Southern California studies, it appears that coastal regulation tends to raise the price of coastal developed property and to depress the price of coastal undeveloped property. Although much of the difference between coastal and inland property values may reflect the scarcity of coastal homes or the desirability of living near the sea, some of it undoubtedly derives from coastal regulation. It is unclear what the difference might be in less rapidly growing areas.

A 1976 survey of assessors in California coastal counties, conducted by the California Assembly Select Committee on Coastal Zone Resources, found that since the 1972 coastal law had been in effect, sales of undeveloped coastal property had declined drastically. The committee attributed this effect to uncertainty about both the eventual shape of the 1976 legislation and the course of coastal regulation generally. The assessor from rural Sonoma County north of San Francisco told the survey that the 1972 program "brought the sale of larger parcels to a virtual halt," and the Los Angeles County assessor said that the law's "apparent effect" had been "to impair the value of vacant undeveloped land."[19]

At the same time, land parcels that were developed or had received permits from the coastal commissions quickly increased in value. The assessor from rural Humboldt County near the Oregon border said that the program had increased values "approximately 20 percent to 40 percent"; the Los Angeles assessor said "uncertainty as to what future uses can be made of vacant land in the Los Angeles County Coastal Zone has created a premium in existing improved properties in that zone."[20] This uncertainty may have contributed to the steep speculative rises in house prices in southern California in 1976–1979.[21]

The effects of bureaucratic red tape and of regulatory conditions on costs are sometimes confused. An early, somewhat impressionistic study of the Vermont program, conducted by a University of Vermont economist for the Vermont Natural Resources Council, an environmental group, lumped the two costs together and concluded that they increase prices "on the order of 10%."[22] And yet more recent and careful studies that distinguished between the two types of costs have reached approximately the same conclusion.

An Urban Institute examination of the records of the builders of twenty-two residential DRIs in southeast Florida in 1973–74 indicated that the DRI process added an average of $444 to the cost of constructing a single-family house.[23] Of this amount, $223 resulted from bureaucratic obstacles: $31 went for preparing and presenting the DRI application and $192 for delay costs such as interest charges and property taxes while the application was being processed. The remaining $221 resulted from regulatory requirements originating in the DRI process: land donations, construction of public facilities, and other environmental requirements. Using the standard developers' and appraisers' rule of thumb of multiplying all regulatory costs for single-family units by eight to arrive at their effect on market value,[24] the researchers estimated that the Florida land-use program added roughly $3500 to the price of a home. They also estimated that the DRI process added an average of $348 to the cost of constructing an apartment.[25] The rule of thumb for calculating effect on the market value of apartments is to multiply regulatory costs by six;[26] hence, the state land-use program added about $2100 to the value of an apartment.

An examination of regulatory costs in Dover Township, New Jersey, in 1975 came up with somewhat lower estimates. Dover Township, in rapidly growing Ocean County, accounted for nearly a third of the development applications to the state coastal zone management program from 1973 to 1975.[27] In eleven single-family-home developments, state regulations added an estimated average of $135 to the cost of constructing each house: $50 for meeting substantive regulatory requirements, $64 for carrying costs for preparing and presenting the state application, and $21 for the delay costs of interest charges and property taxes.[28] According to the rule of thumb, state coastal regulations added roughly $1100 to the value of a home. State regulations added an average of $125 to the cost of constructing each unit of nine apartment developments examined: $33 for meeting regulatory requirements, $70 for application costs, and $22 for interest charges and property taxes.[29] Again, the rule of thumb suggests that state regulations added about $750 to the value of an apartment.

Part of the reason why regulatory costs in Florida seem to be roughly three times as great as those in New Jersey may be that New Jersey developers had to submit local and state applications at about the same time; the state was thus involved in the regulatory process from its inception, and the builders had to devote relatively little time and money to the satisfaction of state requirements specifically. By contrast, in Florida the review of DRIs by the regional planning council usually began later in the regulatory process and often resulted in a situation where the process was lengthened and made more expensive solely because of the DRI requirements.

Before 1975, the New Jersey coastal program had experimented with later submissions to the state, and it found that these had produced much greater costs and delays. If, for instance, the state submissions took place only after local bodies had approved the project, the state regulatory costs for a single-family house amounted to an average of $534, increasing the market value of the house by nearly $4300. The state regulatory costs for an apartment averaged $241, increasing its market value by over $1400.[30] The house figures for New Jersey under these conditions were higher than those for Florida, and the apartment figures were almost as high.

The Florida and the New Jersey studies took place during recessionary periods and dealt with only large residential projects. The studies do not state total prices for the homes and apartments in question, or how many of them there were. But their findings suggest that state regulation added some 5 to 15 percent to the cost of homeownership. With the effects of regulation on land prices, the total increase in costs for some developments might be in the range of 10 to 20 percent. Both developers and public officials generally agree with this estimate. A series of studies, some of them conducted in Pennsylvania, of the total costs of strip-mine reclamation programs have come up with comparable estimates of the percentage cost increase to buyers per ton of coal.[31] No similar studies of power-plant siting programs are available.

Increasing the Costs to Buyers

Developers always try to pass on to buyers as much as they can of the increases in their costs. If buyers have no substitutes for the developers' products—if, in the language of economists, demand is inelastic or supply elastic—then the developers will succeed in their attempts to pass along the costs; the buyers will end up bearing the increases themselves. There have been no empirical econometric studies of how the cost increases produced by state land-use regulation are distributed between developers and their customers. But home buyers have relatively few substitutes for the developers' products (and sometimes cannot remain living where they are) and so must pay much of the increase. Buyers of energy also typically lack substitutes (at least over the short term) for the products of coal operators and power companies, and must pay nearly all of the increase.

The state land-use programs also may raise costs for buyers in more indirect ways. For example, the cost increases the programs create may on occasion slow the rate of construction, compel developers to move to unregulated areas or build smaller projects, or otherwise reduce the availability of some types of building—thereby upping its cost. The programs also may penalize buyers by in effect forcing them to accept housing or other construction of lower quality or smaller size than they would like. But economists have never measured these effects of the programs.

The programs also seem to encourage developers to build less dense, more expensive projects. Another Urban Institute study of south Florida DRIs found that this tactic alone increased selling prices by an average of 11 percent.[32] The study did not examine the effects of DRI regulation on the rest of the local and regional development market, but presumably it both diminishes the supply of land that can be developed and increases the number of potential buyers for less expensive residential (and other) projects. These projects, too, therefore become more expensive. As the price of new development rises, the price of existing development, whether rental or owned, inevitably rises as well.

The total increases in costs for buyers as a result of state land-use regulation have never been precisely measured and may not be measurable. But they are obviously real. On the other hand, these costs have fallen on developers and their customers during a period when many of the other costs of development have risen even more. Nationally, between 1970 and 1974 the wages of construction workers went up 39 percent, the costs of building materials 36 percent, and the price of land 62 percent.[33] Increases in interest rates, inflation, equipment prices, and overhead costs (most notably for energy) also took their toll. All these costs are still rising. The costs of the state land-use programs, although substantial, do not appear to represent a relatively large share of increments in the overall costs to developers and their customers in the past decade.

And yet, a 5 percent increase in the price of a $50,000 house raises the price to $52,500; a 20 percent increase raises it to $60,000. The young couple unable to afford a first home, the older family unable to move to a new one, the industry unable to put up a locally desired plant, and the builder unable to provide the housing, the plant, or employment can focus their frustrations on what is wrong with state land-use regulation. For the programs, even as minor contributors to overall price increases, are under direct political control in a way that the causes of larger increases—inflation, housing demand, interest rates, energy prices, urbanization itself—all too evidently are not. The programs are visible. Unlike local zoning, they are new and experimental. They can be influenced and changed more readily than inflation.

Moreover, the price increases the programs produce fall hardest on those portions of society least able to bear them—the poor and minorities, and in fact all those who are economically situated beneath the upper middle class that originates the programs. As Phyllis Myers wrote of Florida in 1974:

> Florida's housing industry has been hard hit by the woes of financing and inflation. Developers have scurried around to serve the luxury second-home condominium market while many residents live inadequately in first homes. Although developers in their DRI review are supposed to relate their project to the region's needs, very few of them are coming forward with single-family housing below $40,000. There are no incentives, financial or otherwise, to build for the low- or moderate-priced market.
>
> Some housing experts, such as Jay Janis, head of the Governor's Task Force on Housing [later undersecretary of the U.S. Department of Housing and Urban Development and chairman of the Federal Home Loan Bank Board] argue that the DRI process is exacerbating the housing shortage by raising the price of housing. Since the DRI thresholds are set so high (especially in the more populous counties where the need is), says Janis, the assessment process now offers no counterbalancing relief.[34]

Nor, for the most part, do the other state land-use programs offer such relief.[35] The California coastal commissions have from time to time made decisions deliberately to protect low- and middle-income housing—preventing, for instance, the construction of an industrial warehouse in a San Diego low-income Chicano neighborhood and the demolition of a set of Santa Monica single-story middle-income rental buildings in favor of a high-rise, high-priced condominium building.[36] In a few higher-income developments, the commissions also have successfully insisted on the provision of low- and middle-income housing.[37] In January 1980, the state commission adopted a policy requiring that a quarter of the nonrental units in any new residential development with 16 or more units be priced so that middle-income buyers could afford them. But such decisions and policies are exceptional for the state land-use agencies. Presumably, land-use regulation inevitably raises costs for the customers of the regulated development; if it did not, profit-minded developers might spontaneously adopt many of the measures necessary for regulatory approval and eliminate the need for governmental action.

Housing costs have risen so high and so quickly as to solve, in a perverse sense, the problem of exclusionary zoning.[38] In the past ten years, many of the victims of exclusionary zoning—minorities and the poor—have found themselves simply priced out of the housing market. A California coastal commissioner stated: "It was the farthest thing from our minds to make it harder for the poor to live on the coast. But as I look back, that was the first and most obvious thing we did" (ATI, San Diego, California, June 1978). As a result, measures to deal with exclusionary zoning have been quietly allowed to disappear from the agencies' agendas. The programs have reinforced the social homogenization they were intended, in part, to undo. The urban slumdwellers who regard the programs with indifference and the rural poor who regard them with hostility are not without justification. To these groups, land-use reform must appear as, to put it politely, just another well-intentioned but ineffectual liberal gesture that dissipated when times became tough or when conservative political pressure was applied.

The programs also have had unfavorable economic effects on groups that are wealthier but still not affluent. The programs have impeded the efforts of elderly farmers to subdivide marginal farms and to retire on the profits, have forced young couples to move into trailer camps thirty miles from work because they cannot afford to live in the towns where they grew up, and have compelled retirees on a fixed income to move away from an increasingly expensive coast; these are social costs that no environmental cleanup can really offset. A Vermont developer fumed: "The state land-use people are the living end. They keep me from hiring people, they keep the projects I'd build from pumping money into the community, they decimate the construction market, they kick Vermonters out of Vermont or to its least attractive parts, and they make a lot of people's lives unbearable. Then they tell you how they've saved the warthog or something" (AI, Essex Junction, Vermont, June 1976). Even if state land-use regulation is responsible for only a small portion of the cost increases for which it is blamed, it has to bear a great deal of opprobrium. The constituency that it antagonizes economically is often much larger than that which supports it politically.

Favoring Large Developers

Developers are a mixed breed in a complex setting. Some are enormous established corporations, such as utilities and large manufacturing concerns. Some are low-capital, high-risk companies, such as those found in much of the homebuilding and coal industries. Some are tiny, often part-time family operations that put up a handful of houses or other small projects. Most developers work in highly volatile, decentralized markets with steep, roller-coaster cycles that depend on broad economic factors—interest rates, recessions, energy prices, inflation—which are essentially beyond the developers' control. Homebuilders are particularly vulnerable to economic cycles; their market is more competitive than that of say, utilities, and their prosperity more closely tied to the health of the overall economy, particularly to the level of deposits at savings and loan associations. But all forms of development demand a high tolerance for entrepreneurial competitiveness and uncertainty. Development is not a line of work for those seeking peace and quiet.

The state land-use programs, for the most part, favor large developers over small ones. To be sure, the programs give some competitive advantages to small developers. A small Florida developer does not build developments of regional impact and so need not be concerned with how DRIs are regulated. A small California developer cannot afford to build on large coastal tracts, and so does not have to worry if coastal regulation effectively removes them from the market. In general, the state agencies seem to scrutinize large projects more closely than small ones. But the larger firms are more likely than the small ones to be able to afford the specialists and the paperwork that the programs necessitate. Most large firms already have such specialists on their staffs and so do not have to hire them at consultants' expensive daily rates to do the paperwork. Similarly, because large firms typically have more capital and larger, more secure profit margins than smaller firms—and because large firms also pay lower interest rates to their lenders—large firms can absorb the costs of the bureaucratic delays and regulatory conditions the land-use programs impose with relatively little pain. Large firms generally have or can get the front-end money necessary to deal with the programs; the smaller firms cannot. Thus the large firms, unlike the small ones, can wait out the programs.

In addition, large firms are more likely than small ones to have several projects under way at any one time. They can afford to spread the risk of regulatory refusal over a number of projects, as small firms cannot. And the financial costs that the programs produce represent a lower percentage of the total for large projects than for small ones. For example, in Vermont: "Many of the added expenses were semi-fixed costs (including architect's fees, engineering design and others). . . . the $50,000-or-so added expense on a $500,000 development might rise to $60,000 on a $1 million development. The hours of consulting, testimony, and design effort, as minimal examples, might not change that significantly (in some cases, not at all) for a much larger project."[39]

If these changes are not significant, then the per-unit cost of the programs will be lower for large projects than for small ones. This difference may lower the prices or raise the profits of the larger firms, in either case further increasing their competitive advantage. The more expensive the units in question, the larger the advantage. The point is made in a William Hamilton cartoon showing one prosperous builder telling another: "I've been for quality development ever since way back when it first became profitable."[40]

Large firms as a rule have more political influence at the state level than small ones. They probably account for more jobs, tax revenues, campaign contributions, public construction, and economic and urban growth than their smaller competitors. They can threaten to go elsewhere or to stop building unless they receive the regulatory treatment they want, and be taken more seriously than small firms, most of which cannot make good on such threats, or cannot do much economic damage if they do. The large firms can therefore strike more advantageous bargains with the state land-use programs than are available to the small firms.

Even state land-use programs that inspect for compliance with their orders or otherwise try to enforce them still tend, for political reasons, to favor large operations. In 1974, according to one study, the Pennsylvania Bureau of Surface Mine Reclamation used its power to suspend licenses disproportionately against the smaller coal operators—disproportionately, that is, in terms of the number of smaller companies, the tonnage they produced, and the frequency and severity of the violations they apparently committed. The study also documented numerous instances of repeated serious violations by large operators, including the biggest coal company in the state, of which the bureau was aware and on which it took no punitive action.[41]

A big Florida developer whose company had spent half a million dollars on planning a large project before construction even began commented: "The little guy can no longer be in the development business."[42] Of course, "the little guy" can and does build projects smaller than DRIs, in unregulated areas, or otherwise exempt from regulation. But some small and ruggedly individualistic builders respond to any regulation so irritably as to make their own problems worse. A younger Vermont developer of medium-size projects explained:

The older guys especially can't deal with the state bureaucracy because they don't expect it, they weren't brought up with it. Sure, when the state tells me what to do, I get mad, but then after a while I go do it. Or I trot back for another meeting to see if I can smooth over the problems. A lot of the small older builders get told what to do, stay mad, and never get around to building the project. They run small operations. There's no big-time board of directors to keep them in line. They build because they like to build. I sympathize, but I can't make a living that way, and neither can they. Sometimes they just drop out of the market. (AI, Burlington, Vermont, September 1975)

A former consultant to the Vermont Environmental Board wrote of Act 250: "Many of the larger developers have been strongly supportive of the Act because they feel it protects their projects from undesirable development on adjoining lands."[43] A big Massachusetts developer who had built two second-home condominium projects in Vermont wrote to the secretary of the Vermont Development and Community Affairs Department, which contains the Vermont Environmental Board:

It is our opinion that the law [Act 250] complements our particular business approach, since it allows us to achieve the standards we set for ourselves without the risk of being undercut by less circumspect development. Our only major complaint is that the law subjects a proposed development to prolonged (sometimes harassing) delays through its appeals process. However, even this fault is sometimes more an issue of judicial backlog than the function of Act 250 itself.

You should also know that these comments are against the background of our company experiencing severe financial problems with our last condominium project. It would perhaps be convenient to blame these problems on Act 250, but that would be self-deluding.[44]

In 1973, *Florida Trend*, an influential business-oriented magazine, editorialized that the state land-use law "will help the developer who really wants to do a good job. Today, if he does that good job, he may find the houses in his subdivision difficult to sell because the developer across the county line wasn't all that interested in quality and, as a result, can sell his homes cheaper."[45]

The small builders make equally self-serving comments, but from a different perspective. "I wouldn't want to say there's a conspiracy," a small Adirondack Park builder confided, "but the APA ends up screwing me and my friends much worse than any of those bigger guys who complain so much and then take the bite off the top" (AI, Lake Placid, New York, June 1976). A small California contractor explained: "The coastal commissions aren't deliberately trying to hurt the small operator, and sometimes they'll lean over backward for him. But day-in, day-out he'd be better off if they'd go away, leave him be" (AI, Montara, California, August 1975). "Getting approval from the state," a big Vermont developer commented, "is like getting a license or a patent. You're in, they're out. Amazingly often, it seems it's large builder who's in and the small one who's out" (AI, Bolton, Vermont, September 1975). Another large Vermont builder said: "The law inconveniences me a lot of ways, and there are a lot of ways I'd change it, but for me the basic thing about it is that it helps keep the competition down" (ATI, Brattleboro, Vermont, June 1979).

The Question of Economic Benefits

The programs also produce substantial economic savings and benefits. But they are not immediately evident, and are extremely difficult to measure against the losses and costs. It is virtually impossible to arrive at a defensible judgment that a particular program is a net economic plus for society or a specific regulatory action a net economic minus. In general, economists find it easier to measure the costs of regulation than its benefits.[46] Many economists, perhaps a majority of them, are philosophically predisposed in favor of unrestrained markets and against regulation.[47] Consequently, little empirical research has been done on the economic benefits that state land-use regulation offers society.

Yet the benefits unquestionably exist. State land-use programs may raise the initial price of a house, but they lower the overall lifetime cost of operating or repairing it by even more. They may increase the value of the house by compelling nearby houses to be built to higher standards or by limiting the amount of housing that is built. They may lower the cost of energy and other utilities for the house, and if they alter its location substantially they may also lower its owner's driving and commuting costs. They can improve the environmental and aesthetic quality of its surroundings, and perhaps make them healthier as well, again increasing the value of the house.[48]

The programs offer the same economic benefits to developers, who can charge their customers for them. In addition, the programs typically force builders to plan their projects in greater detail, a process that often generates gains that surprise them. The market-stiffening effects of the programs also may eventually make developers less vulnerable to speculative crazes and the boom-and-bust cycles that squeeze many builders. The programs' application and hearing requirements may make public specific information about particular projects, allowing competitors (and their lenders) to make more rational, accurate economic decisions. In Florida and Pennsylvania in particular, many builders, coal operators, bankers, and government officials have praised the programs for revealing previously unavailable information about the actual competitive situation in the building and coal industries.[49]

The program also can provide economic benefits for local and state governments. Raising property values is an obvious benefit. By preventing sprawl, the programs also may prevent governments from overextending themselves in the building of public facilities, thus restraining capital budgets. In addition, although the programs may raise the cost of constructing public facilities, they may lower the overall, long-run costs of operating and maintaining them by a greater amount. And if the programs in fact improve or protect the environment, they may promote economic growth in the locality or state in question by attracting economically desirable, environmentally conscious migrants: some kinds of high-technology corporations (for instance, electronics plants and research firms) and their employees, as well as high-income retirees and tourists.

Finally, the programs may produce economic benefits for society at large. Cleaner air and water, avoidance of sprawl, frugal energy consumption, and improved public health confer tangible as well as intangible benefits.[50] The programs also may, directly or indirectly, foster economic growth by generating employment. William Toner, a professor of environmental planning at Governors State University near Chicago, noted:

The "cost" of regulation, every regulation, shows up in a job for someone—a bureaucrat, a lawyer, a planning consultant, a construction worker, a banker, a ditchdigger. In one case [in California] a developer's "cost" was raised by about $75–100,000 on a $500,000 project. But these "costs" showed up in a retaining wall (70' × 3'), in an improved flood control structure, a differing street layout, and so forth. Thus the "costs" of regulation turned into jobs for construction and allied industries. This is the reverse side of regulation.[51]

The federal Council on Environmental Quality (CEQ) has attempted to estimate how many jobs are created not by state land-use regulation, but by environmental controls generally. In 1973, the Census Bureau estimated that there were more than 225,000 government jobs associated with pollution control.[52] A private study for CEQ estimated that for every billion dollars of expenditure on local sewage-treatment plants—nearly $10 billion was so spent by all levels of government in 1975—20,000 people are directly employed in construction.[53] Perhaps as many as an additional 62,000 are indirectly employed through multiplier effects—for example, persons in the private sector providing goods and services for the construction workers or for the manufacturers of pollution-control equipment.[54] This figure may overstate the case, for many of these jobholders would be employed elsewhere in the absence of the programs. But CEQ also estimates that the national unemployment rate is often lower by 0.3 or 0.4 percent because of the programs, and the reduction in unemployment is usually greater in recessionary periods.[55] If these figures are valid, environmental controls, among them state land-use regulation, can be a positive force in the national economy.

CHAPTER 10

The Environmental Effects of the Programs

The primary achievements of the land-use reform movement have been, as they were intended to be, environmental. State land-use regulation has prevented objectionable development and has succeeded in improving the quality of the development that has occurred. It has helped to slow urban growth and to make it less harmful. It also has contributed to the diminution of air and water pollution. It has preserved agricultural land, scenic vistas, and public access to shorelines and other recreational areas. It has both conserved energy and prevented energy production from harming the environment. It has raised environmental consciousness.

But these improvements have been slighter, slower to arrive, and more difficult to achieve than reformers, eight or ten years ago, might have hoped. The environmental benefits of the state land-use programs are difficult to verify. Evidence is scarce in part because the programs have not been under way for long. Environmental effects take time to show up and are hard to measure. Very little research, apart from a few governmental surveys,[1] has been done on the environmental effects of state land-use programs. Moreover, the state land-use agencies have generally lacked funds to do or support such research, even though it might justify or improve their own activities.

Of course, designing research to show a link between the agencies' activities and changes in the environment poses difficult problems of methodology and causation. If, for instance, a state's or region's air becomes less polluted or its urban growth rate slows, the state land-use program may be less responsible for the change than the area's economic or population growth, interest rates, or other state, local, or federal environmental laws, including those of adjoining states. And yet, from their different perspectives developers, environmentalists, and state and local officials generally believe that the programs have made a difference.

Improvement in the Quality of Development

Observers agree that the state land-use programs are raising the level of development practice. Melvin Mogulof of the Urban Institute found that the California coastal commissions "have worked well":

The provision of [beach] access, the protection of recreation areas, the concern for solid and liquid waste treatment, and the minimization of adverse effects from altered land forms have all been ongoing and successfully pursued concerns of much commission action. The State Commission—more often than the regional commissions—has guarded these specific objectives consistently and well.[2]

Similarly, Phyllis Myers concluded that, in Vermont:

On the whole, the district commission system seems to be working remarkably well for a sparingly funded institution in a totally new field of regulation. In just a few years, most Vermonters agree, it has improved the quality of growth. Examples abound, from turndowns of massive second-home developments to a summer resident's observation that "cheesy development along Lake Champlain has been halted." Lots are bigger, septic systems are carefully watched over, trees are protected from bulldozing. For a vision of pre- and post-Act 250, says a Vermonter, "Look at the ski development at Mt. Snow and then look at Stowe."[3]

Robert Healy wrote that as a result of Florida's regulation of developments of regional impact "density was slashed in several south Florida planned unit developments; a shopping center near Tampa was greatly reduced in size and another in Ocala turned down completely; a mangrove area was saved from destruction south of Fort

Myers; and public access was assured along an Atlantic ocean beach.''[4]

The continual complaints from development interests, local governments, and other state agencies about the demands of the state land-use agencies and the conjectures about particular projects or firms being deterred from construction or going elsewhere because of the agencies' activities suggest that state land-use regulation has not proved entirely toothless.

The agencies place heavy environmental conditions on most of the projects they approve. Most agencies annually place hundreds of conditions on dozens of projects. The California coastal commissions, for example, have required developers to preserve more open space, to install additional drainage and sewer systems, to construct smaller buildings and less dense projects, to allow public access to beaches on project sites, and to donate land for parks.[5]

These conditions can be quite burdensome in particular cases. In 1974, a proposed inn at Muir Beach in Marin County was turned down by the comparatively stringent San Francisco area regional commission. The developer appealed the decision to the state commission, which then approved the project—conditionally. Final plans for building, grading, and landscaping had to be approved by the executive director of the regional commission before construction could begin. The inn's bar and restaurant could have a maximum capacity of only fifty seats. No trees were to be cut or removed from the site. All utility lines had to be placed underground (a standard condition for all the coastal commissions). The developer was to provide sewage treatment and drainage systems of tightly specified size and design. Procedures for checking on sewage treatment, drainage, and water pollution were spelled out, and the regional commission's executive director had to approve any contracts the inn's proprietors made with sewage or drainage contractors. The local zoning board, which had approved the proposal before it went to the regional commission, had not dealt in much detail with any of these matters.[6]

The other state land-use programs have imposed similarly difficult conditions. The Maryland Public Service Commission, for instance, at the urging of the state's Power Plant Siting Program, required Baltimore Gas and Electric Company's Brandon Shores plant on

Chesapeake Bay to meet demanding air-pollution standards and to install fuel stacks of specified height, from which gas would exit at a specified minimum temperature. The plant's noise could not exceed 45 decibels in surrounding residential areas, nor could the annual salt fallout from its cooling towers exceed 100 pounds per acre of ground more than a mile from the towers. The plant's intake of water from the bay was limited, and the utility had to plant shrubbery and put up screens around the plant so that it could not be seen from the surrounding countryside or from the bay.[7] If the state land-use programs did not exist or did not impose such conditions, the Maryland power plant, the California inn, and many other projects would have caused far more environmental harm than they have.

The agencies also are achieving improvements in development practice through the special attention they devote to large projects— that is, to the projects with the greatest potential environmental consequences. This attention offsets to some extent the advantages enjoyed by developers of large projects in dealing with the state land-use agencies. In Vermont and the Adirondacks, for instance, it is widely acknowledged that big leisure home, skiing, shopping-center, and manufacturing developments get tighter regulatory review from the state agencies than small motel, restaurant, or store projects, whose regulation is more in the hands of local land-use boards. Along the California coast, the regional commissions examine large condominiums and apartment-house projects more closely than single-family houses. Large Pennsylvania strip mines attract much more state regulatory attention than small ones.

No such size differentiation occurs in the regulation of power plants, in Maryland or anywhere else, because all plants qualify as large developments. In Florida, the DRI threshold is so high as to exclude relatively small developments entirely from regulatory consideration. But in the states where the objects of regulation vary in size, the state agencies review large projects more intensively than small ones and much more intensively than the localities do.

The relation between the size of a project and its chances for state regulatory approval has been investigated only in California, and information is limited. Nonetheless, the Construction Industry Research Board, an organization of southern California developers, found that from 1973 to 1975 the average dollar value of the projects approved by the coastal commissions was $216,500, while the value of those denied by the commissions was over $900,000. The denied projects represented about 3 percent of the total number of projects, but over 12 percent of their dollar value.[8] In a more detailed examination of the Los Angeles–Orange County regional commission, three University of Southern California investigators found that in 1973 and 1974 only 1.5 percent of the applications for single-family houses were denied, while 13.3 percent of the applications for multi-family developments and 7.3 percent of the applications for commercial developments (many of them shopping centers) were turned down. Public hearings were held for only about 7 percent of the applications for single-family housing but for over 45 percent of the multi-family applications, 31 percent of the commercial ones, and 35 percent of the industrial ones.[9] The same relations held when the proposed projects were analyzed in terms of construction costs, acreage, and number of housing units.[10] Similar relations have been found in the procedures of the Santa Barbara area regional commission.[11]

Regional commission decisions may be appealed to the California state coastal commission, which has the option of ruling on them or letting them stand by declining to rule. From 1973 to 1975, according to Paul Sabatier, the state commission chose to rule on 66 percent of the proposals for residential projects of fifty units or more, 49 percent of the projects with five to forty-nine units, and 18 percent of the projects with two to four units.[12] Sabatier added:

> As about 80% of the large multi-unit residences came from the already urbanized areas of Los Angeles, Orange, and San Diego counties, the commission generally restricted its attention to very large projects that would have effects on environmental quality and public access commensurate with their size. In these areas, small apartments and single-family residences were not considered to raise substantial issues.[13]

Of course, the benefits of this focus may be counterbalanced by the cumulative effects of many small projects that do not receive close regulatory scrutiny.

In recent years, many developers have begun to use the state regulatory requirements, particularly the applications describing them, as a primary guide in laying out their projects. The developers typically do not use local zoning applications for guidance because they are considered less complete and less rigorous than the state ones. "I don't want you to think I like state regulation," a large Florida builder said, "but there are times when that state application is the best planning tool I've got" (ATI, Boca Raton, Florida, November 1977). The applications function as checklists for what needs to be done, for what has been done, or simply for pitfalls to avoid.

In this context, the length and detail of the applications are no longer perceived merely as bureaucratic bugaboos. They have deprived the development business of some of its freewheeling charm and spontaneity, but also have led developers to an appreciation of the virtues of detailed planning. The cost of employing consultants—planners, lawyers, hydrologists, and other intermediaries—to fill out the applications and otherwise deal with the state agencies has paid off not only in approval of projects but also in improved project design. It may be expected to result as well in some substantial environmental improvement.

Robert Healy wrote that in Vermont

district commissions have required so much information from developers that they have had to markedly improve the quality of their site plans. For example, for one large recreational-residential complex it was estimated that it cost at least $100,000 to do the groundwork leading up to the formal presentation of fact at the district hearing. For that hearing, the applicant has to have pinpointed building lots, roads and their grades, water supply lines, types of structures and their designs, sewage systems and water system details, financing arrangements, and even the legal setup of a homeowners' association, if there is to be one.[14]

Similarly, after the Adirondack Park Act went into effect, the average width of new shoreline lots in the park increased, in some areas by more than half—a sign that builders in the park were generally complying with the minimum shoreline lot requirements of the act by designing so as to minimize environmental strain on Adirondack lakes.[15] Shortly after the California coastal commission began operations, the state's power companies suddenly started locating most of their new plants inland, away from the environmentally vulnerable coast.[16]

It is not clear that the conditions imposed by the state agencies are always either adequate or necessary to protect the environment. Several Maryland environmentalists, for example, have criticized the noise-level and salt-fallout conditions placed on the Brandon Shores power plant. It is entirely possible that for the plant's environmental impact to be seriously muffled, the Maryland Public Service Commission should have fixed the maximum noise level at, say, 35 decibels rather than 45, and the maximum annual salt fallout at 75 pounds per acre rather than 100. But objective experiments measuring the effects of these different restrictions would have been quite complex, expensive, and hypothetical before construction of the plant. And the agency can do little to remedy the effects of its decisions now that the plant has been constructed.

The imposition of essentially meaningless conditions seems to be fairly common; many permit orders include conditions that both developers and state regulatory officials are reluctant to discuss with outsiders. Many of the programs' other weaknesses—exempted development, high thresholds, inadequate enforcement, low staffing, and reliance on bargaining with opposed interests also limit their ability to improve development practices.

The programs have largely eliminated the worst, most flagrant, and most environmentally harmful development practices.[17] In Vermont a project can no longer be designed without thoroughly working out its road access and parking arrangements in advance. In Pennsylvania coal companies can no longer ignore the water-pollution effects of their stripping operations. Yet more remains to be done. For example, having cited the "successes" of the Florida land-use program, Robert Healy wrote that "at least as numerous have been the failures—the projects allowed to go forward even though ill-conceived and ill-located and environmental problems left uncorrected, or even unappreciated."[18] He cited a number of instances where, because of the political weakness of the regional planning councils and the reluctance of local governments to take their advice into account, projects were approved that would drastically and obviously increase traffic, pollute water, or contaminate the Floridan Aquifer.[19]

The Pennsylvania strip-mining program, whose provisions are simpler and stronger than Florida's and whose environmental results are easier to examine with the naked eye, shows a similarly uneven record. Reclamation of stripping sites is often poor in the anthracite region of eastern Pennsylvania, especially where the site in question is in the midst of land unreclaimed by previous stripping. In such cases the site probably cannot be restored to its previous state without vast expense. Thus, the anthracite regions are dotted with pathetic plantings of hardy Scotch pine that have taken root atop debris heaps where nothing else ever will grow.

In the bituminous regions of western Pennsylvania, reclamation is generally better, and the Bureau of Surface Mine Reclamation is happy to take visitors to excellent showcase projects, one of which has become a state park.[20] Because bituminous seams are level, unlike anthracite seams, continued bituminous stripping does not involve increasingly deep cuts in the earth. The bituminous companies tend to be larger, better financed, more technologically adept, less racketeer-infested, certainly more conscious of public relations, and generally more sophisticated in corporate style than their eastern Pennsylvania counterparts. One western company gives each visitor to its headquarters a golf tee to suggest (with some pardonable exaggeration) how well it grooms the land it restores.

In addition, to take advantage of rising coal prices, many wealthy farmers in the bituminous regions have strip-mined their own land and therefore reclaimed it well. A Pennsylvania strip-mining official said:

A farmer can make maybe three hundred dollars a year per acre if he just farms his land. If he strip-mines it, he can make perhaps fifty or sixty thousand dollars an acre. But that is usually on a one-shot basis; he can't count on that money next year. And he's got to restore the land if he wants to keep farming it or to sell it to someone else. Sometimes by stripping and reclaiming the land, he can actually improve it for agricultural or other purposes—say, if he smooths out a ridge line or a depression in the earth. That's fine with us. (AI, Harrisburg, Pennsylvania, October 1975)

But even in western Pennsylvania, not far from the showcase projects, a number of supposedly reclaimed sites display extremely meager and perfunctory revegetation, unrestored gullies, and left-over highwalls from excavation, all of which indicate no serious attempt to restore the land to the approximate-original-contour standard. On some sites there are abandoned bulldozers and other mining equipment, as well as unrepaired mining roads. Ongoing stripping operations that supposedly conform to state regulations nonetheless have obvious water-discharge violations, cuts in the earth longer than 1500 feet, and topsoil set aside so improperly as to make it useless for revegetation. Some of these operations may have taken place on slopes steeper than the allowed forty degrees or illegally close to such slopes.[21]

The available evidence suggests that the California coastal program is relatively effective in protecting the environment, apparently because it has popular support and precise standards. Healy described these results of the California program:

> In general there was modest growth, taking the form mostly of infilling of semideveloped areas or slow increases in intensity of land use in older, built-up areas. No new large-scale subdivisions were allowed in the near-coast area. Owners of lots in existing residential or recreational subdivisions were generally allowed to build, provided they built structures no larger than those on nearby lots. . . .
>
> Energy facilities were by no means barred from the coastal zone, but they frequently faced tough and detailed conditions. Some of the huge projects discussed during the period, however, never reached the point of submitting definite permit applications. . . .
>
> In several parts of the state, the commissions prevented projects that would have caused urban development to spill onto agricultural land. They also limited subdivision of farmland or timber land into parcels that they considered too small to be economically productive. The commissions also tended to turn down applications for single-family homes on undeveloped parts of the coastline or where they might interfere with views from the coastal highway. In some cases, this denial of a low-intensity use was followed by state purchase of land for park purposes.
>
> The commissions devoted a good deal of attention to matters of design and aesthetics and to ensuring beach access through new projects. The commissions used bulk and design restrictions to ensure that new construction was of a size, style, and character not greatly different from other buildings in the neighborhood. Applicants who sought to build several units or a commercial structure near the beach were almost inevitably required to provide a public accessway. Requirements for access from the road to the water or along the dry sand portion of the beach were also commonly attached to permits for new single-family dwellings in areas where access had been limited. . . .
>
> In short, the commissions exercised their interim permit powers quite vigorously, citing frequently the law's uncompromising mandate to protect coastal resources. In some cases, the commissions went beyond the letter of the law, as when they imposed conditions concerning energy conservation or low-cost housing.[22]

Raising of Environmental Consciousness

Environmental and growth-management considerations today influence governmental and developer actions in a way that they did not ten or fifteen years ago. They have become an accepted part of day-to-day decision-making in both the public and private sectors. Many large government agencies and corporations now have some sort of environmental department. Many small cities and counties are hiring urban planners and land-use lawyers for the first time, and many large localities are hiring additional ones. As John Adams, executive director of Natural Resources Defense Council, said, "There is solid, permanent strength on the environmental side. . . . Every state is looking at land use."[23] The land-use reform movement and the programs it engendered can take a considerable part of the credit for this change.

At least at the level of rhetoric, neither developers nor local government officials wish to go on record as opponents of environmental or growth-management goals. No one, whether in interviews or in public or in print, dismisses such goals as trivial or misguided. Debate focuses on measures to achieve them, and particularly on the compatibility of environmental goals with other important objectives—keeping the economy strong, defending private property, maintaining the autonomy of local government, providing energy, and restraining bureaucracy. People with other interests do not suggest neglecting environmental goals but merely keeping them in their proper place—as one set of public goals among a number of others. Those who formerly opposed land-use regulation no longer question the essential legitimacy of concern for the environment:

> Before the last decade's surge of popular interest in the environment, most developers neither knew much about the more subtle ecological consequences of their actions, nor cared. And, in that, they were little different from the average citizen. Now that the public's consciousness has been raised, it is not surprising to find that the same is true for many responsible builders. There is no reason to suppose that home builders are more callous than anyone else toward wildlife and wetlands. And even if they were, their keen sense of the market's pulse would tell them that environmental—or at least aesthetic—sensitivity can sell homes.[24]

Concern for the environment has become publicly acceptable—at times, almost a motherhood issue. We are all environmentalists now.

In 1974, Kent State University political scientists Steven Brown and James Coke surveyed 199 local government officials, businessmen, developers, farmers, environmentalists, and members of the general public (most of them Ohio residents) regarding their attitudes toward land use. Brown and Coke expected to find pro-development and pro-environmental attitudes that were directly opposed to each other. But they could find no one who seriously favored development regardless of the cost to the environment. The only conflict they found was between environmentalism and localism—that is, some respondents preferred to have local government rather than state government regulate land use and growth. All but ten of the respondents considered some form of environmental regulation desirable. And none was opposed to localism.[25] Many respondents with localist views also favored environmentalist goals and regulatory measures.

Brown and Coke therefore concluded that environmentalist and localist attitudes "are not diametrically opposed—only different." They noted:

Both groups are skeptical about new development. The localists do not believe that growth automatically brings about a healthy local economy and a sound tax base. By the same token, the environmentalists do not believe that growth itself is a curse.

Both groups reject the laissez-faire view that a person should have the right to do as he pleases with his property. . . .

Externalities [i.e., the negative spillovers of development] are the main concern of the environmentalists, local control and accountability of the localists. Both sides recognize a need for some change to take into account the needs of society. . . . There is a guarded willingness to cooperate and discuss the issues because the motives of those who want change in the present system are not thought devious.

Both the laissez-faire view of property rights and the uncritical acceptance of the desirability of growth are ideas that have lost their power. In their place is a widely shared concern for protecting communities from unchecked and uncontrolled development.[26]

This concern is being incorporated into governmental policy and practice. For example, citizen participation, especially for environmentalists, has become an accepted feature of land-use programs at all levels of government.[27] A California woman environmentalist commented on the change:

Even a couple of years ago, a lot of politicians treated us like kooks, bird-and-bunny fanatics. There've always been a lot of women in the movement, and we'd get typed as little old ladies in tennis shoes, only younger and on the left. Now that we've been around a while and won some fights, we get treated better. There's usually not much danger of any of our own people becoming one of the boys, but we're legitimate, accepted. (AI, San Rafael, California, August 1975)[28]

Public officials at both state and local levels consistently exhibit increased environmental sophistication. A California regional coastal commissioner who had also been a mayor and city councilwoman reflected on her experience with coastal regulation:

I'd never understood before how wetlands work and that you've got to preserve some of them to give fish places to spawn. So I'd never caught on that if you lose the wetlands, you lose the fish and eventually sport fishing, tourism, and the fishing industry all suffer. The same way, I'd never realized how fragile marshes and sand dunes are, or how if you build the wrong way on a beach you're going to affect offshore ocean currents and hurt the fish supply another way. (AI, Pacifica, California, August 1975)

Even officials of development-minded agencies have acquired a similar, if grudging, appreciation for the environment. "Of course the district commissions are a pain," a Vermont state highway official said: "But they make us do our homework and if we slip up, they'll catch us and embarrass us in public. They make us think about things like drainage cuts and fitting with local plans, things we wouldn't get involved with otherwise. All in all, the commissions are good for us" (AI, Montpelier, Vermont, September 1975).

Local land-use planning and regulation appear to have become more environmentally demanding in recent years, partly as a result of efforts by the states. Many communities, while resisting state intervention, have at the same time been rethinking their attitudes toward growth and growth control. Among Vermont's 246 localities, for example, between 1972 and 1975 the number that had adopted land-use plans went from 110 to 195; the number with zoning ordinances grew from 98 to 172; and the number with subdivision regulations increased from 38 to 98.[29] In the Adirondacks, between 1971 and 1977, many of the same towns, villages, and counties that refused to submit land-use control programs for Adirondack Park Agency approval were nonetheless undertaking new land-use control programs. Of the 107 localities in the park, only 41 had active planning boards in 1971. By 1977, 90 localities had such boards. In the same period, 44 made new master plans; 27 enacted new subdivision regulations; 24 enacted zoning ordinances; 16 sanitary codes, 14 building codes, and 35 floodplain ordinances.[30] In 1976, Mary Prime, a former APA commissioner, marveled: "I saw a sign that said, 'Lots for sale. Beautiful view. Zoning.' Five years ago you'd never have seen a sign like that here."[31]

Some localities surpass the state agencies in environmental rigor. For example, near Miami and Tampa a number of fast-growing cities and counties that had sought the passage of Florida's land-use law in the first place have since instituted review procedures modeled on the state's process for evaluating developments of regional impact. Because these local "mini-DRI" reviews typically have much lower size thresholds than the state DRI process, they can examine much smaller projects. The Tampa-area city of Clearwater, for instance, demands an extensive "community impact statement" for all proposed projects whose total value, including both land and buildings, will exceed $500,000. In contrast, to qualify as a DRI for state review in a county as large as Clearwater's Pinellas County, a proposed residential development must have at least 3000 dwelling units; the total value of such a development runs to millions of dollars. Florida's DRI applications demand a huge amount of information from developers, but Clearwater's demand still more, getting into such environmental details as the proposed project's interference with scenic views, production of shadows, and design compatibility with existing structures.[32] Several Florida cities and counties are developing mini-DRI procedures more stringent than Clearwater's.[33]

All this increased governmental awareness of the environment is compelling development interests to acquire a similar perspective if they want their projects approved. But some progressive developers are actually coming to believe in the value of environmental awareness, especially in financial terms. Some are willing to say so. A Maryland power company executive commented:

> We used to try to handle environmental complaints by sending in the public relations department, but we learned better. Then we set up a special environmental department, which has helped some. But the real solution, which we've tried to adopt, is for everyone in the company to think en-

vironmentally. Not that we want them to obstruct our projects on company time, but we want them to be able to see what the environmentalists are getting at, to pick up on their objections ahead of time, and to be able to separate the situations where they've got a point from the ones where they don't. (AI, Baltimore, Maryland, December 1975)

A lawyer who has served as a consultant to both Vermont's Environmental Board and its State Planning Office also reported:

There is agreement that the main effect of Act 250 has been to improve the quality of those major subdivisions and developments which are subject to it. . . . In addition, Act 250 has probably helped to improve the quality of those subdivisions and developments that are *not* subject to it by raising public awareness and consumer expectations. Although one can still find subdivisions and developments in Vermont which violate even the most basic standards of site planning, construction, and environmental protection, they are normally the handiwork of individuals and small contractors.[34]

In some cases these changed attitudes have practical political consequences, and influential developers and local governments that previously opposed the state land-use laws join with environmentalists to defend them. In 1979, the Florida Home Builders Association and the County Commissioners Association were part of the coalition that preserved the critical-areas provision of the state law; the previous year, they, together with environmentalists, successfully opposed a one-stop-shopping bill that would have consolidated DRI reviews with those for water-consumption and dredge-and-fill permits.[35] In 1972, the League of California Cities opposed coastal legislation; in 1976, it came to support it.[36]

Society's tolerance for shoddy development has clearly diminished; all parties, the public included, seem to have accepted a higher standard for protection of the environment. But this standard may not be as high as it could or should be, and developers and regulatory agencies seem less than totally committed to meeting it. Much remains for the land-use reform movement to do.

CHAPTER 11

Making Land-Use Reform
Work Better

The land-use reform movement has not triumphed completely. Neither has it deteriorated completely, nor have its programs become the creatures of its opponents.[1] In these respects, it has plainly outperformed any number of past regulatory endeavors.

One of the most impressive achievements of the movement is that it survived the 1970s at all. New state agencies had to establish themselves among existing local governments and other state agencies that in the main had resisted their creation. The new agencies had to regulate active, politically powerful development industries that objected strenuously to state regulation. Absentee land ownership, development, and leasing are notoriously troublesome; state regulation, based hundreds of miles from most of its objects, could not be expected to be easy. In the face of the nation's unforeseen economic and energy problems and the political pressures they produced, the movement might well have dissipated entirely in the middle and late 1970s.

Instead, the movement managed to adapt both to the conditions that it found and to the new ones that emerged. In political terms, it narrowed the scope of the programs for which it campaigned and sought to involve local governments more in them. Under extreme pressure and without real alternatives, it succeeded in operating primarily through bargains. When its bureaucratic red tape came to be widely regarded as objectionable, it simplified and streamlined its procedures. In intellectual terms, it shifted its focus from narrow biological and ecological concerns to broad growth-management issues that turned out to have a much wider constituency. This constituency, in fact, sustained the movement during the time it took to educate government officials, developers, and the public at large about its original ecological concerns.

On the other hand, through its very successes the movement has raised the price and reduced the availability of new housing and other development. It has frequently given large developers an advantage over their smaller competitors. It has done little to eliminate and may even have reinforced exclusionary zoning. Sometimes it has promoted the environmental deterioration, sprawl, poor development, speculation, design homogenization, and inadequate local land-use regulation it originally sought to prevent.

Moreover, the inevitable concessions and bargains, the bureaucratic accommodations to the opposition, the unexpected economic effects, the partial environmental results, and the continual necessity throughout of struggling with a frequently adamant opposition—all these features of the practical political setting of the programs have served to disenchant and alienate a number of those who supported land-use reform most enthusiastically in the first place. "I look at a lot of the APA's recent decisions," a well-known Adirondack environmentalist says, "and I think: we worked for this? This is what we knocked outselves out for? Maybe we would have been better off putting in the same effort to organize nature walks" (ATI, Lake George, New York, July 1979).

The sense of fatigue and futility underlying this statement is noteworthy in part because the Adirondack Park Agency has a relatively *strong* land-use reform program.[2] Other programs have been much weaker; some have failed completely. In early 1979, for instance, the federal coastal zone management program suspended funding for the Illinois, Minnesota, and Virginia state coastal programs as a result of their inadequate, virtually nonexistent performance. The coastal programs of Connecticut, New York, Florida, Georgia, and Indiana also seemed likely to be suspended eventually.[3] The California–Nevada Lake Tahoe Regional Planning Agency was apparently dying.[4]

The Causes of the Shortfall

Under the favorable economic conditions of the late 1960s, the movement, despite the claims of its opponents, fundamentally threatened no one. Centralized regulation might put developers, homeowners, and local governments to some trouble over the short run, but it never really put their economic prospects or survival in jeopardy. In the occasional poverty-stricken rural regions where it seemed to do so—the Adirondacks, for instance, or California's North Coast or Vermont's Northeast Kingdom—the local opposition quickly proved able to take care of itself. But in most cases it was precisely because urban growth was powerful, had frequently discomfiting consequences, and, above all, seemed likely to last that so many people and politicians favored regulatory intervention by state government to restrain it.[5]

But the economy did not stay benevolent. Within five years, the movement had outlived much of the urban growth that produced it and even some of the societal tolerance that nurtured it. Economic abundance and overabundance gave way to recession, inflation, mounting housing costs, high interest rates, and depleted public treasuries. The urgent quest for domestic sources of energy took priority over the environment and growth-management considerations. The loss of spending power and of unlimited access to fuel combined with such highly publicized debacles as Vietnam and Watergate, as well as the dissipation of such governmental efforts as the War on Poverty and Model Cities programs, to generate anti-government sentiment. Conservatism revived, further undermining the land-use reform movement. The bureaucratic operations of the state land-use agencies proved particularly vulnerable to attack from the right. The movement also was constrained by the enormous power of the interests it opposed—interests that, when the economy began its decline, perceived themselves as fighting for their survival.

The movement often seemed to have little more going for it than aesthetic revulsion, the bright idea of centralized regulation, and, occasionally and transiently, high mobilized citizen action. By contrast, the movement's opponents had stable and effective interest groups, legislative influence at the state level, control of local government, and control of state agencies that were the rivals of the new land-use bodies. The opponents of land-use reform owned great amounts of land, controlled large numbers of jobs, and were the source of much of the state's tax revenues, campaign contributions, public construction, urban growth, and general economic growth. They also were closer to the land, better able to concentrate their energies, and more adept at estimating and publicizing the costs of the new land-use programs than the reformers were at explaining their benefits.

In addition, the land-use reform movement had to contend with a whole range of characteristically American attitudes—the spirit of individualism, the private-property ethic, the prestige of the corporation and the entrepreneur, the veneration of the market and its judgments, the contempt for bureaucracy, the desire to limit government, and the persistent localism of the federal system. The movement seemed inherently, congenitally unable to grasp the extent of the opposition's power; its proposals for change always had an air of willful innocence. In particular, the movement never understood how different, even alien, its own approaches were from those that most Americans, if they thought about the matter, would have preferred. Land-use reformers rarely seemed to grasp the force of the opposed private-property sentiment or the depth of the enmity they were arousing until it was too late.[6]

Most Americans instinctively dislike the idea of shifting governmental power upward from the local level to the state or federal level. They believe, with Jefferson, that government should be close to the people and limited in scope. Many also regard such places as Washington, Sacramento, and Albany as insulated company towns with little awareness of or interest in the way the population in the provinces actually lives. Americans, it seems, will accept centralization only if it seems substantively justified. But almost by definition, land use is local, and in the United States it has generally been treated as a local issue. Many people—perhaps most people—felt that the solutions for its problems were still to be found only at the local level. The centralization of land-use regulation often left large powers in the hands of local government officials who might subvert or ignore the goals of the state.

Regulation also implied more government. Worse still, regulation promised to abridge land ownership. Ownership interests—whether large developers or industry or small homeowners or local governments serving their landowning constituency—always resist the introduction of measures that even vaguely infringe on ownership or its economic rewards. Ownership interests have resisted other regulatory measures, such as zoning and, more recently, federal air and water pollution controls,[7] until or unless those measures proved themselves to ownership interests by producing, for example, quieter neighborhoods, improved property values, exclusion of unwanted minorities, cleaner air and water, and reductions in the risks of development.[8]

Yet many localities and many people still resist zoning over fifty years after it was first introduced. Many more resist the newer pollution controls. And resistance to land-use reform at times seems nearly universal. The regulatory measures have simply not been strong enough, or in effect long enough, for their environmental and economic benefits to be widely appreciated or attributed to them.

In the late 1960s, during the period of economic boom, one of the most spectacular and instructive failures of land-use planning in modern times occurred in Pennsylvania. A team of experts from the University of Pennsylvania designed an imaginative and equitable package of land-use and environmental controls to preserve the Brandywine Creek watershed, near Philadelphia.[9] The team diligently promoted the regulatory package among the small farmers who populated the watershed and among local governments. As a result of these efforts, the local residents came to understand that the package would both increase their property values and improve their surroundings. But in a nasty series of public meetings, they rejected it anyway.

Why? A township supervisor explained to Ann Louise Strong, the leader of the team: "I think there is a great sincerity when people say they want the objectives of the plan. The paradox is that they are not willing to take the initiative or endanger their self-interest." Another local official said: "The people don't understand communal responsibility for the land because they are the lords of the land." A local resident said: "If a man's home is his castle, then his land is his fertility. To take away his rights in the land is nothing less than castration."[10]

Strong was reluctant to accept the symbolic meaning of land ownership as the primary reason for the rejection of her regulatory package.[11] Yet Brandywine is by no means the only place where people have invoked land ownership as a reason for opposing land-use regulation. Such sentiments are constantly voiced not just by small farmers but also by small suburban and urban homeowners, developers of middle- and large-sized projects, and the gigantic corporations that hold huge stretches of the country. Nonetheless, the proponents of regulation never seem to understand what they hear.

The various ownership groups express and act on their sentiments in different ways, and they continually compete with each other for land, but their essential message is the same. Owners feel that their land is theirs, to do with as they please. They resent regulation. If absolutely necessary, they will accept it—in the weakest form they can arrange. It is not a matter of disliking change or paperwork. Nor is it invariably a matter of liking money or security. It is simply a manifestation of an impulse toward land as property that is reinforced by the American tradition of free-enterprise individualism. The proponents of regulation rarely seem to comprehend either the emotional strength of the impulse or the political strength of the tradition. The land-use reform movement certainly has not done so.

The movement has never effectively dealt with the purely material, self-aggrandizing, economic interest in land. The movement wanted land to begin to be treated primarily as a resource that was subject to stringent centralized regulation. The opposition wanted it to continue to be treated primarily as a loosely and locally regulated commodity on which its owners could make a profit—with luck, a killing. A Vermont developer explained: "Nine out of ten people speculating in land never really make it big. But the promise that they might hit the jackpot is what keeps them at it. And the biggest defenders of the right to get all you can out of land will not be the one winner, but the nine losers, who can always hope that someday they'll score. Our land-use law seems to take away that hope, so of course it has tough sledding" (AI, Bolton, Vermont, September 1975). "Ninety percent of land use," a Maryland farmer told Robert Healy, "is making a buck."[12] It remains so for virtually all Americans, and seems unlikely to change in any fundamental way.

Even land-use reformers and environmentalists feel the urge to profit from land and are reluctant to be regulated. Not long ago, a prominent Chicago city planning consultant with solid environmentalist credentials was making unofficial inquiries about California's regional coastal commissions to find out which was the least demanding. He wanted to build a house along the California coast, use it on vacations, and rent it out the rest of the year with a minimum of regulatory bother. Such behavior has not gone unnoticed by the land-use reform movement's opponents, to whom it smacks of hypocrisy or self-delusion.

Because of the movement's narrow upper-middle-class social base, in most land-use disputes the opponents of reform have outnumbered its supporters, who could be depicted as wealthy busybodies trying to impose their own incomprehensible, bureaucratic preoccupations on a poorer, less educated, local population. Moreover, the movement's adherents often were condescending and dogmatic. "Well, you know these blue collars," a California coastal planner remarked. "All they want out of the coast is a place to park their campers and run their dune buggies and motorcycles" (AI, San Rafael, California, August 1975). The movement's adherents frequently acted as if their reform programs were inherently and patently virtuous; anyone who opposed them was assumed to be a knave or a fool. They never seemed to realize how offensive their approach was to people who were not securely in the upper middle class. A small California building contractor complained:

All these people pushing the coastal operation have nice high regular incomes. A lot of them seem to own maybe 10 acres in Woodside [a noncoastal high-income suburb of San Francisco]. But me and my friends have to make out living out of the dirt. If we can't move that dirt, we don't eat. But here are all these nice rich people with their nice fancy charts telling us we have to starve or make less money. Of course we won't go for that. (AI, Half Moon Bay, California, August 1975)

The speaker of the Vermont House of Representatives attacked the 1974 state land-use plan as coming from the "stratosphere of the elite."[13]

In the late 1960s, Ann Strong was largely unable to sympathize with the Brandywine farmers' reluctance to serve as guinea pigs for the untested, complex schemes of academic outsiders, some of whom had long hair, acted patronizing, or could not bring themselves to appreciate the profit motive of the local population. The farmers complained that her project's local representative was too aggressive, didn't know local customs, went to the front door rather than around the house, and "dressed too well to. do the job right. People here like a fellow who's been shovelling manure for ten years." The local residents trusted no government more remote than their own township.[14] But, at least by 1975, she could admit the opposition's legitimacy: "We *were* technocrats from the outside, as they charged. Our lives, our future expectations of income, and our personal control were *not* affected by the plan. Theirs were, and we owed them more than they received."[15]

The grace and humility of this admission have rarely been matched by other land-use reformers. A Montpelier lawyer who was active in drafting the Vermont land-use law reminisced:

I remember in 1973 this young fellow from the State Planning Office presenting an early draft of the plan to some committee of the legislature. He was nervous and from out of state and talked very fast, very technically, and of course the committee was mainly old-time Vermont farmers and lawyers and small businessmen—down-to-earth people. The kid showed a map of some area with a line running down the middle of it. On one side of the line a lot of development was permitted, on the other side much less. So the land on one side became more valuable, but not the parcels on the other side. Then some old guy on the committee asked why the line was drawn there. He said he knew the area well, that the line separated a series of practically identical farms. One set of farmers could count on a windfall if they sold out, but it would be tough luck for the other guys. It seemed awfully unfair. So why had they drawn the line that way? "Well," said the state planner, bright as could be, "We had to draw it somewhere." I think the plan lost four votes on the committee right there. (AI, Montpelier, Vermont, September 1975)

The land-use reform movement consistently antagonized or ignored those who would be most affected by its program. It seems never to have tried to make any contact with blacks or the poor or people on fixed incomes or small farmers or other deprived groups it said it was trying to help; nor did it even try to convince less deprived, more powerful groups such as developers, businessmen, homeowners, construction-union members, and large farmers that it was not trying to hurt them. It simply wrote off the support of all such groups, and then was surprised by the inevitable political consequences.

The Regulatory Implications of the Shortfall

It is not surprising that the land-use laws contain large concessions to their opponents, that the state land-use agencies have to regulate primarily by means of bargains, or that the agencies' bureaucratic operations are open to counterattacks. Nor is it surprising that the development market has adapted easily (if sometimes undesirably) to the new land-use programs, that the programs' environmental accomplishments are thus far less than hoped, or that some of the results of the programs have been perverse. Under such circumstances and with such disadvantages, the land-use reform movement has done quite well to achieve a standoff against its opposition.

The land-use reform programs seem to have encountered all the difficulties of centralized regulation predicted by its critics. The programs have frequently been influenced by the economic interests they were supposed to restrain. They have often been out of touch with the public at large, especially the less privileged portions of it. The programs have raised prices for consumers and made markets less competitive. They have fostered faraway, unwieldy bureaucracies. They have hindered the introduction of new development methods and designs. They have largely failed to plan effectively.

More specifically, as Milton Friedman might have predicted, the obtuse bureaucracies of the programs have inadvertently elicited socially objectionable economic responses from the development market. By threatening to crush private initiative, the bureaucracies have forced private-sector interests and their allies in local and state government to take political measures against them. Since the private-sector and local government forces are roughly as powerful as the state bureaucracies, the bureaucracies' programs have been at least partly neutralized.

Or, as Theodore Lowi might have predicted in accordance with the tenets of interest-group liberalism, all the relevant organized interests participated in formulating the land-use laws. To avoid confronting the disagreements among these interests, the drafters of the legislation watered it down. In particular, the laws rarely set specific standards. Instead, they delegated discretionary power to the programs' administrators, who were able to carry out the laws only by bargaining with the organized interests. In these bargains, the political power of the ownership interests quickly emerged.

From the perspective of Ralph Nader, the programs frequently amounted to a lost opportunity. The entrenched opposition simply weakened the programs in the legislature and then achieved substantial representation in the agencies that were to implement them. The popular outcry that produced the programs and acted as a spur to their implementation rarely endured in strength much past the passage of the laws. Adverse external economic conditions reduced public support somewhat. But more important, ownership interests usually made certain that the programs discouraged citizen participation. As a result, the new Nader-style regulation typically ended up suffering from many of the same defects as the old Roosevelt-style centralized regulation that it sought to replace. These defects testify both to the inadequacy of Nader's critique and to the practical import of Friedman's and Lowi's critique.

The defects of state land-use reform agencies turned out to be much the same as those of the local zoning agencies they were intended to supplement. Like the local agencies, the state agencies were both understaffed and underfinanced, and they did not have jurisdiction over large amounts of important development. Like those of the local agencies, their arrangements for citizen participation were often inadequate and their planning was often meaningless. Like the local agencies, they frequently favored developers, especially the large, powerful ones best able to infiltrate and otherwise deal with a state-level regulatory body. Like those of the local agencies, the state agencies' bureaucracies have been criticized, although the state agencies have been accused of being cumbersome, arbitrary, and uncertain rather than corrupt and procedurally sloppy. Like local regulation, state regulation has raised the costs of development—thereby harming low-income groups—and led to physical and social homogenization.

It is now plain that the opponents of land-use regulation—the ownership interests and their allies in government—can usually exert enough control over centralized bodies to weaken their effectiveness. Centralized regulation cannot attain more than a portion of its objectives because it must deal with these ownership interests. Thus the land-use reform movement would seem to be at an impasse. The country is evidently not completely ready for land-use reform, at least in the form in which the movement has presented it, and indeed may never be ready for such reform.

Meanwhile, what needs reforming in land use is not any single general problem but rather an array of separate problems. These include the new growth, the economics of rapid development, energy projects, the decline of small-scale agriculture, and the deficiencies of zoning. Each problem is different; each is complex in itself; and each relates to the others in intricate, perhaps unknowable ways. Centralized regulation may be a suitable approach for some of these problems, but cannot reasonably be expected to solve all of them.

Legislative measures—for example, more specific and stringent physical and procedural standards, stronger enforcement activities and penalties, fewer exemptions, lower thresholds, more citizen participation, more representation on regulatory boards for environmentalists and less for ownership interests, more substantial staffing and financing for the regulatory agencies, better information-gathering about proposed projects, more elaborate planning efforts, stronger coordination efforts with other agencies, and the like—might help to make state regulation more effective. Many supporters of land-use reform have recommended such improvements.[16] Most of these measures are, however, politically unfeasible at present or would be watered down in enactment or implementation. Programs of centralized regulation made good political sense in 1970 and accorded with the Nader-inspired orientation of the reformers. But the programs have gone as far as they can go in the current political climate; today their limitations are quite clear.

A large number of plausible programs to alter the nation's land-use practices do not employ centralized regulation. These programs appear politically feasible. They have been available all along; some have been put into effect successfully. And they do not conflict with established programs of centralized regulation.

Land Consumerism

The land-use reform movement can reposition itself more attractively in the marketplace of public-policy ideas.[17] In its present form, the movement suffers from a problem of image that has become a problem of substance. To the extent that it considers the issue, the general public understands land-use reform as being upper-middle-class and white in its constituency; suburban and rural in its emphasis; liberal or radical in its perspective; and technocratic, bureaucratic, and inter-

loping in its style. Its true interests seem to be not so much the
environment, growth management, or resource conservation; instead, they seem to be aesthetics. So the movement appears essentially out of touch with the economic, energy, housing, racial, and
class issues that actively concern most Americans about their country
and, if they make the connection, about how its land is used.

The movement need not accept this characterization. It can break
out of the isolation in which it has, in large part, placed itself. Other
Nader-inspired reform efforts have focused with great success on
consumer protection. Similarly, instead of seeking to reform land-
use practices, the movement should seek to represent the interests of
the users—that is, the consumers—of land. Everyone is a consumer
of land, and in a large number of capacities: not just as an owner or
renter but also as a taxpayer, a user of public services, and a cus-
tomer of utilities and other businesses. All economic units—
individuals, families, corporations, and governments—are consumers of land.

As land consumers, they have many desires in common. They
want land that is as cheap as possible, and on which the taxes are as
low as possible. They want land that gives good value for the purposes to which it is put. They want land that yields a fair return on
the investment, both financial and emotional, they place in it. They
want land that suffers minimally from the spillovers of environmentally degrading or socially expensive ways others consume their
land. And they want land that is subject to public decisions made in
an equitable manner that embodies these other perspectives. The
interest of land consumers in land is primarily economic.

Yet this universal economic interest rarely receives organized
political or governmental attention. Land-use regulatory bodies have
not been particularly concerned with it, development forces have
overridden it by concentrating mainly on their own profits, and the
land-use reform movement has generally treated it as a dirty little
secret. As a result, the economic interests of land consumers have
not played a part in public decisions about land use, and land consumers as a group have suffered economically—through increases in
land prices, housing and construction costs, taxes, utility bills, and
other prices.

The environmental focus of land-use reform activists has seemed downright frivolous to people confronting large stacks of bills for their basic household expenses each month. But in the long run, better land use is a way of saving money and protecting property investments; a means of both producing and conserving energy; a measure to encourage economic growth, create jobs, lower inflation, build housing, revitalize the inner city, and reduce racial and economic inequality. In other words, better land use should pay, especially in economic terms. Today, energy difficulties and inflation, among other pressures, are bringing about changes in land-use patterns—such as reductions in sprawl and highway construction, less wasteful building practices, and migrations back to the city— that the reform movement was largely unable to attain through centralized regulation.[18] A movement for better land use should work with these pressures.

More precisely, such a movement should join forces with other groups that share goals which are part of better land use. For example, keeping housing as affordable and the suburbs as accessible as possible are even now goals that many liberal consumer-protection, low-income, minority, inner-city, fair housing, tenant, and good-government groups espouse. The goals of expanding the availability of low- and middle-income housing, keeping taxes and land prices low, and making government services cheaper and more efficient also are shared by conservative developers, business people, construction and other unions, homeowners, farmers, local government, and taxpayer groups.

Both sets of potential allies, liberal and conservative, have in the past shown at least as much strength and staying power as the land-use reform movement. And the conservative groups have frequently beaten the movement in their confrontations. The movement should realize that it will not get much further on its own, that it has a large number of concerns in common with many stronger groups, including some it has considered its enemies. In the same way that coalitions of environmentalists, developers, and local governments have recently emerged to defend state land-use laws, previously hostile groups might often see political and economic advantages for themselves in joining the land-use reform movement in pursuing land consumerism.

Land-consumer coalitions would free the movement from the inevitably losing position of challenging all the strong ownership interests simultaneously. They would allow the movement to exploit differences between the ownership interests, so as to induce some of them to work with it to promote land-consumer ends. Union members, for instance, particularly those not in the building trades, want to keep the cost of new housing down in a way that most developers do not. Homeowners, as California's Proposition 13 showed dramatically, may want to set property-tax rates lower than local government officials would prefer.

In addition, the land-consumer approach would allow the movement to take constructive advantage of differences *within* particular ownership interests. The issue of the price of housing, for example, presents obvious political opportunities. Developers of luxury and leisure homes will not be greatly concerned about the price of new homes, but the more numerous developers of middle-income housing, along with the construction unionists who build it, will want to see such housing kept affordable for the bulk of the middle class so as not to price themselves out of business. Homeowners who do not intend to move will be happy to see home prices rising, while those who know they will move will be uneasy about the increases; the profits on selling their present houses will not always cover the higher cost of their new ones. First-time home buyers, as well as their parents who frequently help them make their purchases, will definitely be unhappy about the increases.

These examples suggest why some ownership interests, or portions of them, would support land consumerism, even though they have opposed land-use reform. Those ownership interests that may in the future be compelled to make major land purchases they may barely be able to afford—the have-nots, from a consumer perspective—will support land consumerism. Those more comfortably situated—the haves, from a consumer perspective—will oppose land consumerism or be indifferent to it. Fortunately for land consumerism, the have-nots now seem to outnumber the haves. Given the nation's economic and energy difficulties, they may well outnumber them by a wider margin in the future. Moreover, the have-nots evidently care about their disadvantages. This politically favorable situation for land consumerism contrasts strikingly with that of the land-use reform movement, which even at its height was plainly never able seriously to interest more than a minority of the population.

The changeover from land-use reform to land consumerism ought to benefit the public. During the 1970s, when the demand for land, housing, and energy was increasing rapidly, the land-use reform movement was often able to decrease the supply of those resources. This "success" naturally raised prices further and hurt the movement politically. By contrast, land consumerism would have responded to the rising demand for land, housing, and energy by attempting to increase or hold constant their supply, thereby restraining the price increases. These efforts would have been both more socially desirable and politically popular than those achieved by the land-use reform movement.

Put another way, land-use reformers and environmentalists often complain that newspapers do not devote much attention to land use.[19] The complaint is misguided. Newspapers may not adequately cover land use from an environmental perspective, yet they give it, and always have given it, an immense amount of space in their real-estate sections, and also to some extent in their home and leisure-living sections. These large, popular sections cater primarily to consumer impulses rather than reform or public-interest ones. From a purist standpoint, the sections sometimes caricature the latter, more noble impulses. Five or ten years ago, for instance, one selling point in a real-estate listing was that the home in question did not harm the environment; in the same way, houses today are frequently sold on the basis of their energy efficiency or otherwise economical operation. This consumer approach works: homes are successfully bought and sold (and large amounts of paid-for newspaper space are filled). The consumer perspective plainly has a popular appeal that the reform one does not.

To introduce this perspective into public policy, land-consumer coalitions might press for the creation of public or private units that would represent the interests of land consumers at the deliberations of state and local regulatory land-use bodies. Several state public-service commissions—those of Connecticut, Maryland, Minnesota, New Hampshire, Rhode Island, Vermont, and Washington—have appointed "people's counsels" who act as advocates for utility customers by trying to keep the rates they pay as low as possible.[20]

Similar advocacy groups would extend this concept by pointing out to the land-use bodies in question the consequences of the alternative decisions before them for housing prices, land prices, utility rates, other prices, tax rates, governmental costs, and job opportunities, in both the short and the long term.[21]

Similarly, the coalitions might work for the appointment to the state land-use agencies of representatives of groups that have been economically harmed by the agencies' past operations—for example, blacks, Latinos, the elderly, the poor, middle-income people, small business people, small developers, marginal farmers, unionists, and other blue-collar people. Land-use reform and other environmental organizations should also do more to obtain their own members from these groups, whose interests have been at best neglected over ten years of state land-use regulation.

In addition, land-consumer coalitions might support some attempts to simplify the bureaucratic procedures of state and local land-use agencies. Although past campaigns for simplification have been covert attempts to weaken or undermine the agencies, the agencies may in fact be imposing regulatory requirements that are superfluous or uneconomical. The costs of unnecessary paperwork, consultant employment, multiple hearings, or procedural delays for developers usually are borne by land consumers. Some evidence suggests that in Vermont the district environmental commissions consistently use only about half of the ten state regulatory standards—primarily those pertaining to air and water pollution, soil erosion, and aesthetics—to deny permits or to place conditions on them.[22] The presence of extraneous standards may add substantially to the cost of building without improving the product or protecting the environment. If so, they probably should be dispensed with entirely.

Additional costs can also result from technical construction requirements and on- and off-site improvements that may be little more than frills. Martin Mayer described Charles Rutenberg, head of the Florida-based development conglomerate U.S. Homes, as "bleeding inside but privately" because, in Rutenberg's words:

More and more towns have decided that sidewalks have to be five feet rather than four feet wide. No problem—it just adds eighty-eight cents per month for the rest of the homeowner's life. And it doesn't matter to us if the village demands—at a time when cars are getting lighter and speed limits lower—that streets where trucks are prohibited must be designed to state highway standards. It's just another $1.70 a month on the cost of the house.[23]

Land consumer groups could usefully try to determine which development regulations lead to such unproductive, environmentally unnecessary costs, and strive to alter or eliminate them.[24]

Land-consumer groups also might undertake politically significant applied-research projects. They might, for example, try to determine whether a particular development is genuinely needed by the community or region for which it is proposed; such research might focus on who would benefit economically from it and who would not. In an urban or suburban area where a large new residential project is proposed, the research might focus on the project's probable effects on the local housing market, especially middle- and low-income home buyers and renters. In a rural coastal area threatened by urban or industrial development, the research might examine what the proposed projects would do to tourism, commercial fishing, or other local enterprises. Or in a rural area under pressure from energy development, the research might concentrate on its likely effect on hunting, fishing, or other kinds of locally profitable recreation. (The Pennsylvania Federation of Sportsmen's Clubs has long been known as one of the state's most effective environmental groups, especially in its opposition to strip mining.) Other applied-research projects might ascertain, perhaps in the absence of any proposals, what kinds of development a given community or region actually needs, or what kinds offer the most (or most widespread) economic benefits to residents.

Still other projects might examine the economic or environmental impacts of particular land-use regulations. The projects might investigate, for instance, the validity of the costs imposed by application requirements, multiple-hearing procedures, or permit conditions— that is, whether or not these procedures result in significant environmental benefits that justify their effects on the price of housing or other construction.[25] Other economic projects might examine in detail whether the regulations in fact produce overall, long-term public or private savings, unduly favor the large developer, harm the poor, or stiffen the development market. Environmental research projects might take a closer look at the environmental benefits the regulations actually produce, the regulatory bodies' use of conditions to obtain the benefits, or the changes in development practice that the regulations induce.

Land consumerism is not incompatible with environmentalist principles, and a movement that responds to individual economic self-interest can gain more political support and effectiveness than one that fights or ignores it. Environmentalism can succeed only by addressing the public's concerns—land prices, jobs, housing availability, tax rates, public service levels, utility bills, and other prices. It can achieve little by calling for esoteric improvements in air- and water-pollution control, garbage disposal, or landscape design, and then suggesting that the costs of these amenities are too trivial or demeaning to discuss.

Alternatives to Centralized Regulation

Land use has always been affected by taxation, public-works policies, and government subsidies. New measures in these areas can change land use in some ways more effectively than can centralized regulation. Such measures can be more precise than centralized regulation in terms of both geographic scope and functional content, and can be more responsive to the specifics of particular land-use situations.

In addition, such legislation would not be simply reactive. Under a regulatory system, a developer proposes a project to which a regulatory body must respond. But tax laws, for example, once enacted, remain in play and give some of the initiative to government rather than all of it to development interests. Moreover, unlike the bulk of centralized land-use regulation, they apply not only to proposed projects but also to existing ones. Regulatory bodies, in contrast, have to rule conclusively on projects before they are built—often on the basis of inevitably sketchy information provided by their developers—and have almost no control over them afterward.

Changes in tax laws could, for example, mitigate the dispossessing effects of the economics of rapid growth. Even large landowners and the local governments whose tax systems produce these effects eventually regret them. Income-keyed local property tax laws could relieve the burden that rising assessments impose on low-income, land-poor persons. These laws could exempt from property taxes those with incomes below a specified figure, so that rising taxes would not force them to sell their holdings. In addition, a number of state governments have successfully experimented with "circuit breaker" or "homestead exemption" tax provisions that give relief on humanitarian grounds to elderly or unusually poor residents. The provisions, which are administered through the state income tax, can fairly easily be altered to give similar relief on environmental grounds to the rural and urban land-poor.[26]

Local property-tax rates also might depend on the way in which the owner uses the land in question. Today, the tax rates in most states are based on what assessors call "the highest and best use" of the land—that is, the use that in their judgment yields the largest economic return. So, for example, agricultural land that might become a suburban subdivision is taxed at the same high rate as land that has in fact been subdivided. Instead, the rates could be tied, as they are in some states, to the intensity of the land use, so that farmland would be taxed at a lower rate than subdivided land.[27] Alternatively, tax rates could be tied to the environmental damage produced by the land use, again so as to favor farmland or other less heavily used land rather than subdivided land.[28]

The destructive competition in property-tax rates between localities vying for desirable developments would be diminished if states were to enact uniform statewide rates, or were to set ranges within which localities might determine the actual rates they wished to employ.[29] Alternatively, some variant of the Twin Cities tax-sharing arrangement, under which each city in the Minneapolis–St. Paul area shares a portion of the property-tax revenues from development in its jurisdiction with all the other cities,[30] might be adopted by other metropolitan areas, regions, or states.

State and federal tax systems also could be used to curb land speculation. For some years, Connecticut has had a conveyance tax on real estate sales that varies inversely with the number of years the seller has held the property. The tax, which the seller pays, ranges from 10 percent if the property has been held a year or less down to 1 percent if it has been held ten years or more.[31] In 1973, Vermont introduced a comparable capital-gains tax on land sales. It does not apply to structures built on the land, and it now exempts gains on up to twenty-five acres if the property is used as a principal residence; but it does tax land profits at a rate that depends both on how long the seller, who pays the tax, has had the land and on how much the land has increased in value since the seller bought it. Sellers who have held their land more than six years pay no tax; sellers who have held it less than a year and at least tripled their money pay a tax of 60 percent of their gain.[32]

State public-works investments are often the main determinants of community growth, but they have typically been located and built with little consideration for their local environmental, social, and economic effects. In the last few years, however, a number of states, harassed by urban sprawl and the financial and energy pressures it produces, have begun to take these effects into account. California and Massachusetts are now trying to direct their state capital investment—state roads, sewer and water lines, housing projects, office buildings, and so forth—away from suburban, exurban, and rural areas and toward older central-city areas.[33] Vermont is trying to ensure that the state's public-works investments do minimal environmental and economic damage and conflict with one another as little as possible.[34] Maryland, Montana, and Pennsylvania are making comparable efforts,[35] which should be encouraged elsewhere.

The land-use reform movement arose in response to the shortcomings of local regulation, and it has rarely considered measures that were primarily local. But today, partly because of the movement, working from within local government to improve land use makes sense. Environmentalists are much more widely represented in local zoning boards, planning commissions, and governments than they were ten years ago. According to one estimate, more than three hundred of the citizens who actively worked for the passage of the 1972 California coastal initiative had been elected to local public office by 1976.[36]

In a large number of places the local level now appears to be more fertile ground for land-use reform than the higher levels. The local level has always had more practical knowledge and public trust in land-use matters; today, local officials also may be well informed about environmental issues. The Brown and Coke opinion survey that found environmentalist and localist attitudes similar at many points and united in their skepticism about new growth concluded: "The contemporary climate of public opinion is therefore more open to innovation in land use policy than many would have expected."[37] Thus many measures that are politically unfeasible at the state level—such as more specific and stringent standards in land-use laws, stronger enforcement powers for them, more citizen participation, and increased staffing and financing—may now be politically acceptable at the local level. Assertive land-use regulation by several key localities in a state can produce roughly the same environmental results as statewide land-use regulation, and with fewer political and economic difficulties.[38]

In recent years, a number of states, mainly in the West, have required their localities to enact planning, zoning, or subdivision ordinances, with results that are as yet unclear.[39] But if the states were also to offer their localities financial and technical aid in devising and carrying out the ordinances—probably more on the scale of what California now offers its coastal communities than what New York offers localities in the Adirondacks—the states could then effectively insist on rigorous physical and procedural requirements in the ordinances and on local attainment of the requirements. The states might also be able to induce localities to allow more low-income housing. And they might be able to make developers hire as many local people as possible and to pay for good consulting studies—the consultants to be chosen by the locality—of the actual economic costs and benefits of the proposed project.

Higher-level governments also might offer special subsidies to communities with particular land-use problems. The federal coastal zone management program already has an Energy Impact Fund that gives states grants, loans, and bond guarantees to try to alleviate the difficulties experienced by coastal communities when they undergo rapid energy development.[40] Montana and North Dakota, among other states, levy special minerals severance taxes on coal companies and use the revenues to help their boom towns cope with energy development.[41] Other federal and state agencies could give more financial and technical assistance to communities experiencing energy booms.[42] Or they could offer such help to communities with public works or even general construction booms; this, in fact, is roughly what Florida's Bureau of Land and Water Management has been doing in the Apalachicola and Charlotte Harbor regions as an alternative to designating them as areas of critical state concern. (In the Keys, which were so designated, the bureau also helped local governments get federal and state aid to undertake road, bridge, and water-supply projects.[43]) State and federal agencies also might conceivably be able to help communities suffering from extreme declines in small-scale agriculture, as Minnesota now does by offering qualified young agricultural families low-interest loans to enter farming.[44] In many cases, state or federal provision of land-use funds and expertise to localities or individuals may prove more politically feasible than direct state land-use regulation.

Improving Centralized Regulation

Land consumerism, tax measures, public-works policies, government subsidies, and changes in local land-use regulation should not replace centralized regulation. The many functioning and contemplated programs of centralized regulation should not be written off. They have achieved some real successes and remain the primary engine of land-use reform. But they also may benefit from a number of new approaches. For example, single-purpose or single-area land-use legislation tends to arouse less opposition, to be easier to pass, and to result in more demanding environmental legislation than comprehensive state laws.

Many states have passed single-purpose laws; many have rejected comprehensive laws. As Don Benninghoven of the League of California Cities told *Planning* in 1977: "There is no interest in statewide land-use planning in California. None. Not by cities, not by counties, not by the state. . . . We've given up on the grand scheme of doing anything statewide. Instead, we concentrate on legislation on specific problems, such as coastal protection, prime agricultural land, and preserving Lake Tahoe."[45]

The land-use reform movement has recognized the many possibilities for single-purpose and single-area regulatory legislation—not just coastal, strip mining, power plant, and regional laws, but also wetland, shoreland, floodplain, industrial siting, land sales, farmland preservation, environmental impact statement, and pollution laws. In any one state, the combination of even a few such laws can easily be more effective than a comprehensive land-use law.[46]

Similarly, statewide land-use plans have proved less than satisfactory as a tool of land-use reform. The plans, most of which take the form of maps, are too abstract or technical to convey much real information to the public. They also make ownership interests uneasy or rebellious by suggesting that the state has bold designs on their property and its value. Such plans apparently originate because the city planners and lawyers working for land-use reform both inside and outside the state land-use agencies feel uncomfortable without them. But they do little for the cause of land-use reform that centralized regulation, for all its flaws, does not do better by itself.[47]

If state land-use plans are legally required or administratively necessary, they should not cover the entire state—only selected portions of it. The maps of the plans should, if possible, be mainly white space where the plans do not apply. Such white space would go a long way toward reassuring ownership interests not affected by the plans. Alternatively, the state land-use agencies might publish lists of environmentally fragile areas they did not want to see developed. These lists could be accompanied by specification of what kinds of development would be particularly objectionable in the fragile areas. Other lists might designate environmentally sturdy areas in which the agencies welcomed development, and specify preferred kinds of development for those areas. By publishing these lists, the state regulatory agencies would be taking the initiative and informing developers about where they might build with a minimum of regulatory difficulty. The lists also would not pose the political problems inherent in the production of state land-use plans and maps, and they would take out of the regulatory process some of the uncertainty that has led to charges of arbitrariness.[48]

The state land-use agencies should strive to appoint to their memberships representatives of such groups as blacks, Latinos, the elderly, the poor, small developers and other small-business people, marginal farmers, unionists, and others whom their operations have heretofore harmed. They should appoint people's counsels, and they should, wherever possible, give preference in their hiring to qualified persons who are already residents of the state, especially if they have genuine roots in the regulated areas. Such persons usually regulate both more effectively and more sympathetically than out-of-staters, particularly those with impressive technocratic credentials.

In addition, the agencies should do what they can to defuse opposition by simplifying their bureaucratic procedures without tilting them in favor of ownership interests. For instance, they could allow developers, as the Florida program now does, to make specified small changes in their projects without having to return to the agencies for reapproval. The programs also could use a shorter application form for relatively small or simple projects. They could make certain that the state regulatory process begins as early as possible, so as to minimize complex, expensive, time-consuming confusions within and among different state and local agencies. They could, in consultation with other state agencies, designate a "lead agency" for particular projects or classes of projects; this agency would then be responsible for seeing that the projects in question received a timely but thorough review from the other relevant state agencies, and if possible from the local and federal ones as well.

Such an arrangement—involving only state agencies—seems to have worked satisfactorily in the State of Washington.[49] More informally, the state agencies could, as they do in Vermont, meet periodically to discuss the most important development applications before them and reach agreement on a unified, expeditious state-level response to each.[50] These simplification measures also would make small developers more nearly equal to large ones as objects of government regulation.

In addition, some of the economic and environmental research proposed earlier for land-consumer groups—the studies, for example, on unnecessary or redundant development requirements, the impacts of the land-use programs on home buyers and small developers, the environmental benefits of the programs, or the alterations in development practice they produce—could as easily be done by the state land-use agencies, which might then be better situated to act on the findings.[51] The agencies also might publish simple-English handbooks or establish toll-free telephone numbers where developers, builders, homeowners, environmentalists, and public agencies could learn what state, local, and federal permits were needed for particular projects or what actions would be necessary to obtain them.[52]

Finally, the state land-use agencies might want to consider giving payments to some applicants whose projects are rejected or heavily conditioned. The possibility of such payments would reduce the psychological and political pressures that now force agency members to approve some projects they would rather not, or to impose lighter conditions than they would prefer. Melvin Mogulof wrote that the California commissions

could only erratically and infrequently bring themselves to block action because, in the absence of compensation, they often saw the denial of a permit as unfair. . . . The grossest consequences of regulation, where it compromises value acquired in good faith, must be in some way compensable. . . . Over the longer term, the availability of compensation is particularly crucial in dealing with the small property owners who would suffer hardship from restrictions on the use of their land. Without compensation, accommodation or outright permit [denial] become the only really practicable and acceptable regulatory actions for these cases.[53]

The state land-use agency members would be more likely to enforce their environmental mandates if they could compensate such applicants for the burden their directives imposed. The applicants also would have less reason to feel that they were suffering an unjustified arbitrary taking of their property.

Any compensation system, of course, needs safeguards to prevent abuses. The regulatory agency would have to make sure the project in question was a genuine, financially feasible proposal, not simply a sham to gain compensation. Preference for compensation would be given in the case of proposed land uses that were permitted when the property in question was purchased by the owner. The owner could in any event only be paid once for any piece of property. The system would set a maximum amount for such payment. It would be a serious, not merely token, compensatory amount, but less than the full after-tax profit the owner would have made had the project been completely approved. If the owner later received approval for a project on the property, the approval would be conditioned on the owner's returning at least a portion and perhaps all of the previous payment to the land-use agency.

Corporations or owners above a specified size could not receive payments. Payees would have to have held the property for a specified period. The agency would have to establish procedures to ensure that it treated applicants equitably. Under such procedures, hardship cases—the farmer or motel owner, for example, whose retirement is jeopardized because the state land-use agency will not allow him to subdivide his property—would get priority. Within this framework, compensation systems could both strengthen and humanize land-use regulation.[54]

It was not a mistake for the land-use reform movement to rely almost totally on centralized regulation; or if it was a mistake, it was one made inevitable by the movement's political and intellectual origins. But today, more than a decade after the advent of the movement, there clearly are better ways, as suggested above, for it to pursue its goals. There are also, as suggested, better ways for it to approach centralized regulation. The American political and economic scene has changed dramatically since the late 1960s, and the land-use reform movement must change as well.

CHAPTER 12

Afterword:
The Lessons for Other Fields

Centralized regulatory programs, as efforts at reform, have spread to many governmental fields in recent years. In 1978 Paul MacAvoy, a Yale University economist, wrote that the domain of direct federal price controls and health-and-safety regulations—"the control sector of the American economy"—had "probably grown from something like 7 percent [of the economy] to close to 30 percent in the last decade. Elsewhere, the extent of controls is now not as great by any means, but it is also not negligible. All of industry now undertakes pollution and safety-related investments, checks price increases, [and] monitors output quality, with a federal agency in mind."[1]

Moreover, despite the current attacks on centralized regulation and the occasional efforts to deregulate, Nader-influenced programs such as land-use reform are far from losing momentum. In the environmental area alone, for example, the federal government has within the last two years begun major new efforts, largely taking the form of grants to states that create regulatory programs, to control the pollution caused by solid wastes, hazardous substances, and toxic chemicals.[2] A similar federal effort to regulate power-plant siting seems likely to get underway in the next few years.

But the experience of the land-use reform movement suggests that centralized regulation is not always and forever the most desirable public approach to social problems. The value that our society places

233

on individual rights, especially property rights, as well as the power of local and other lower-level governments in our federal system, inevitably limit what centralized regulation can accomplish.

Centralized regulation can achieve important, positive results, but because its legislative formulation and administrative implementation are always likely to be compromised, its achievements tend to be partial, uncertain, yoked with negative results, and not at all what either its supporters or its opponents originally expected. The political bread of reformers necessarily consists of half-loaves or even single slices—the normal diet of democratic pluralism.

Attenuated and sometimes nonexistent benefits have been the products of a large number of innovative programs, regulatory and nonregulatory.[3] No large-scale reform program seems to sweep the field before it. Given the astonishing diversity, complexity, and tenacity of American political and economic behavior, it is unrealistic and unfair to expect any single reform program, or even any group of them, to achieve night-and-day changes within a few years. Many programs never achieve any solid or lasting benefits. The history of centralized regulation has always been a history of disappointment. But in the case of the land-use reform movement, it has been a creative, productive disappointment—one that has kept most land-use reformers from giving up and should encourage them to try new strategies in the future.

The experience of the land-use reform movement is actually reassuring. Contrary to conventional administrative wisdom and the bulk of political science and economic literature, programs of centralized regulation need not be captured by the interests they are intended to restrain.[4] Similarly, they need not inevitably undergo some cycle of secular decline into ineffectuality or desuetude. They need not wither in the face of adverse economic or other external circumstances. They may influence the thinking and action of the corporations, governments, and individuals they regulate. They can, in short, make a difference. The difference may not be enormous, but in the case of the land-use reform movement, it has certainly been perceptible.

The comparative success of land-use reform appears to be due in part to the movement's flexibility—its shift in focus from ecological to growth-management concerns. A more important source of the movement's success was its continued public support. The population at large has favored land-use reform at least in principle, and often in practice as well.[5] Naturally, both principle and practice typically had to be accommodated to other public values.

The land-use reform movement's experience offers more pessimistic lessons. Programs of centralized regulation, as well as other devices for reform, virtually always confront a powerful, well-financed, entrenched conservative opposition that can often block, weaken, subvert, pervert, or ignore them, but whose help will nonetheless be needed to carry them out. So before choosing to pursue such programs in any field, reformers should carefully examine their political assets and those of their opponents. Programs of centralized regulation are unlikely to succeed if their active supporters represent only a relatively narrow social stratum and especially if they try to change the traditional and personally profitable habits of much of the population. Instead, they should try to find more isolated, discrete, particular targets whose activities the public finds objectionable. They will succeed to the extent that they can neutralize, co-opt, or join forces with portions of the interests that would otherwise oppose them. They will be more likely to attain their goals if they either do not challenge lower-level governments or can enlist or compel their support.

They will be more effective, too, if they can devise and impose clear standards for the behavior they are restraining, and less effective if they cannot. They will perform better if they can keep their bureaucratic operations from becoming so complex and unwieldy as to give their opponents an obvious point of attack. They will be more successful if they do not benefit large, established enterprises at the expense of small new ones, or the affluent at the expense of minorities, the poor, and blue-collar and middle-income people. Their chances of survival will improve if they can produce specific, substantial economic savings and improvements in industrial practices and then convincingly demonstrate them to the public. On the other hand, they will encounter problems if the public comes to see their economic costs as large or their benefits as unclear or negligible. If a proposed or existing effort at centralized regulation cannot pass most of these tests, it will probably falter and perhaps fail completely.

Reference Matter

Notes

Chapter 1: A Regulatory Experiment

1 See, for instance, Jens Sorensen, *State-Local Collaborative Planning: A Growing Trend in Coastal Zone Management* (Washington: U.S. Department of Commerce, Office of Coastal Zone Management and Office of Sea Grant, 1978).

2 See, for instance, Nelson Rosenbaum, "Private Property and the Public Interest: Citizen Involvement in State Land Use Control" (Washington: Urban Institute Working Paper, 1977).

3 See, for example, Nelson Rosenbaum, *Land Use and the Legislatures: The Politics of State Innovation* (Washington: Urban Institute, 1976).

4 See, for instance, Robert Ditton, John Seymour, and Gerald Swanson, *Coastal Resources Management: Beyond Bureaucracy and the Market* (Lexington, Massachusetts: Lexington Books, 1977), and Joseph Heikoff, *Coastal Resources Management: Institutions and Programs* (Ann Arbor, Michigan: Ann Arbor Science Publishers, 1978).

5 See, for example, Daniel Mandelker, *Environmental and Land Controls Legislation* (Indianapolis: Bobbs-Merrill, 1976). A supplement to this volume appeared in 1978.

6 See, for example, Fred Bosselman and David Callies, *The Quiet Revolution in Land Use Control* (Washington: Government Printing Office, 1972), and Robert Healy, *Land Use and the States* (Baltimore: Johns Hopkins University Press, 1976). A second edition of the latter book, co-authored by John Rosenberg, was published in late 1979, too late for extensive citation.

7 See, for example, Dan Richardson, *The Cost of Environmental Protection: Regulating Housing Development in the Coastal Zone* (New Brunswick, New Jersey: Rutgers University Center for Urban Policy Research, 1976).

8 See, however, Nelson Rosenbaum, "The State Role in Wetlands Protection," *Environmental Comment*, July 1978, as well as the larger forthcoming study cited there.

Chapter 2: Land-Use Regulation as a Public Issue

1 Barry Bruce-Briggs, "Land Use and the Environment," in Institute for Contemporary Studies, *No Land Is an Island: Individual Rights and Government Control of Land Use* (San Francisco: ICS, 1975), p. 2. For what homeownership means to homeowners, see Constance Perin, *Everything in Its Place: Social Order and Land Use in America* (Princeton, New Jersey: Princeton University Press, 1977), pp. 32–162.

2 For more on corporate landholders, see Frank Popper, "We've Got to Dig Deeper into Who Owns Our Land," *Planning*, October 1976, and Peter Meyer, "Land Rush," *Harper's*, January 1979.

3 Robert Boxley, *Land Ownership Issues in Rural America* (Washington: Department of Agriculture, Economic Research Service, 1977), pp. 2, 3.

4 Meyer, "Land Rush," pp. 47–48, citing figures of the Conference Board of New York.

5 For extended discussions of how the patterns of land use reveal the character of its users, see Perin, *Everything in Its Place*, and Paul Goodman and Percival Goodman, *Communitas: Means of Livelihood and Ways of Life* (Chicago: University of Chicago Press, revised edition, 1960).

6 The material in this section and the following one is documented in greater detail in Chapters 3 and 4. For general documentation, see Richard Babcock, *The Zoning Game: Municipal Practices and Policies* (Madison: University of Wisconsin Press, 1966); Robert Burchell and David Listokin, eds., *Future Land Use: Energy, Environmental, and Legal Constraints* (New Brunswick, New Jersey: Rutgers University Center for Urban Policy Research, 1975); John DeGrove, *Land Management: New Directions for the States* (Columbus, Ohio: Academy for Contemporary Problems, 1976); Healy, *Land Use and the States*; Samuel Kaplan, *The Dream Deferred: People, Politics and Planning in Suburbia* (New York: Seabury, 1976); R. Robert Linowes and Don Allensworth, *The States and Land Use Control* (New York: Praeger, 1975); Noreen Lyday, *The Law of the Land: Debating National Land Use Legislation, 1970–75* (Washington: Urban Institute, 1976); Ralph Nader's Study Group on Land Use in California, Robert Fellmeth, Project Director, *Politics of Land* (New York: Grossman, 1973); National Commission on Urban Problems, *Building the American City* (Washington: Government Printing Office, 1968; New York: Praeger, 1969); National Resources Defense Council, Elaine Moss, ed., *Land Use Controls in the United States: A Handbook on the Legal Rights of*

Citizens (New York: Dial Press/James Wade, 1977); and William Reilly, ed., *The Use of Land: A Citizens' Policy Guide to Urban Growth* (New York: Crowell, 1973).

7 On the multiplicity of federal policies and programs that affect land use, see Council of State Governments, *Land: State Alternatives for Planning and Management* (Lexington, Kentucky: CSG, 1975), pp. 18–23; Charles Little, *Shifting Ground: New Priorities for National Land Use Policy* (Washington: Library of Congress, Congressional Research Service, 1976), pp. 8–9; Meyer, "Land Rush," pp. 55–58; and Aspen Systems Corporation, *Land and Natural Resources Management: An Analysis of Selected Federal Policies, Programs, and Planning Mechanisms* (Washington: Council on Environmental Quality and U.S. Geological Survey, 1979).

8 Reilly, ed., *The Use of Land*, p. 27.

9 See, for example, ibid., pp. 19–31.

10 Ibid., pp. 219–23, 246–61.

11 See Kermit Parsons and Harriet Budke, *Canadian Land Banks* (Chicago: American Society of Planning Officials, 1972); Neal Roberts, ed., *The Government Land Developers* (Lexington, Massachusetts: Lexington Books, 1976); and Ann Strong, *Land Banking: European Reality, American Prospect* (Baltimore: Johns Hopkins University Press, 1979).

12 Reilly, ed., *The Use of Land*, pp. 213–14.

13 Ibid., pp. 236–37.

14 See, for example, ibid., pp. 19–26, 103–208.

15 See, for example, ibid., pp. 26–31, 208–304.

16 "Proposal for the Future: A Research Center on Regulation," *Bulletin of the Kennedy School of Government*, Winter 1977, pp. 22–23. For some further figures on the growth of regulation, see William Lilley III and James Miller III, "The New 'Social Regulation,'" *The Public Interest*, Spring 1977, pp. 49–52.

17 Stanley Marcus, "Can Free Enterprise Survive Success?" in J. Jeffrey Leonard, J. Clarence Davies III, and Gordon Binder, eds., *Business and Environment: Toward Common Ground* (Washington: Conservation Foundation, 1977), pp. 70, 71.

18 For a defense of centralized regulation by Hubert Humphrey, see his presentation in American Enterprise Institute for Public Policy Research, *Government Regulation: What Kind of Reform?* (Washington: AEIPPR, 1976).

19 For a comparison of the three positions, see Benjamin Ward, *The Ideal Worlds of Economics: Liberal, Radical, and Conservative Economic World Views* (New York: Basic Books, 1979).

20 For expositions of the Friedman position, see Milton Friedman and Rose Friedman, *Capitalism and Freedom* (Chicago: University of Chicago Press, 1962); Milton Friedman, *There's No Such Thing as a Free Lunch* (La Salle, Illinois: Open Court, 1976); and George Stigler, *The Citizen and the State: Essays on Regulation* (Chicago: University of Chicago Press, 1975). *The Journal of Law and Economics*, the *Bell Journal of Economics and Management Science*, and *Regulation* frequently contain articles and case studies with this point of view.

21 For expositions of the Nader position, see Ralph Nader, Mark Green, and Joel Seligman, *Taming the Giant Corporation* (New York: Norton, 1976), and the Nader presentation in American Enterprise Institute for Public Policy Research, *Government Regulation: What Kind of Reform?* For some evidence on federal regulation, see the six-volume Senate Committee on Governmental Affairs, *Study on Federal Regulation* (Washington: Government Printing Office, 1977); the Subcommittee on Oversight and Investigation of the House Committee on Interstate and Foreign Commerce, *Federal Regulation and Regulatory Reform* (Washington: Government Printing Office, 1976); and Common Cause, *With Only One Ear* (Washington: CC, 1976).

22 See Theodore Lowi, *The End of Liberalism: Ideology, Policy, and the Crisis of Public Authority* (New York: Norton, 1969), especially pp. 55–97, 125–56. A second edition of the book, now subtitled *The Second Republic of the United States*, appeared in late 1979, too late for extensive citation.

23 Milton Friedman, "Special Interests and the Law," *Chicago Bar Record* (1970), p. 434, quoted by M. Bruce Johnson, "A Critique of the Concept of Federal Land Use Regulation," *Environmental Law*, Spring 1975, p. 585.

24 Ronald Coase, "Economists and Public Policy," *Reason*, December 1974, pp. 22–23, quoted by Johnson, "A Critique of the Concept of Federal Land Use Regulation," p. 585. For a collection of the kinds of studies Coase cites, see Institute for Contemporary Studies, *Regulating Business: The Search for an Optimum* (San Francisco: ICS, 1978).

25 For some Friedman-like treatments of land use, see Bernard Siegan, *Land Use without Zoning* (Lexington, Massachusetts: Lexington Books, 1972); Siegan, *Other People's Property* (Lexington, Massachusetts: Lexington Books, 1976); Robert Nelson, *Zoning and Property Rights: An Analysis of the American System of Land-Use Regulation* (Cambridge: MIT Press, 1977); and John McClaughry, "The Land Use Planning Act—An Idea We Can Do Without," *Environmental Affairs*, Volume 3, Number 4, 1974.

26 Lowi, *The End of Liberalism*, p. 155.

27 Ibid., p. 156.

28 Ibid.

29 Ibid., pp. 89–90. The last sentence is emphasized in the original.

30 Ibid., p. 154, quoting Jaffe, "The Effective Limits of the Administrative Process: A Reevaluation," *Harvard Law Review*, May 1959, p. 1134. For another view of centralized regulation from a left-wing perspective, see Gabriel Kolko, *The Triumph of Conservatism* (Glencoe, Illinois: Free Press, 1963).

31 The elements of a Lowi approach to land use described in this paragraph are extrapolated from Lowi, *The End of Liberalism*, pp. 287–314.

32 Ralph Nader's Study Group on Land Use in California, *Politics of Land*, pp. ix, viii.

33 Ibid., p. 215.

34 Ibid., pp. 210–15, 349–50, 456–92.

35 For other views of centralized regulation from a liberal centrist perspective, see Marver Bernstein, *Regulating Business by Independent Commission* (Princeton: Princeton University Press, 1955); Stephen Breyer, "Analyzing Regulatory Failure: Mismatches, Less Restrictive Alternatives, and Reform," *Harvard Law Review*, January 1979; A. Myrick Freeman III and Robert Haveman, "Clean Rhetoric and Dirty Water," *The Public Interest*, Summer 1972; Samuel Huntington, "The Marasmus of the ICC: The Commission, the Railroads, and the Public Interest," *Yale Law Journal*, April 1952; Simon Lazarus, *The Genteel Populists* (New York: Holt, Rinehart and Winston, 1974; revised edition, 1976); Grant McConnell, *Private Power and American Democracy* (New York: Knopf, 1966); Roger Noll, *Reforming Regulation: An Evaluation of the Ash Council Proposals* (Washington: Brookings Institution, 1971); Charles Schultze, *The Public Use of Private Interest* (Washington: Brookings Institution, 1977); James Wilson, "The Politics of Regulation," pp. 135–68, in James McKie, ed., *Social Responsibility and the Business Predicament* (Washington: Brookings Institution, 1975); and the section "About Regulation" in *The Public Interest*, Fall 1977.

36 Richard Babcock, "Regulating Land Development: Some Thoughts on the Role of Government," in Soil Conservation Society of America, *Land Use: Tough Choices in Today's World* (Ankeny, Iowa: SCSA, 1977), pp. 40–41. See also Babcock, "On Land-Use Policy," *Planning*, June 1975, and Babcock and Duane Feurer, "Land as a Commodity 'Affected with a Public Interest,'" *Urban Land*, November 1977.

Chapter 3: The Birth of an Issue

1 Bosselman and Callies, *The Quiet Revolution in Land Use Control*, p. ii.
2 For some examples near New York and Philadelphia respectively, see Reilly, ed., *The Use of Land*, pp. 39–43, and Ann Strong, *Private Property and the Public Interest: The Brandywine Experience* (Baltimore: Johns Hopkins University Press, 1975), pp. 175–77.
3 See Reilly, ed., *The Use of Land*, p. 85.
4 Peter Morrison, *Migration and Rights of Access: New Public Concerns of the 1970s* (Santa Monica, California: Rand Corporation, 1977), p. 6.
5 For more on the new nonmetropolitan migration, see Calvin Beale, *The Revival of Population Growth in Nonmetropolitan America*, U.S. Department of Agriculture, Economic Research Service Report No. 605 (Washington: Government Printing Office, 1975); Glenn Fugitt, Paul Voss, and J. C. Doherty, *Growth and Change in Rural America* (Washington: Urban Land Institute, 1979); Richard Lonsdale and H. Seyler, eds., *Nonmetropolitan Industrialization* (Washington: Winston and Sons, 1979); Peter Morrison, "The Current Demographic Context of National Growth and Development," *Environmental Comment*, July 1976; and William Alonso, "Metropolis without Growth," *The Public Interest*, Fall 1978. For some case studies, see Alvin Sokolow, "The Redistribution of California's Population: New Growth in Nonmetropolitan Areas," *California Data Brief*, February 1978; University of Wisconsin, University-Industry Research Program, *Small City Growth* (Madison: U-IRP, 1977); and Gene Summers and Arne Selvik, *Nonmetropolitan Industrial Growth and Community Change* (Lexington, Massachusetts: Lexington Books, 1979).
6 Richard Lamm, "Winter Games: An Opponent's View," *State Government*, Summer 1973, p. 139.
7 Ibid., p. 140.
8 See U.S. Department of Commerce, Bureau of the Census, *Statistical Abstract of the United States, 1977* (Washington: Government Printing Office, 1977), p. 5.
9 For the Florida figures in this paragraph, see Healy, *Land Use and the States*, pp. 11, 24.
10 Ibid., pp. 11, 24.
11 Memorandum from Joseph Bodovitz, Executive Director, San Francisco Bay Conservation and Development Commission, to all commissioners and alternates, October 22, 1971, p. 1. I obtained a copy of the memorandum at the commission's office in San Francisco.

12 See Jane Jacobs, *The Death and Life of Great American Cities* (New York: Vintage paperback, 1961), pp. 68–71.

13 Ed McCahill, "They Don't Want Clean Air; They Want Pure Air," *Planning*, March/April 1973, p. 35. For a different opinion on the effects of cars, see Barry Bruce-Briggs, *The War against the Automobile* (New York: Dutton, 1977).

14 John Costonis, *Space Adrift: Saving Urban Landmarks through the Chicago Plan* (Urbana: University of Illinois Press, 1974), p. 4.

15 Ben Funk, "Miami: Kissing the Good Life Goodbye," *Tallahassee Democrat*, March 21, 1971, quoted by Luther Carter, *The Florida Experience: Land and Water Policy in a Growth State* (Baltimore: Johns Hopkins University Press, 1974), pp. 146–47.

16 Carter, *The Florida Experience*, p. 147.

17 Urban Systems Research and Engineering, *The Growth Shapers: The Land Use Impacts of Infrastructure Investments* (Washington: Government Printing Office, 1976), p. 3. See also Bill Boyarsky and Nancy Boyarsky, *Backroom Politics: How Your Local Politicians Work, Why Your Government Doesn't and What You Can Do about It* (Los Angeles: Tarcher, 1974), pp. 152–63.

18 See, for example, Ben Kelley, *The Pavers and the Paved* (New York: Brown, 1971), especially pp. 21–63; and Helen Leavitt, *Superhighway—Superhoax* (New York: Ballantine paperback, 1971), especially pp. 106–78. Kelley was the first director of the Federal Highway Administration's office of public affairs in the U.S. Department of Transportation. For an outstanding example of runaway local and state highway building, see Robert Caro, *The Power Broker: Robert Moses and the Fall of New York* (New York: Knopf, 1974).

19 Urban Systems Research and Engineering, *The Growth Shapers*, p. 28.

20 For a study of a proposed Richmond, Virginia, beltway that comes to similar conclusions using the experience of beltways in San Antonio, Indianapolis, and Columbus, Ohio, see Thomas Muller, Kevin Neels, John Tilney, and Grace Dawson, *The Impact of Beltways on Central Business Districts: A Case Study of Richmond* (Washington: Urban Institute, 1978).

21 For examples and bibliography, see Urban Systems Research and Engineering, *The Growth Shapers*, pp. 30–31, 38. See also R. M. Pope, Jr., and J. Stepp, *Effects of a New Interstate Highway on Traffic-Oriented Enterprises in a Rural Area* (Clemson, South Carolina: Clemson University Agricultural Experiment Station, 1970).

22 Urban Systems Research and Engineering, *The Growth Shapers*, pp. 48–49, 53, 55. For further discussion, see Richard Tabors, Michael

Shapiro, and Peter Rogers, *Land Use and the Pipe: Planning for Sewage* (Lexington, Massachusetts: Lexington Books, 1976).

23 For further discussion, see Urban Systems Research and Engineering, *The Growth Shapers*. For a case study of the effects of siting an Atomic Energy Commission accelerator in a rural Illinois village, see Theodore Lowi et al., *Poliscide* (New York: Macmillan, 1976).

24 Morrison, *Migration and Rights of Access*, p. 1.

25 Lawrence Livingston, Jr., and John Blayney, *Foothill Environmental Design Study: Open Space v. Environment* (San Francisco: Livingston and Blayney, 1971). For a different view of the Palo Alto finding and the city's subsequent experience with the land it purchased, see Bernard Frieden, *The Environmental Protection Hustle* (Cambridge, Massachusetts: MIT Press, 1979), pp. 107–18.

26 Richard Appelbaum, Jennifer Bigelow, Henry Kramer, Harvey Molotch, and Paul Relis, *The Effects of Urban Growth: A Population Impact Analysis* (New York: Praeger, 1976). For the results of more such studies that come to similar conclusions, see Nelson, *Zoning and Property Rights*, pp. 155–57.

27 For more on the public and private costs of development, see Earl Finkler, William Toner, and Frank Popper, *Urban Nongrowth: City Planning for People* (New York: Praeger, 1976), pp. 82–148. For more general treatments of the economics of development, see Thomas Muller, *Fiscal Impacts of Land Development: Employment, Housing, and Property Values* (Washington: Urban Institute, 1976), and the October 1976 issue of *Environmental Comment*, on "Analyzing the Impact of Development." For a more technical treatment, see Robert Burchell and David Listokin, *The Fiscal Impact Handbook: Estimating Local Costs and Revenues of Land Development* (New Brunswick, New Jersey: Rutgers University, Center for Urban Policy Research, 1978).

28 See John Holdren and Peter Herrera, *Energy* (San Francisco: Sierra Club, 1971), p. 11.

29 See National Academy of Sciences, *Rehabilitation Potential of Western Coal Lands* (Cambridge, Massachusetts: Ballinger, 1974), pp. 11–12.

30 See, for example, Ora Spaid, "Forecast: Doubled Coal Production in Appalachia," *Appalachia*, June-July 1975.

31 See Real Estate Research Corporation, *The Costs of Sprawl* (Washington: Government Printing Office, 1974). For a skeptical examination of this study, see Duane Windsor, "A Critique of *The Costs of Sprawl*," *Journal of the American Planning Association*, July 1979.

32 Quoted in Environmental Policy Institute, *The Need for Energy Facility*

Sites in the United States: 1975–1985 and 1985–2000 (Washington: EPI, 1975), p. 1.

33 Florida Energy Committee, *Energy in Florida* (Tallahassee: FEC, 1974), pp. 96–113.

34 Little, *Shifting Ground*, p. 14.

35 For such an argument, see Environmental Policy Institute, *The Need for Energy Facility Sites in the United States*, particularly pp. 35–46.

36 For documentation of the employment figures in this paragraph, see David Myrha, "Energy Development," *Practicing Planner*, September 1976, p. 18; Illinois Institute of Environmental Quality, *Power Plant Siting in the State of Illinois, Part II—Environmental Impacts of Large Energy Conversion Facilities* (Chicago: IIEQ, 1975), pp. 144–45; and John Baldwin, "Socio-Economic Impact of Power Plant Construction: A Case History," *Record of the Maryland Power Plant Siting Act* (Annapolis: Maryland Department of Natural Resources), June 1975, p. 2.

37 The text's account is drawn from K. Ross Toole, *The Rape of the Great Plains: Northwest America, Cattle and Coal* (Boston: Atlantic Monthly–Little, Brown, 1976), pp. 93–113; John Gilmore and Mary Duff, *Boom Town Growth Management* (Boulder, Colorado: Westview Press, 1975); and William Curry, "A Time to Choose" (Johnstown, Pennsylvania: Laurel Highlands Conservation and Development Project, 1975), pp. 1–2.

38 See Michael Coakley, "Murder Angers Tough Boom Town," *Chicago Tribune*, October 20, 1978, p. 1–4.

39 See Gerald Seib, "Debate on Exploiting Mineral Riches Focuses on Remote Red Desert," *Wall Street Journal*, November 9, 1978, p. 1.

40 On western energy development generally, see National Academy of Sciences, *Rehabilitation Potential of Western Coal Lands*; Council on Economic Priorities, *Leased and Lost: A Study of Public and Indian Coal Leasing in the West* (New York: CEP, 1974); Suzanne Dean, "How to Kill a Land-Use Bill," *Planning*, January 1976; John Krutilla and Anthony Fisher, *Economic and Fiscal Impacts of Coal Development—Northern Great Plains* (Baltimore: Johns Hopkins University Press, 1978); and the section on Alaska in the February 1978 issue of *Planning*. For a study of the effects of a completed eastern power plant, the controversial Calvert Cliffs nuclear plant in southern Maryland, see Baldwin, "Socio-Economic Impact of Power Plant Construction: A Case History." On the effects of drilling for coastal oil and gas, see Robert Bendiner, "Taking Oil Off the Shelf," *The New York Times Sunday Magazine*, June 29, 1975; Resource Planning Associates, *Po-*

tential Onshore Effects of Oil and Gas Production on the Atlantic and Gulf of Alaska Outer Continental Shelf (Washington: Government Printing Office, 1974); Arthur D. Little, Inc., *Potential Onshore Effects of Deepwater Oil Terminal-Related Industrial Development* (Springfield, Virginia: National Technical Information Service, 1973); and Council on Environmental Quality, *Oil and Gas in Coastal Lands and Waters* (Washington: Government Printing Office, 1977).

41 For more documentation of the points in this paragraph, see American Society of Planning Officials, *Subdividing Rural America: Impacts of Recreational Lot and Second Home Development* (Washington: Government Printing Office, 1976), pp. 5–6, 17–20, 27. I participated in this study.

42 Ibid., pp. 89–93. See also Barbara Page, "The Land of Enchantment Is Also the Land of Ripoffs," *Planning*, April/May 1977.

43 "Violations by Land Developer Result in Consumer Refund," *Land Use Planning Report*, January 31, 1977, p. 33.

44 "FTC Reaches Largest Land Sales Refund Agreement in Its History," *Land Use Planning Report*, May 14, 1979, p. 153. For an emerging case that seemed likely to result in still larger refunds, see "FTC Cites Horizon Corp. in $370-Million Land Fraud," *Land Use Planning Report*, October 8, 1979, p. 319.

45 See David Mosena and Frank Popper, "Leisure Homes Urbanize the Countryside," *Planning*, August 1973, p. 19, and William Shands, *The Subdivision of Virginia's Mountains* (Washington: Conservation Foundation, 1974).

46 For examples from southern Vermont, see Healy, *Land Use and the States*, p. 38. See also Carter, *The Florida Experience*, pp. 27–34, 138–86, 228–63; David Stuart et al., *Impacts of Large Recreational Developments upon Semi-Private Environments: The Gallatin Canyon Case Study* (Bozeman: Montana State University, Center for Interdisciplinary Studies and Montana Agricultural Experiment Station, 1974); and from Appalachia, James Branscome and Peggy Matthews, "Selling the Mountains," *Southern Exposure*, Fall 1974.

47 Vermont Public Interest Research Group, *Downhill in Warren* (Montpelier: VPIRG, 1972). For further discussion of the economics of leisure home development, see American Society of Planning Officials, *Subdividing Rural America*, pp. 61–79.

48 On several such Arizona developments, see Mary Leonhard, "Growing Old Gracefully Can Be Easy in Arizona," *Planning*, April/May 1977.

49 For additional discussions of leisure homes, see the three-volume study by INFORM, *Promised Lands* (New York: INFORM, 1976–78);

Alfred Parker, *Second Home Development in the Southwest: Trends and Perspectives* (Albuquerque, New Mexico: Southwest Regional Project, University of New Mexico, Department of Economics, 1975); Charles Prentice, Donald Schink, and Ayse Somersan, *Large Recreational Home Developments in Wisconsin's Coastal Zone* (Madison: Wisconsin Coastal Zone Management Development Program, 1976); and Reilly, ed., *The Use of Land*, pp. 263–93.

50 Henry Dill and Robert Otte, *Urbanization of Land in the Western States* (Washington: U.S. Department of Agriculture, Economic Research Service, 1970). For other such results, see Kathryn Zeimetz et al., *Dynamics of Land Use in Fast Growing Areas* Report (Washington: U.S. Department of Agriculture, Economic Research Service, 1976); Pennsylvania Land Policy Project, *A Land Use Strategy for Pennsylvania* (Pittsburgh: PLPP, undated), pp. 19–21; Benjamin Huffman, *The Vermont Farm* (Montpelier: Vermont State Planning Office, 1973); *Report of the Blueprint Commission on the Future of New Jersey Agriculture* (Trenton: Blueprint Commission, 1973); and Michigan Department of Agriculture, *Agricultural Land Requirements: A Projection to 2000 A.D.* (Lansing: Michigan Department of Agriculture, 1973).

51 "Continued Farmland Losses Seen in EIC Report," *Land Use Planning Report*, August 21, 1978, p. 268, which cites *Land Use Planning Abstracts* (New York: Environment Information Center, 1978).

52 See, for example, Melvin Cotner, Melvin Skold, and Orville Krause, *Farmland: Will There Be Enough?* (Washington: U.S. Department of Agriculture, Economic Research Service, 1975); Melvin Cotner, *Land Use Policy and Agriculture: A National Perspective* Report (Washington: U.S. Department of Agriculture, Economic Research Service, 1976); National Task Force on Research Related to Land Use Planning and Policy, *Land Use* (Pullman: Washington State University, College of Agriculture, 1976), pp. 7–15; Healy, *Land Use and the States*, pp. 17–18; Meyer, "Land Rush," pp. 53–55; George Peterson and Harvey Yampolsky, *Urban Development and the Protection of Metropolitan Farmland* (Washington: Urban Institute, 1975); and Zeimetz et al., *Dynamics of Land Use in Fast Growing Areas*. For a contrary opinion, see Roger Blobaum, *The Loss of Agricultural Land* (Washington: Council on Environmental Quality Citizen's Advisory Committee on Environmental Quality, 1974).

53 Healy, *Land Use and the States*, p. 17.

54 California Legislature Joint Committee on Open Space Lands, *State Open Space and Resource Conservation Programs for California* (Sacramento, California: CLJCOSL, 1972). For a contrary opinion, see

Kaleb Nelson, "Despite Hearsay, California Isn't Losing Farmland," *Planning*, January 1979.

55 On Vermont, see Huffman, *The Vermont Farm*.

56 Morton Paulson, "What Should Be Done to Improve Consumer Protection in Land Sales?" *Urban Land*, July/August 1974, p. 23.

57 See Gilmore and Duff, *Boom Town Growth Management*; Curry, "A Time to Choose"; Council on Economic Priorities, *Leased and Lost*; Toole, *The Rape of the Great Plains*; David Myrha, "Energy Development"; Northern Plains Resource Council, *Stripping Montana*, a special edition of *The Plains Truth* (Billings, NPRC, May/June 1976); and John Doyle, Jr., *Strip Mining in the Corn Belt: The Destruction of High Capability Agricultural Land for Strip-Minable Coal in Illinois* (Washington: Environmental Policy Institute, 1976).

58 For an example from California's Santa Clara Valley near San Jose, see Kaplan, *The Dream Deferred*, pp. 23–24.

59 For leisure home examples, see American Society of Planning Officials, *Subdividing Rural America*, pp. 45–95. For energy-development examples, see Toole, *The Rape of the Great Plains*, especially pp. 80–125.

60 Gene Wunderlich, *Who Owns America's Land* (Washington: U.S. Department of Agriculture, Economic Research Service, 1974), pp. 11–12. See also Robert Bildner, "Southern Farms: A Vanishing Breed," *Southern Exposure*, Fall 1974.

61 U.S. Department of Agriculture, Economic Research Service, *Our Land and Water Resources: Current and Prospective Supplies and Uses* (Washington: USDA, 1974), p. 25.

62 On this point, the best source is still the President's Commission on Rural Poverty, *The People Left Behind* (Washington: Government Printing Office, 1967).

63 For further discussion, see Wendell Berry, *The Unsettling of America: Culture & Agriculture* (San Francisco: Sierra Club, 1977).

64 See, for example, Richard Hofstadter, *The Age of Reform: From Bryan to F.D.R.* (New York: Vintage paperback, 1955), pp. 23–59.

65 For documentation, see Reilly, ed., *The Use of Land*, pp. 75–101.

66 Martin Mayer, *The Builders: Houses, People, Neighborhoods, Governments, Money* (New York: Norton, 1978), p. 251. Emphasis in original.

67 For a brief history of the rise of zoning, see National Commission on Urban Problems, *Building the American City*, pp. 199–201.

68 This accomplishment and the others in this paragraph are drawn from pp. 35–36 and 41–42 of Norman Williams, Jr., "The Future of Land Use Controls," in Burchell and Listokin, eds., *Future Land Use*.

69 For an example from the Appalachian portion of New York State, see Dick Robbins, "New York Towns Squelch Local Zoning Laws," *Planning*, September 1974. For examples from Ozark portions of Missouri and Arkansas, see Sylvia Lewis, "Antiplanners Are Coming, Antiplanners Are Coming," *Planning*, February 1976.

70 John McPhee, *Pieces of the Frame* (New York: Farrar, Straus and Giroux, 1977), p. 258.

71 Richard RuBino and William Wagner, *Supplement* to *The States' Role in Land Resource Management* (Lexington, Kentucky: Council of State Governments, 1972), pp. 9, 12, 16. See also Allen Manvel, National Commission on Urban Problems Research Report No. 6, *Local Land and Building Regulation: How Many Agencies? What Practice? How Much Personnel?* (Washington: Government Printing Office, 1968).

72 Ralph Nader's Study Group on Land Use in California, *Politics of Land*, p. 369. For other examples, see National Commission on Urban Problems, *Building the American City*, pp. 323–33, and Ralph Richardson, Jr., and Gilbert Tauber, eds., *The Hudson River Basin: Environmental Problems and Institutional Response*, Volume 1 (New York: Academic Press, 1979), pp. 65–77.

73 National Commission on Urban Problems, *Building the American City*, pp. 210, 213.

74 Ibid., p. 210. See also Manvel, *Local Land and Building Regulation*.

75 For specific examples of these shortcomings, see Williams, "The Future of Land Use Controls," p. 42 n. 12, and Perin, *Everything in Its Place*, p. 185.

76 There are no good studies of the memberships of planning commissions or zoning boards, but for some suggestive insights, see Frederick Bair, Jr., *Planning Cities* (Chicago: American Society of Planning Officials, 1970), especially "Boards of Adjustment and How They Got That Way," pp. 486–91, and Mark Gottdiener, *Planned Sprawl: Private and Public Interests in Suburbia* (Beverly Hills, California: Sage Publications, 1977).

77 Perin, *Everything in Its Place*, pp. 148, 149.

78 For an anatomy of an instance of local conflicts of interest that produced governmental incompetence rather than corruption, see Carter, *The Florida Experience*, pp. 240–42.

79 McCahill, "Stealing: A Primer on Zoning Corruption," *Planning*, December 1973, p. 6.

80 See respectively Philip Ross, *The Bribe* (New York: Harper and Row, 1976); Boyarsky and Boyarsky, *Backroom Politics*, pp. 49–70; and Kaplan, *The Dream Deferred*. For a more general study of zoning corruption, see John Gardiner and Theodore Lyman, *Decisions for*

Sale: Corruption in Local Land-Use and Building Regulation (New York: Praeger, 1978).

81 See Ralph Nader's Study Group on Land Use in California, *Politics of Land*, pp. 393–95.

82 For examples of haphazard annexation, mainly from San Jose, California, see Kaplan, *The Dream Deferred*, pp. 23–27, and Ralph Nader's Study Group on Land Use in California, *Politics of Land*, pp. 351–53, 369–80 (especially the outline map of San Jose on p. 373), 400–401.

83 Bair, *Planning Cities*, p. 132. Emphasis in original. See also Duane Windsor, *Fiscal Zoning in Suburban Communities* (Lexington, Massachusetts: Lexington Books, 1979).

84 Healy, *Land Use and the States*, p. 20.

85 For an example from the Los Angeles area, see William Bulkeley, "Commerce, Calif., Lives Up to Name with a Vengeance," *Wall Street Journal*, January 31, 1978, p. 1.

86 Anonymous student author, "Large Lot Zoning," *Yale Law Journal*, July 1969, p. 1418.

87 See National Commission on Urban Problems, *Building the American City*, pp. 211–17.

88 Ibid., pp. 211–17, 225–26.

89 Perin, *Everything in Its Place*, p. 87. For similar quotes, see ibid., pp. 86, 134, 135, 138, 187.

90 See, for example, Potomac Institute, *Environment and Equity: A Survey of Metropolitan Issues* (Washington: PI, 1976), and Mary Brooks, *Housing Equity and Environmental Protection: The Needless Conflict* (Washington: American Institute of Planners, 1976), pp. 9–12, 36–76.

91 Seymour Toll, *Zoned American* (New York: Grossman, 1969), p. 29.

92 Norman Karlin, "Land Use Controls: The Power to Exclude," *Environmental Law*, Spring 1975, pp. 536–40.

93 See, for example, Toll, *Zoned American*, pp. 3–210, and National Commission on Urban Problems, *Building the American City*, p. 200.

94 For further discussion of exclusionary zoning, see Kaplan, *The Dream Deferred*, pp. 87–136; Ralph Nader's Study Group on Land Use in California, *Politics of Land*, pp. 395–400; Richard Babcock and Fred Bosselman, *Exclusionary Zoning: Land Use Regulation and Housing in the 1970s* (New York: Praeger, and Chicago: American Society of Planning Officials, 1973); Michael Danielson, *The Politics of Exclusion* (New York: Columbia University Press, 1976); and Perin, *Everything in Its Place*, pp. 81–209. For more on zoning in general, see Don Allensworth, *The Political Realities of Urban Planning* (New York: Praeger, 1975); Babcock, *The Zoning Game*; Richard Babcock, "Zon-

ing" in Frank So, Israel Stollman, Frank Beal, and David Arnold, eds., *The Practice of Local Government Planning* (Washington: International City Management Association, 1979); National Commission on Urban Problems, *Building the American City*, pp. 199–234; National Commission on Urban Problems Research Report No. 2, *Problems of Zoning and Land-Use Regulation* (Washington: Government Printing Office, 1968); Allan Jacobs, *Making City Planning Work* (Chicago: American Society of Planning Officials, 1978); Robert Leary, "Zoning," in William Goodman and Eric Freund, eds., *Principles and Practice of Urban Planning* (Washington: International City Managers' Association, 1968); R. Robert Linowes and Don Allensworth, *The Politics of Land Use: Planning, Zoning and the Private Developer* (New York: Praeger, 1973); Julian Moynahan, *Garden State* (Boston: Little, Brown, 1973); Nelson, *Zoning and Property Rights*; T. William Patterson, *Land Use Planning: Techniques of Implementation* (New York: Van Nostrand Reinhold, 1979); Reilly, ed., *The Use of Land*, pp. 182–92; John Reps, "Requiem for Zoning," in American Society of Planning Officials, *Planning 1964* (Chicago, ASPO, 1964); Irving Schiffman, *The Limits of the Local Planning Commission* (Davis, California: University of California, Davis Institute of Government Affairs, 1975), and Schiffman, *The Politics of Land-Use Planning: A Review Essay and Annotated Bibliography* (Davis, California: University of California, Davis Institute of Governmental Affairs, 1977); Siegan, *Land Use without Zoning*, and Siegan, *Other People's Property*; John Tarrant, *The End of Exurbia: Who Are All These People and Why Do They Want to Ruin Our Town?* (New York: Stein and Day, 1976); Toll, *Zoned American*; and Donald Wolfe, "Zoning Is Doing Planning In," *Practicing Planner*, June 1976.

Chapter 4: The Land-Use Reform Movement

1 Babcock, *The Zoning Game*, pp. 153–85.
2 National Commission on Urban Problems, *Building the American City*, pp. 235–53.
3 Reilly, ed., *The Use of Land*, pp. 19–33.
4 Ralph Nader's Study Group on Land Use in California, *Politics of Land*, pp. 210–15, 349–50, 401–5.
5 David Heeter, *Toward a More Effective Land-Use Guidance System: A Summary and Analysis of Five Major Reports* (Chicago: American Society of Planning Officials, 1969), and American Bar Association Advi-

sory Commission on Housing and Urban Growth, Richard Fishman, ed., *Housing for All under Law: New Directions in Housing, Planning, and Land-Use Law* (Cambridge, Massachusetts: Ballinger, 1977).

6 American Law Institute, *a Model Land Development Code: Official Draft* (Philadelphia: ALI, 1977). For an explanation of an early draft of the code by one of its principal drafters, see the *Transcript* of the National Association of Home Builders' *Conference on State Land Use Legislation* (Washington: NAHB, 1973), pp. 56–103. See also Peter Brown, *The American Law Institute Model Land Development Code, the Taking Issue, and Private Property Rights* (Washington: Urban Institute, 1975). For a discussion of the code, see Mandelker, *Environmental and Land Controls Legislation*, pp. 63–126.

7 Council of State Governments, *State Growth Management* (Lexington, Kentucky: CGS, 1976), pp. 23–26. See also Healy, *Land Use and the States*, pp. 139–60; American Institute of Planners Research Staff, "Most States Are Making Progress on the Land Use Element," *Practicing Planner*, April 1976, which is drawn from American Institute of Planners, *Survey of State Land Use Activity* (Washington: Department of Housing and Urban Development, 1976); DeGrove, *Land Management*; and Charles Lamb, *Land Use Politics and Law in the 1970's* (Washington: George Washington University Program of Policy Studies in Science and Technology, 1975). On how these programs have diffused from state to state, see Rosenbaum, *Land Use and the Legislatures*.

8 James Coke and Steven Brown, "Public Attitudes about Land Use and Their Impact on State Policy-Makers," *Publius*, Winter 1976, p. 128. See also Richard Mann and Mike Miles, "State Land Use Planning: The Current Status and Demographic Rationale," *Journal of the American Planning Association*, January 1979.

9 See Rosenbaum, *Land Use and the Legislatures*, pp. 81–82.

10 The text's discussion of the Oregon law is drawn from Charles Little, *The New Oregon Trail: An Account of the Development and Passage of State Land-Use Legislation in Oregon* (Washington: Conservation Foundation, 1974).

11 Ibid., p. 11.

12 Ibid., p. 7.

13 Land Use Planning Reports, Michael Arnold, ed., *A Summary of State Land Use Controls* (Washington: LUPR, 1976), p. 35.

14 For more on this legislation, see Natural Resources Defense Council, *Land Use Controls in the United States*, pp. 98–120; Fred Bosselman, Duane Feurer, and Tobin Richter, *Federal Land Use Regulation* (New

York: Practising Law Institute, 1977), pp. 212–23; and Mandelker, *Environmental and Land Controls Legislation*, pp. 223–46.

15 For more on this legislation, see Frank Popper, "The 1977 Surface Mining Act: The Lessons from Land-Use Regulation Elsewhere," *Environment*, forthcoming.

16 For the $3 billion estimate, see Council on Environmental Quality, *Environmental Quality, 1976: The Seventh Annual Report of the Council on Environmental Quality* (Washington: Government Printing Office, 1976), p. 355. For an explanation of the air- and water-quality amendments, their land-use implications, and their effects on a particular state, see Natural Resources Defense Council, Elaine Moss, ed., *Land Use Controls in New York State: A Handbook on the Legal Rights of Citizens* (New York: Dial Press/James Wade, 1975), pp. 181–232. For national expansions of this material, see Natural Resources Defense Council, *Land Use Controls in the United States*, pp. 40–97; Bosselman, Feurer, and Richter, *Federal Land Use Regulation*, pp. 9–32; and Mandelker, *Environmental and Land Controls Legislation*, pp. 169–221.

17 For analyses of the act's defeats, see Lyday, *The Law of the Land*, and John Whitaker, *Striking a Balance: Environmental and Natural Resources Policy in the Nixon-Ford Years* (Washington, and Stanford, California: American Enterprise Institute for Public Policy Research and Hoover Institute on War, Revolution and Peace, 1976), pp. 155–66. For a discussion of the provisions of one version of the act, see Luther Carter, "Land Use Law (I): Congress on Verge of a Modest Beginning," *Science*, November 16, 1973.

18 See David Myrha, "Will the Public Have More Say in Power Plant Siting?" *Planning*, July 1978.

19 On this act and its effects on land use in one state, see Natural Resources Defense Council, *Land Use Controls in New York State*, pp. 167–80. See also Natural Resources Defense Council, *Land Use Controls in the United States*, pp. 18–39, and Mandelker, *Environmental and Land Controls Legislation*, pp. 127–68.

20 Council on Environmental Quality, *Environmental Quality, 1976*, pp. 135–37. See also Mandelker, *Environmental and Land Controls Legislation*, pp. 127–68.

21 On this act and its effects on land use in one state, see Natural Resources Defense Council, *Land Use Controls in New York State*, pp. 268–80. See also Natural Resources Defense Council, *Land Use Controls in the United States*, pp. 121–32, and Bosselman, Feurer, and Richter, *Federal Land Use Regulation*, pp. 92–111.

22 Fred Bosselman, "Commentary," pp. 136–37, in Harvey Perloff, ed., *Agenda for the New Urban Era* (Chicago: American Society of Planning Officials, 1975).

23 On the California body, see Bosselman and Callies, *The Quiet Revolution in Land Use Control*, pp. 108–35; Ditton, Seymour, and Swanson, *Coastal Resources Management*, pp. 147–65; and Rice Odell, *The Saving of San Francisco Bay* (Washington: Conservation Foundation, 1972). On the New Jersey body, see Bosselman and Callies, *The Quiet Revolution in Land Use Control*, pp. 136–63; John Fischer, *Vital Signs, U.S.A.* (New York: Harper and Row, 1975), pp. 57–74; Oliver Byrum and Robert Hoffman, "Development Framework Guides Required Land Use, Public Facilities," *Practicing Planner*, March 1977; and on a recent strengthening of the body, "Metropolitan Land Planning Bill Signed in March for Twin Cities," *Practicing Planner*, April 1976. On the Massachusetts body, see Martin Jaffe, "Regional Planning Comes of Age on Martha's Vineyard," *Planning*, February 1977.

24 See Bosselman and Callies, *The Quiet Revolution in Land Use Control*, pp. 291–93; Edmond Constantini and Kenneth Hanf, *The Environmental Impulse and Its Competitors: Attitudes, Interests, and Institutions at Lake Tahoe* (Davis, California: University of California, Davis, Institute of Governmental Affairs, 1973), and Kenneth Davis, *Land Use* (New York: McGraw-Hill, 1976), pp. 208–37.

25 See Peter Bradford, *Fragile Structures: A Story of Oil Refineries, National Security, and the Coast of Maine* (New York: Harper's Magazine Press, 1975).

26 Urban Systems Research and Engineering, *The Growth Shapers*, p. 37. For a similar effort in Greenburgh, New York, see V. Ferrandino, "Greenburgh's New Zoning May Clean Up the Strip," *Planning*, June 1977.

27 On local managed-growth efforts, see Finkler, Toner, and Popper, *Urban Nongrowth*; Earl Finkler and David Peterson, *Nongrowth Planning Strategies* (New York: Praeger, 1974); Michael Gleeson et al., *Urban Growth Management Systems* (Chicago: American Society of Planning Officials, 1975); David Godschalk et al., *Constitutional Issues of Growth Management* (Chicago: American Planning Association, revised edition, 1979); the four-volume series by the Urban Land Institute, *Management & Control of Growth: Issues, Techniques, Problems, Trends* (Washington: ULI, 1975 and 1978); California Office of Planning and Research, *Growth Management Practices in California* (Sacramento: Office of the Governor, 1976); Grace Dawson, *No Little Plans: Fairfax County's PLUS Program for Managing Growth*

(Washington: Urban Institute, 1977); and the June 1979 issue of *Environmental Comment* on a "Growth Management Workshop" conducted by the Urban Land Institute. For negative views of these efforts, see Nelson, *Zoning and Property Rights*, pp. 154–66; Frieden, *The Environmental Protection Hustle*; and Potomac Institute, *Controlling Urban Growth—But for Whom?* (Washington, PI, 1973).

28 For a legal analysis of the taking question, see Fred Bosselman, David Callies, and John Banta, *The Taking Issue: An Analysis of the Constitutional Limits of Land Use Controls* (Washington: Government Printing Office, 1973). See also Reilly, ed., *The Use of Land*, pp. 145–75.

29 Little, *The New Oregon Trail*, p. 26. For the description of Macpherson, see p. 10.

30 See "Land Use Bill Dies with a Whimper—This Year," *Planning*, July 1974, p. 4.

31 Healy, *Land Use and the States*, p. 163, quoting an unidentified story in the *Washington Post*, March 21, 1973. The brackets are in Healy's quote.

32 For an example of this agrarian approach, see *National Land for People*, the monthly publication of a Fresno-based organization of the same name that has been active in the 160-acre controversy. For a good review of the issues in the controversy, see E. Philip LeVeen, "Reclamation Policy at the Crossroads," *Public Affairs Report* (Berkeley: University of California, Berkeley, Institute of Government Studies), October 1978.

33 See, for example, Peter Barnes, ed., *The People's Land: A Reader on Land Reform in the United States* (Emmaus, Pennsylvania: Rodale Press, 1975); Walter Goldschmidt, *As You Sow: Three Studies in the Social Consequences of Agribusiness* (originally published in Glencoe, Illinois: The Free Press, 1947; reissued with much additional material in Montclair, New Jersey: Allanheld, Osmun, 1978); and Frank Popper, "Who Owns the Midwest? Who Cares?" *Acorn*, December 1978–January 1979.

34 See Frank Popper, "Ownership: The Hidden Factor in Land-Use Regulation," in Richard Andrews, ed., *Land in America: Commodity or Natural Resource?* (Lexington, Massachusetts: Lexington Books, 1979), reprinted as "What's the Hidden Factor in Land-Use Regulation?" *Urban Land*, December 1978.

35 Warren Weber, "Rockefeller Report: Land Use Planning for Whom?" *People & Land*, Winter 1974, p. 17.

36 For more on this position as it emerged during the struggle over the National Land Use Policy Act, see Lyday, *The Law of the Land*, espe-

cially pp. 44–45, 49–53. See also Jack Doyle, "Centralizing Power," *Environmental Action*, May 10, 1975.

37 See "West Tells U.S. What It Wants," *State Government News*, November 1979, p. 5. For a western case in which the local and state officials' reservations about the federal government seem to have been justified, see Peter Van Alstyne, "Utah Wishes It Hadn't Scuttled Statewide Planning," *Planning*, December 1978. See also William Shands, "The Feds Can't Manage All That Land Alone," *Planning*, August 1979.

38 Meyer, "Land Rush," pp. 57–58. Emphasis in original.

39 William Reilly, "National Land Use Planning: A Legislative Agenda," in Soil Conservation Society of America, *Land Use*, pp. 13–14.

40 Ibid., p. 14.

41 For a historical exploration of the social origins and political development of the reform impulse in America, see Hofstadter, *The Age of Reform*, especially pp. 131–214. For discussions of the contemporary social bases of reform movements supporting centralized regulation, see Lazarus, *The Genteel Populists*, pp. 121–66, and Paul Weaver, "Regulation, Social Policy, and Class Conflict," in Institute for Contemporary Studies, *Regulating Business*.

42 Jon Margolis, "Land of Ecology," *Esquire*, March 1970, quoted in Healy, *Land Use and the States*, pp. 181–82.

43 For documentation, see Potomac Institute, *Environment and Equity*, pp. 13–27, and Ellen Hall, *Inner City Health in America* (Washington: Urban Environment Foundation, 1979).

44 Little, *Shifting Ground*, p. 10.

45 See, for example, Potomac Institute, *Controlling Urban Growth—But for Whom?*

46 Frank Graham, Jr., *The Adirondack Park: A Political History* (New York: Knopf, 1978), p. 239.

47 Healy, "Environmentalists and Developers: Can They Agree on Anything?" (Washington: Conservation Foundation, 1977), p. 12.

48 See also A. Lawrence Chickering, "Land Use Controls and Low Income Groups: Why Are There No Poor People in the Sierra Club?" in Institute for Contemporary Studies, *No Land Is an Island*; John Allen, *A Study of Public Knowledge and Awareness Concerning Land Use in Ohio* (Columbus: Academy for Contemporary Problems, 1974); Lloyd Hudman and Richard Jackson, *Attitudes and Perceptions of Residents of [Utah's] Southeastern Association Region of Land-Use Planning and Land-Use Decisions* (Provo, Utah: Brigham Young University, Geography Department, undated); and Healy, *Land Use and the States*, pp. 181–86.

49 For a clear case of this "last-one-in" tendency at work, see Boyd Gibbons III, *Wye Island* (Baltimore: Johns Hopkins University Press, 1977). For a discussion of the tendency in leisure home areas, see American Society of Planning Officials, *Subdividing Rural America*, p. 88. See also Gene Wunderlich, *Land along the Blue Ridge: Ownership and Use of Land in Rappahannock County, Virginia* (Washington: U.S. Department of Agriculture, Economic Research Service, 1975), pp. 20–21.

50 William Tucker, "Environmentalism and the Leisure Class," *Harper's*, December 1977, pp. 49, 50. See also Frieden, *The Environmental Protection Hustle*, especially pp. 119–38.

51 For an expansion of this argument, see Berry, *The Unsettling of America*, pp. 17–38.

52 For some poll evidence on this peaking and dropoff, see Jones, *Clean Air: The Policies and Politics of Pollution Control* (Pittsburgh: University of Pittsburgh Press, 1975); pp. 152–53, and Louis Harris, "Economy Is Public's Top Worry," *Chicago Tribune*, January 1, 1976, op-ed page. See also John Mitchell, *Losing Ground* (San Francisco: Sierra Club, 1975).

53 See, for example, John Quarles, *Cleaning Up America: An Insider's View of the Environmental Protection Agency* (Boston: Houghton Mifflin, 1976), and Robert Sansom, *The New American Dream Machine* (Garden City, New York: Anchor Press/Doubleday, 1976), pp. 1–92. For a contrary view, see Whitaker, *Striking a Balance*.

54 Lou Cannon, "President Advised on Talk," *Washington Post*, December 19, 1974, p. 1.

55 For a discussion of the arrangements possible in such programs, see Sorensen, *State-Local Collaborative Planning*.

56 See, for example, Rosenbaum, *Land Use and the Legislatures*, pp. 31–78, 85–89.

57 Meyer, "Land Rush," p. 58. Emphasis in original. For some future possibilities for federal land-use legislation, see Little, *Shifting Ground*, and Reilly, "National Land Use Planning."

58 Healy, *Land Use and the States*, p. 217. See also the annual Land Use Planning Report, *A Summary of State Land Use Controls* (Silver Spring, Maryland: LUPR, reports of 1976 and 1977).

59 For documentation and case studies, see Gleeson et al., *Urban Growth Management Systems*.

60 For further discussion, including documentation, see Reilly, ed., *The Use of Land*, pp. 33–73.

61 Healy, "Environmentalists and Developers," pp. 2, 3. See also Urban Land Institute, *Management & Control of Growth*, especially Volume 4.

62 Dennis Farney, "Whether Coloradans Hate Pollution or Red Tape More Vehemently May Decide Governorship Race," *Wall Street Journal*, October 31, 1978, p. 48.

Chapter 5: The Six State Programs

1 For descriptions of these other programs, see Land Use Planning Report, *A Summary of State Land Use Controls*.

2 On the Hawaii law, see Bosselman and Callies, *The Quiet Revolution in Land Use Control*, pp. 5–53; Mandelker, *Environmental and Land Controls Legislation*, pp. 269–322; Phyllis Myers, *Zoning Hawaii: An Analysis of the Passage and Implementation of Hawaii's Land Classification Law* (Washington: Conservation Foundation, 1976); R. Robert Linowes and Don Allensworth, *The States and Land Use Control*, pp. 53–75; Shelley Mark, "It All Began in Hawaii," *State Government,* Summer 1973; Kem Lowry and Michael McElroy, "State Land Use Control: Some Lessons from Experience," unpublished paper presented to the 1975 annual conference of the American Institute of Planners, held in San Antonio; and Thomas Creighton, *The Lands of Hawaii: Their Use and Misuse* (Honolulu: University of Hawaii Press, 1978).

3 I also decided to concentrate on programs that: provided for comprehensive regulation of all large projects, for statewide planning, and for state review of local regulatory decisions; regulated land use in a particular environmentally fragile region; controlled development in coastal areas; created a mechanism for siting power plants; and regulated strip mining.

I then had to choose specific state programs to examine in my fieldwork. To see comprehensive programs in action, I decided to go to Vermont and Florida. Next to Hawaii, Vermont has the nation's oldest comprehensive program (enacted in 1970). Vermont is a small state (mid-1975 estimated census population: 471,000, larger only than Alaska and Wyoming) and a relatively homogeneous one. Florida, on the other hand, is the nation's fastest-growing big state and is comparatively diverse; moreover, its land-use program is quite similar to those proposed by the National Land Use Policy Act and the American Law Institute Model Code. To look at a regional land-use program, I went to upstate New York, where the Adirondack Park Agency regulates development in the largest state-regulated region in the country, a wilderness area the size of Vermont, comprising about a fifth of New York State.

To examine a coastal program, I went to California, the nation's most populous state; it has an 1100-mile coast with both big cities and quite rural areas, and its coastal program originated with a 1972 popular initiative. To observe a power plant siting program, I went to Maryland, a state that not only regulates the location and operation of power plants from an environmental perspective, as many other states do, but also, unlike other states, buys environmentally suitable sites to hold for eventual purchase by utilities.

To look at a strip-mine regulation program, I went to Pennsylvania, whose operation had the reputation of being by far the toughest in the country. (See, for example, the frequent references to the Pennsylvania program in National Academy of Sciences, *Rehabilitation Potential of Western Coal Lands*; John Doyle, Jr., *Strip Mining in the Corn Belt*; Doyle, *State Strip Mining Laws: Alabama, Colorado, Kansas, Ohio, Texas, and Virginia* [Washington: Environmental Policy Center, 1976]; Doyle, *State Strip Mining Laws: An Inventory and Analysis of Key Statutory Provisions in 28 Coal-Producing States* [Washington: Environmental Policy Institute, 1977]; the special edition of *The Plains Truth* on "Stripping Montana," May/June 1976; Center for Science in the Public Interest, Albert Fritsch, Director, *The Enforcement of Strip Mining Laws in Three Appalachian States: Kentucky, West Virginia, and Pennsylvania* [Washington: CSPI, 1975]; Genevieve Atwood, "The Strip-Mining of Western Coal," *Scientific American*, December 1975; Stanford Research Institute, *A Study of Surface Mining in West Virginia* [Menlo Park, California: SRI, 1972]; Ford, Bacon, and Davis, Inc., and Mathematica, Inc., *The Design of Surface Mining Systems in Eastern Kentucky Coal Fields* [New York, and Princeton, New Jersey: FBD and Mathematica, 1974]; and Marc Landy, *The Politics of Environmental Reform: Controlling Kentucky Strip Mining* [Washington: Resources for the Future, 1976].) Pennsylvania's program provided a model for the 1977 federal strip-mining law, as well as the first director, the chief lawyer, and the chief scientist of the Interior Department's Office of Surface Mining Reclamation and Enforcement, which administers the law.

During 1975 and 1976, I spent two weeks apiece in five of the six states. I spent only a week in the Adirondacks. The population of the Adirondacks is relatively small—about 120,000, roughly the size of Albany or Pasadena or Savannah. I interviewed about two hundred people: land-use and other officials at all levels of government, developers of various kinds, interest-group representatives, academics, journalists, and citizen activists. Some of these people are quoted but not named in the text, thus preserving the anonymity I promised. I also collected documents, attended public meetings, and drove nearly 20,000 miles looking at the states and visiting the sites in question. Since 1976, I have maintained continual contact with the state programs.

4 For other accounts of the Florida law, see Carter, *The Florida Experience*; Healy, *Land Use and the States*, pp. 103–38, 219–20; Phyllis Myers, *Slow Start in Paradise: An Account of the Development, Passage, and Implementation of State Land-Use Legislation in Florida* (Washington: Conservation Foundation, 1974); and Earl Gallop, "The Florida Environmental Land and Water Management Act of 1972: A Partially Fulfilled Expectation," *Florida Environmental and Urban Issues*, November/December 1978. Another book on the Florida law, Thomas Pelham, *State Land-Use Planning and Regulation: Florida, the Model Code, and Beyond* (Lexington, Massachusetts: Lexington Books, 1979) appeared too late for extensive citation.

5 For other accounts of the Vermont law, see Bosselman and Callies, *The Quiet Revolution in Land Use Control*, pp. 54–107; Healy, *Land Use and the States*, pp. 35–63, 223–24; Phyllis Myers, *So Goes Vermont: An Account of the Development, Passage, and Implementation of State Land-Use Legislation in Vermont* (Washington: Conservation Foundation, 1974); David Heeter, "Almost Getting It Together in Vermont," in Mandelker, *Environmental and Land Controls Legislation*; and Linowes and Allensworth, *The States and Land Use Control*, pp. 76–99. For a more hostile account, see McClaughry, "The Land Use Planning Act—An Idea We Can Do Without," pp. 600–605.

6 For other accounts of the Adirondack law, see Natural Resources Defense Council, *Land Use Controls in New York State*, pp. 106–31; League of Women Voters of New York State, *Land Use: The Adirondack Park Agency* (New York: LWVNYS, 1975); Frank Graham, Jr., *The Adirondack Park*, pp. 219–78; Fred Sullivan, "Adirondack Zoning: A National Experiment in Land-Use Control Faces Local Challenge," *Empire State Report*, December 1975; and Sylvia Lewis, "New York's Adirondacks: Tug of War in the Wilderness," *Planning*, September 1976. Another study of the Adirondack law, G. Gordon Davis and Richard Liroff, *Conflict in the North County: A Study of the Implementation of Regional Land Use Controls by the Adirondack Park Agency* (Washington: Environmental Law Institute, 1979), appeared too late for extensive citation.

7 The plan is Adirondack Park Agency, *Adirondack Park Land Use and Development Plan* (Ray Brook, New York: APA, 1973).

8 Ibid., pp. 23, 19.

9 For other accounts of the 1972 legislation, see Healy, *Land Use and the States*, pp. 64–102, 220–23; Peter Douglas, "Coastal Resources Planning and Control: The California Approach," *Environmental Law*, Spring 1975; Robert Healy, ed., *Protecting the Golden Shore: Lessons from the California Coastal Commissions* (Washington: Conservation Foundation, 1978); Institute for Contemporary Studies, *The California Coastal Law: A Critique* (San Francisco: ICS, 1976); Melvin Mogulof, *Saving the Coast: California's Experiment in Intergovernmental Land Use Control* (Lexington, Massachusetts: Lexington Books, 1975); Stanley Scott, *Governing California's Coast* (Berkeley: University of California, Berkeley, Institute of Governmental Studies, 1975); Scott, "Coastal Planning in California: A Progress Report," *Public Affairs Report* (University of California, Berkeley, Institute of Government Studies), June-August 1978. Another study on the California law, Paul Sabatier and Daniel Mazmanian, *Can Regulation Work? The Implementation of the 1972 California Coastal Initiative* (Davis and Claremont, California: University of California, Davis, Institute of Government Affairs and Pomona College Program in Public Policy Analysis, 1979), appeared too late for extensive citation.

10 The plan is California Coastal Zone Conservation Commissions, *California Coastal Plan* (Sacramento: State of California Documents and Publications Branch, 1975).

11 For other accounts of the 1976 legislation, see Healy, ed., *Protecting the Golden Shore*; California Legislature, Senate Committee on Natural Resources and Wildlife, Subcommittee on Land Use Planning, "A Brief Summary of the California Coastal Act of 1976" (Sacramento: Subcommittee, 1976), and Tom Gorton, "The Debate Rages over California's Coastal Plan," *Planning*, April/May 1977.

12 For other accounts of the Maryland legislation, see Kenneth Perkins and Roy Madgewick, "The Maryland Power Plant Siting Program: Some Planning Perspectives," unpublished paper presented to the 1975 annual conference of the American Institute of Planners, held in San Antonio; Maryland Power Plant Siting Program, *Long Range Plan* (Annapolis: MPPSP, 1975); and Maryland Joint Legislative Committee on Power Plant Siting, "1974 Report," *Record of the Maryland Power Plant Siting Act* (Annapolis: Maryland Department of Natural Resources), February 1975.

13 See U.S. Department of Commerce, Bureau of the Census, *Census of the Population: 1970, Volume 1, Characteristics of the Population, Part A, Number of Inhabitants, Section 1* (Washington: Government Printing Office, 1972), p. 178.

14 For more on the Calvert Cliffs controversy, see Holdren and Herrera, *Energy*, pp. 184–90. On the effects of the plant, see Baldwin, "Socio-Economic Impact of Power Plant Construction."

15 For other accounts of the Pennsylvania legislation, see Center for Science in the Public Interest, *The Enforcement of Strip Mining Laws in Three Appalachian States*, pp. 75–94; David Maneval, "Coal Mining vs. Environment: A Reconciliation in Pennsylvania," and Ernest Preate, Jr., "A New Law for an Old Problem," both in *Appalachia*, February–March 1972; and David Maneval, "Reclaiming Land for Recreational Development," *Coal Mining and Processing*, April 1975, and "Recreational Development on Reclaimed Land," *Coal Mining and Processing*, June 1975.

16 There do not appear to be any good studies of this grip, but for a novel suggestive on the subject, see Harry Caudill, *The Senator from Slaughter County* (Boston: Atlantic Monthly-Little, Brown, 1973).

17 For an examination of the options for Pennsylvania localities in regulating strip mining, see William Curry III and Cyril Fox, Jr., *A Role for Local Governments in Controlling Strip Mining Activities* (Pittsburgh and Harrisburg: Western Pennsylvania Conservancy and the Pennsylvania Departments of Environmental Resources and Community Affairs, 1978).

Chapter 6: The Politics of the State Land-Use Laws

1 For an exception, see 1000 Friends of Oregon, *Four-Year Report, 1975–1979* (Portland: 1000 Friends of Oregon, 1979), and Henry Richmond, "Unique Public Interest Law Group Supports Oregon Land Use Program," *Land Use Law & Zoning Digest*, October 1979. Richmond is the organization's executive director. The California Coastal Alliance, although an umbrella organization, may also qualify as an exception.

2 For documentation in a number of different states, see John Wahlke et al., *The Legislative System* (New York: John Wiley, 1962); Harmon Zeigler, "Interest Groups in the States," in Herbert Jacob and Kenneth Vines, eds., *Politics in the American States: A Comparative Analysis* (Boston: Little Brown, 1965); Zeigler and Michael Baer, *Lobbying: Interaction and Influence in American State Legislatures* (Belmont, California: Wadsworth), pp. 28–35; and Zeigler and Harvey Tucker, *The Quest for Responsive Government: An Introduction to Politics* (North Scituate, Massachusetts: Duxbury, 1978), pp. 85–134.

3 See, for example, Zeigler and Baer, *Lobbying*, pp. 43–45, and Ralph

Nader's Study Group on Land Use in California, *Politics of Land*, pp. 668–82.

4 For discussion of the relationship between large land ownership and political power, see Popper, "Ownership," and "We've Got to Dig Deeper into Who Owns Our Land."

5 Ralph Nader's Study Group on Land Use in California, *Politics of Land*, pp. 20–25, 459–60. For more information on the political influence of developer groups, see ibid., pp. 3–20, 456–86, 515–84, 657–67; Center for Science in the Public Interest, *The Enforcement of Strip Mining Laws in Three Appalachian States*, pp. 12–16; Ralph Nader's Study Group on the Pulp and Paper Industry in Maine, William Osborn, Project Director, *The Paper Plantation* (New York: Grossman, 1974), pp. x, 1–2, 177, 227–28, 230–39, 265–66, 269–71; and Ralph Nader's Study Group on DuPont in Delaware, James Phelan and Robert Pozen, Project Directors, *The Company State* (New York: Grossman, 1973), pp. 1, 12, 119–24, 177–203, 231–321, 375–83.

6 For poll evidence, see Healy, *Land Use and the States*, pp. 54, 116, 165–67. For further poll evidence from Florida, see DeGrove, *Land Management*, p. 130.

7 See Healy, *Land Use and the States*, p. 165.

8 Lawrence Libby, "Comprehensive Land Use Planning and Other Myths," *Journal of Soil and Water Conservation*, May/June 1974, p. 106.

9 For acknowledgment of this fact, see Healy, *Land Use and the States*, pp. 217–18, and Land Use Planning Report, *A Summary of State Land Use Controls*, p. 3.

10 See Myers, *Slow Start in Paradise*, p. 12.

11 See Heeter, "Almost Getting It Together in Vermont," p. 331.

12 For evidence that Vermont's state legislators did not grasp the meaning of Act 250 when they voted for it, see ibid., pp. 330–32.

13 See, for example, Myers, *Slow Start in Paradise*, p. 165.

14 For other accounts of the passage of the Florida law, see Myers, *Slow Start in Paradise*, pp. 15–19, and Carter, *The Florida Experience*, pp. 29–53, 133–37.

15 Myers, *Slow Start in Paradise*, p. 16.

16 Carter, *The Florida Experience*, p. 136.

17 Myers, *Slow Start in Paradise*, p. 19.

18 Carter, *The Florida Experience*, p. 26.

19 U.S. Department of Commerce, Bureau of the Census, *1970 Census of the Population: Detailed Characteristics, Florida* (Washington: Government Printing Office, 1972), p. 11–824.

20 Myers, *Slow Start in Paradise*, p. 19.

21 U.S. Department of Commerce, Bureau of the Census, *1970 Census of the Population: Detailed Characteristics, Florida*, p. 11–994.

22 For more on the aquifer, see Healy, *Land Use and the States*, p. 106.

23 For a similar estimate of the state's development capacity, see the Red Flag Charrette, *Florida: The Seeds of Crisis* (Tallahassee: Florida Chapter of the American Institute of Architects and Florida Defenders of the Environment, 1972).

24 See Carter, *The Florida Experience*, pp. 1–40; Healy, *Land Use and the States*, pp. 104–10; and Myers, *Slow Start in Paradise*, pp. 10–13.

25 Myers, *Slow Start in Paradise*, p. 17.

26 Ibid., p. 17.

27 For other accounts of the passage of the 1972 California law, see Healy, *Land Use and the States*, pp. 69–73; Scott, *Governing California's Coast*, pp. 319–52; Janet Adams, "Proposition 20—A Citizen's Campaign," *Syracuse Law Review*, Summer 1973; and William Duddleson, "How the Citizens of California Secured Their Coastal Management Program," in Healy, ed., *Protecting the Golden Shore*, pp. 3–15.

28 Healy, *Land Use and the States*, p. 69.

29 Quoted ibid., p. 72.

30 For a list of unions that endorsed the law, see Adams, "Proposition 20—A Citizen's Campaign," p. 1029 n. 18.

31 See the study cited by Healy, *Land Use and the States*, p. 73.

32 Even in California, however, there was a rush to begin coastal development before the onset of regulation in 1973. See Duddleson, "How the Citizens of California Secured Their Coastal Management Program," p. 21. Another coastal land rush occurred before the 1977 effective date of the 1976 legislation; see ibid., p. 215 n. 68.

33 On the passage of the 1976 California coastal legislation and the concessions it contained, see Duddleson, "How the Citizens of California Secured Their Coastal Management Program," pp. 48–60; "California Protection Bill Approved by Legislature," *Land Use Planning Report*, August 30, 1976, p. 6; California Senate Committee on Natural Resources and Wildlife, Subcommittee on Land Use Planning, "A Brief History of SB 1277" (Sacramento: California Legislature, 1976), pp. 2–4.

34 Healy, *Land Use and the States*, p. 69, and Adams, "Proposition 20—A Citizen's Campaign," p. 1029.

35 See, for example, Myers, *Slow Start in Paradise*, p. 17.

36 See Duddleson, "How the Citizens of California Secured Their Coastal Management Program," pp. 13, 61.

37 For detailed accounts of other state legislative battles and the concessions they led to, see Graham, *The Adirondack Park*, pp. 242–53;
Myers, *So Goes Vermont*, pp. 13–17; Myers, *Zoning Hawaii*, pp.
19–22; Ralph Nader's Study Group on the Pulp and Paper Industry in
Maine, *The Paper Plantation*, pp. 233–34; Little, *The New Oregon
Trail*, pp. 14–24; and Constantini and Hanf, *The Environmental Impulse and Its Competitors*, pp. 30–38.

38 U.S. Department of Commerce, Bureau of the Census, *1970 Census of
the Population: Detailed Characteristics, Vermont* (Washington: Government Printing Office, 1972), pp. 47–335 to 47–337.

39 U.S. Department of Commerce, Bureau of the Census, *1970 Census of
the Population: Detailed Characteristics, California, Section 1*
(Washington: Government Printing Office, 1972), pp. 6–2009 to
6–2011.

40 On exemption of Oregon power plants, see Little, *The New Oregon
Trail*, p. 20. On exemption of Maine forestry construction, see Ralph
Nader's Study Group on the Pulp and Paper Industry in Maine, *The
Paper Plantation*, p. 234.

41 On the operations of public service commissions generally, see Bar
Association of the City of New York, Special Committee on Electric
Power and the Environment, *Electricity and the Environment* (St. Paul,
Minnesota: West Publishing Company, 1972).

42 For a Vermont case, see Healy, *Land Use and the States*, p. 42. For a
similar situation involving Maine's twenty-acre threshold, see National
Association of Home Builders, *Transcript, Conference on State Land
Use Legislation* (Washington: NAHB, 1973), p. 137.

43 Jonathan Brownell, "State Land Use Regulation: Where Are We Going?" *Real Property, Probate, and Trust Journal*, Spring 1974, p. 30.
See also Heeter, "Almost Getting It Together in Vermont," p. 281.

44 For similar estimates, see Myers, *So Goes Vermont*, p. 24, and Heeter,
"Almost Getting It Together in Vermont," p. 382.

45 Charles River Associates, *The Economic Impact of Public Policy on the
Appalachian Coal Industry and the Regional Economy: Volume II,
Impact of Environmental and Other Policies on the Appalachian Coal
Industry* (Washington: Appalachian Regional Commission, 1973), p.
107.

46 See Adirondack Park Agency, *Adirondack Park State Land Master
Plan* (Ray Brook, New York: APA, 1972).

47 See Carol Rose, "Lake Placid Copes with the Olympics," *Planning*,
August 1979, pp. 10–11.

48 See, for example, Maryland Public Service Commission, *1978 Ten-*

Year Plan of Maryland Public Utilities, Possible and Proposed Power Plants, 1978 through 1987 (Baltimore: MPSC, 1977).

49 For similar penetration by local-government and land-development interests in the Texas coastal zone program, see the Advisory Committee listed on p. 2 of *Texas Coastal Management Program Newsletter* (Austin: General Land Office), Summer 1976. For penetration of the North Carolina coastal zone program, see Arthur Cooper, "North Carolina: The Importance of the Local Role," *Environmental Comment*, November 1976, and Nelson Rosenbaum, "Private Property and the Public Interest: Citizen Involvement in State Land Use Control," p. 63.

50 See Sullivan, "Adirondack Zoning," pp. 466–67.

51 See, for example, Adirondack Park Local Government Review Board, *1976 Annual Report, "A Local Perspective"* (Long Lake, New York: APLGRB, 1976), pp. 7–9. For an example of a similarly local-oriented body attached by law to the California-Nevada Lake Tahoe Regional Planning Agency, see Constantini and Hanf, *The Environmental Impulse and Its Competitors*, p. 36.

52 See Doyle, *State Strip Mining Laws: Alabama, Colorado, Kansas, Ohio, Texas, and Virginia*, p. 6, and Center for Science in the Public Interest, *The Enforcement of Strip Mining Laws in Three Appalachian States*, p. 68.

53 "Vermont Governor Salmon to Press for Land Use Planning with Reduced State Role," *Land and the Environment*, May 16, 1975, p. 78. See also Judy Walke, "Report on Problems in the Practice of Environmental Law in Vermont" (Boston: Conservation Law Foundation of New England, 1973), pp. 4–7.

54 See, for example, Florida Department of Administration, Division of State Planning, *Annual Progress Report on State and Regional Planning, 1977–1978* (Tallahassee: DSP, 1978), p. 39. See also Carter, *The Florida Experience*, pp. 341–42.

55 For a complete list of the programs, see Vermont Environmental Board, *State Permit Procedure Guide: Land Development and Subdivision* (Montpelier: VEB, 1973), p. 4.

56 Heeter, "Almost Getting It Together in Vermont," p. 377 n. 163. See also Myers, *So Goes Vermont*, pp. 22–23.

57 See, for example, Luther Carter, "Land Use Law (II): Florida Is a Major Testing Ground," *Science*, November 30, 1973, pp. 903–4.

58 Florida Department of Administration, Division of State Planning, *Annual Progress Report on State and Regional Planning, 1977–1978*, p. 69.

59 For indication of the range, see ibid., pp. 64–85.

60 Myers, *Slow Start in Paradise*, p. 25.

61 See, for example, Little, *The New Oregon Trail*, pp. 21–24; Ralph Nader's Study Group on the Pulp and Paper Industry in Maine, *The Paper Plantation*, p. 235; Council of State Governments, *Land Use Policy and Program Analysis Number 3: Organization, Management, and Financing of State Land Use Programs* (Lexington, Kentucky: CSG, 1974); and Connecticut Coastal Areas Management Program, "Local Regulation of 'Inland Wetlands' in Connecticut: A Prototype 'Management Program' under the Coastal Zone Management Act of 1972" (Hartford: CCAMP, undated).

62 For these figures, see Center for Science in the Public Interest, *The Enforcement of Strip Mining Laws in Three Appalachian States*, p. 82. For similar problems in Kentucky and West Virginia, see ibid., pp. 19–74. For the same problem in Virginia, see Doyle, *State Strip Mining Laws: Alabama, Colorado, Kansas, Ohio, Texas, and Virginia*, Appendix I, pp. 1–6.

63 See, for example, Nelson Rosenbaum, *Citizen Involvement in Land Use Governance: Issues and Methods* (Washington: Urban Institute, 1976); Rosenbaum, "Private Property and the Public Interest: Citizen Involvement in State Land Use Control"; and Lynton Caldwell, Lynton Hayes, and Isabel MacWhirter, *Citizens and the Environment* (Bloomington: Indiana University Press, 1976), pp. 6–75.

64 See Pennsylvania Department of Environmental Resources, *Commonwealth of Pennsylvania Surface Mining Conservation and Reclamation Act* (Harrisburg: PDER, 1971), Section 18.3, "Remedies of Citizens," p. 12.

65 Preate, "A New Law for an Old Problem," p. 52. See also Center for Science in the Public Interest, *The Enforcement of Strip Mining Laws in Three Appalachian States*, pp. 91–93.

66 On Kentucky, see ibid., pp. 42–43, and on West Virginia, ibid., pp. 70–73. See also Doyle, *State Strip Mining Laws: Alabama, Colorado, Kansas, Ohio, Texas, and Virginia*, p. 2, and Doyle, *State Strip Mining Laws: An Inventory and Analysis of Key Statutory Provisions in 28 Coal-Producing States*, pp. 76–89.

67 On the citizen-participation procedures of the Adirondack Park Agency, see Natural Resources Defense Council, *Land Use Controls in New York State*, pp. 125–29.

68 *Vermont Statutes Annotated* (Oxford, New Hampshire: Equity Publishing Corporation, 1971), Act 250, Subchapter 12a, Section 6086(a), p. 22. See also Brownell, "State Land Use Regulation," pp. 30–32.

69 Adirondack Park Agency, *Adirondack Park Land Use and Develop-ment Plan*, p. 13.

70 See Florida Office of the Attorney General, *1972 Supplement to Florida Statutes, 1971* (Tallahassee: FOAG, 1972), Chapter 380, Subchapter 6, Section 8, p. 389.

71 See Maryland Office of the Attorney General, *Laws of Maryland, 1971* (Annapolis: MOAG, 1972), Chapter 31, Section 765, pp. 90–91.

72 On Hawaii, see Lowry and McElroy, "State Land Use Control," and Meyers, *Zoning Hawaii*, pp. 74–75. On Maine, see Fred Snow, "The Site Location and Development Law: How It Works . . . and Why," *Maine Environnews* (Augusta: Maine Department of Environmental Protection), May 14, 1976, p. 4.

73 California Coastal Zone Conservation Act of 1972, Chapter 5, Article 1, Section 27401, on p. 125 of Mogulof, *Saving the Coast*.

74 On the provisions of state strip-mining laws aside from Pennsylvania's, see Center for Science in the Public Interest, *The Enforcement of Strip Mining Laws in Three Appalachian States*, pp. 13–14; Doyle, *State Strip Mining Laws: Alabama, Colorado, Kansas, Ohio, Texas and Virginia*; Doyle, *State Strip Mining Laws: An Inventory and Analysis of Key Statutory Provisions in 28 Coal-Producing States*; Doyle, *Strip Mining in the Corn Belt*, pp. 22–29; National Academy of Sciences, *Rehabilitation Potential of Western Coal Lands*, pp. 95–100, 140–48; and Edgar Imhoff, Thomas Friz, and James LaFevers, *A Guide to State Programs for the Reclamation of Surface Mined Areas* (Washington: U.S. Department of the Interior, Geological Survey, 1976).

75 For an introduction to the technology, see Maneval, "Coal Mining vs. Environment."

76 See Pennsylvania Department of Environmental Resources, *Common-wealth of Pennsylvania Surface Mine Conservation and Reclamation Act* and *Rules and Regulations, Transmittal Sheet No. 9* (Harrisburg: DER, 1973).

77 See James Rowe, "Surface-Mine Reclamation: The Back-to-Contour Constraint," *Journal of Soil and Water Conservation*, March/April 1977, p. 74.

78 Steven Quarles, Special Counsel, Senate Committee on Interior and Insular Affairs, in National Association of Home Builders, *Transcript, Conference on State Land Use Legislation*, pp. 5–7. For acknowledg-ment of the same balance in the federal Coastal Zone Management Act by its former administrator, see Robert Knecht, "The Coastal Zone Management Act: Incentives for Planning the Water's Edge," *En-vironmental Comment*, November 1976, p. 4. See also U.S. Depart-

ment of Commerce, *U.S. Ocean Policy* (Washington: Government Printing office, 1979).

79 For a similar acknowledgment by the head of the California-Nevada Lake Tahoe Regional Planning Agency, see "No One's Happy about Tahoe," *Planning*, November 1977, p. 77. See also "Texas Land Office Issues Draft of Control Management Program," *Land Use Planning Report*, May 22, 1978, p. 165, and Adirondack Park Agency, *1977 Annual Report* (Ray Brook, New York: APA, 1978), p. 6.

80 For a discussion of the difficulties posed by technical information even in the comparatively simple setting of coastal regulation, see John Clark, "Natural Science and Coastal Planning," in Healy, ed., *Protecting the Golden Shore*.

81 Arthur Davis, "Planning for Natural Space," in Soil Conservation Society of America, *Land Use*, p. 291.

Chapter 7: The Public Implementation Struggle

1 See Myers, *So Goes Vermont*, pp. 19, 21–22. For a weighting of Oregon's coastal commission in favor of opposed interests, see Little, *The New Oregon Trail*, p.9.

2 Judy Rosener, *Environmentalism vs. Local Control: A Study of the Voting Behavior of Some California Coastal Commissioners* (Claremont, California: Claremont Graduate School, 1977), p. 38.

3 Ibid., pp. 20, 25.

4 Ibid., pp. 31, 41.

5 See, for example, "DER Budget Bid Shortchanges Needs," *Pennsylvania Econotes*, March 1977, p. 1.

6 See Florida Department of Administration, Division of State Planning, *Annual Progress Report on State and Regional Planning, 1977–1978*, p. 39. The Florida development market has since revived; see Wayne King, "Real Estate Frenzy Grips Florida Again," *The New York Times*, August 20, 1979, p. 1.

7 For some documentation of these complaints, see Myers, *Slow Start in Paradise*, pp. 28–34, and Barbara Goldsmith, "Delays in Initiating Construction of Energy Facilities in the United States Due to Environmental Review Procedures," an unpublished paper presented at the meeting in Paris of the Group of Experts on the Environmental Impact of Energy Production and Use at the Organization for Economic Cooperation and Development, February 6–8, 1974. The latter paper focuses on the construction of Baltimore Gas and Electric's Brandon Shores plant on Chesapeake Bay.

8 See also Mogulof, *Saving the Coast*, pp. 16–17.

9 Ibid., p. 42.

10 Mark Rosentraub, Robert Warren, and David Gould, *Coastal Zone Development and Coastal Policy in Southern California: A Two-Year Analysis of the South Coast Regional Commission* (Los Angeles: University of Southern California, Sea Grant Program, 1975), p. 12.

11 See California Coastal Zone Commissions, *Annual Report, 1974* (San Francisco: CCZC, 1974), pp. 6–11, and Mogulof, *Saving the Coast*, p. 22.

12 For some indications in other states, see Myers, *So Goes Vermont*, pp. 21–25, and Myers, *Slow Start in Paradise*, pp. 28–34.

13 See, for example, Myers, *So Goes Vermont*, p. 23; Sullivan, "Adirondack Zoning," pp. 471–72; Myra Oliver, "Violator of Coastline Act Going to Jail," *Los Angeles Times*, March 2, 1974; and "Builder Convicted under New York's Tidal Wetlands Act," *Land Use Planning Report*, October 10, 1977, p. 325.

14 On the lack of enforcement until the 1975 assignment, see Judy Walke, "Report on Problems in the Practice of Environmental Law in Vermont," p. 3.

15 See Healy, *Land Use and the States*, p. 131.

16 Philip Fradkin, "Coastal Act—But Not Much Action," *Los Angeles Times*, June 10, 1974, p. 3.

17 Ibid., p. 22.

18 Ibid. See also Mogulof, *Saving the Coast*, p. 23, and John Banta, "The Coastal Commissions and State Agencies: Conflict and Cooperation," in Healy, ed., *Protecting the Golden Shore*, pp. 113–14. For a similar case in Rhode Island, see *Report of the Governor's Wetlands Task Force* (Providence: Office of the Governor, 1976). On the enforcement of state wetlands laws generally, see Nelson Rosenbaum, "The State Role in Wetlands Protection," pp. 11–13, as well as the larger forthcoming study of which the cited article is an early report.

19 Walke, "Report on Problems in the Practice of Environmental Law in Vermont," p. 3. See also Darby Bradley and Richard Mixer, "Act 250 and the Control of Soil Erosion and Sedimentation in Developing Areas in Vermont" (Burlington, Vermont: New England River Basins Commission, 1978), pp. 3, 29–30.

20 For a similar situation leading to a lack of enforcement, see Jaffe, "Regional Planning Comes of Age on Martha's Vineyard," p. 22.

21 Center for Science in the Public Interest, *The Enforcement of Strip Mining Laws in Three Appalachian States*, pp. 81–84.

22 On inspector intimidation as it operates in Pennsylvania, see ibid., p. 84.

23 Ibid., p. 83.

24 For a more critical review of the Pennsylvania program's use of its enforcement powers, see ibid., pp. 84–91.

25 See "DER Focuses on Strip Mine Abuses," *Pennsylvania Econotes*, May–June 1979, p. 1. Pennsylvania's recent enforcement activities are especially striking in view of the current softness of the Appalachian coal market; see Stephen Lynton, "Coal Glut Turns Boom into Slump," *Washington Post*, September 17, 1979, p. 1.

26 Joseph Bodovitz, quoted on p. 385 of John Asbaugh and Jens Sorensen, "Identifying the 'Public' for Participation in Coastal Zone Management," *Coastal Zone Management Journal*, Volume 2, Number 4, 1976.

27 See Duddleson, "How the Citizens of California Secured Their Coastal Management Program," pp. 3, 4, 20–48, and Rosenbaum, "Private Property and the Public Interest: Citizen Involvement in State Land-Use Control," pp. 100–144.

28 This skepticism about citizen participation is, in my experience, justified. In 1975–76 I served on a volunteer citizens' advisory panel on land use for the Illinois coastal zone program. The state has a sixty-mile coast on Lake Michigan, half of which belongs to Chicago, the remainder to the city's suburbs and more rural areas bordering on southern Wisconsin. Four of the seven members of the panel came from Hyde Park, the mostly upper-middle-class neighborhood centered on the University of Chicago, an area that accounts for about a mile and a half of the city's shore. Two of these members lived on the same block. The remainder were from the affluent North Shore suburbs. None of the members came from the nearly fifteen miles of ghetto and lower-middle-class neighborhoods that adjoin Hyde Park along the lakeshore or from any of the rural coastal areas. Our recommendations were uncompromisingly environmentalist and were almost completely ignored. The Illinois coastal program was later suspended from the federal coastal zone program for inadequate performance. So perhaps we were right after all. But on balance, both the effectiveness and representativeness of citizen participation in state land-use programs remain moot.

29 Myers, *Slow Start in Paradise*, p. 33.

30 M. Bruce Johnson, "A Critique of the Concept of Federal Land Use Regulation," p. 578. See also J. P. Taravella, "Coastal Zone Management: A Developer's Perspective," *Environmental Comment*, November 1976, pp. 7–8, and Heeter, "Almost Getting It Together in Vermont," pp. 372–73.

31 See Adirondack Park Agency, *Development in the Adirondack Park: Objectives and Guidelines for Planning and Review* (Ray Brook, New York: APA, 1977).

32 Vermont Environmental Board, *Act 250 Procedure Manual* (Montpelier: VEB, 1978).

33 South Coast Regional Commission, *Interpretative Guidelines/Permits* (Long Beach: SCRC, 1978).

34 Ibid., p. A–4.

35 Ibid., p. 3.

36 Paul Sabatier, "The Use of Technical Information in Land Development Review: The California Coastal Zone Conservation Commissions," a paper presented at the September 1975 annual meeting of the American Political Science Association in San Francisco, p. 34.

37 Vermont Home Builders Association, "Act 250 Analysis" (Essex Junction: VHBA, 1974), p. 2.

38 See the Adirondack Park Local Government Review Board, *1976 Annual Report, "A Local Perspective,"* pp. 7–9.

39 The bill was Senate No. 1569. For the agency's response to it, see Information Bulletin to the New York State Legislature from Robert Flacke, Chairman of the APA, "Bill to Abolish Adirondack Park Agency Repudiates State Interest in Adirondack Park, Ignores Substantial Progress of Past Three Years" (Ray Brook, New York: APA, 1977).

40 See "California Senate Panel Approves Exemption of Large Development from Coastal Zone Rules," *Land Use Planning Report*, July 2, 1979, p. 209. See also Ralph Nader's Study Group on the Pulp and Paper Industry in Maine, *The Paper Plantation*, pp. 240–47, 271–73.

41 For the bases of its opposition, see California Council for Environmental and Economic Balance, *Review and Comment, Preliminary Coastal Plan* (San Francisco: CCEEB, 1975). The reservations also appear in many issues of the council's monthly newsletter, *Environment and the Economy*.

42 Gallop, "The Florida Environmental Land and Water Management Act of 1972," p. 9.

43 For an account of the campaign, see Dean, "How to Kill a Land-Use Bill."

44 See Meyer, "Land Rush," p. 59, and Henry Richmond, "Unique Public Interest Law Group Supports Oregon Land Use Planning Program," p. 8.

45 Adirondack Park Agency, *Second Annual Report, August 1, 1974–July 31, 1975* (Ray Brook, New York: APA, 1975), p. 15. By 1973, the

California–Nevada Lake Tahoe Regional Planning Agency was involved in suits totaling well over $200 million; see Constantini and Hanf, *The Environmental Impulse and Its Competitors*, p. 47.

46 See Adirondack Park Agency press releases of November 5, 1976; April 1 and May 20, 1977; and February 14, 1978. See also Graham, *The Adirondack Park*, pp. 272–73.

47 "Judge Upholds California Coastal Plan Approval, Scores Congress OCZM for 'Befuddled' Programs," *Land Use Planning Report*, September 11, 1978, p. 293.

48 Ibid.

49 Earl Gallop, "Florida Court Kills Environmental Law," *Planning*, February 1979, p. 5. See also Nancy Stroud, "Areas of Critical State Concern: Legislative Options Following the *Cross Keys* Decision," *Florida Environmental and Urban Issues*, March/April 1979. Technically, the Green Swamp designation had already been overturned in 1977 on the procedural grounds that the state had not made the designation within the allowed statutory time limits; see Daniel O'Connell, "Florida Planning and Zoning Case Law: 1974 to Mid-1978," *Environmental Comment*, August 1978, p. 13. In December 1979, the DRI portion of Florida's law received an apparently serious defeat in the state's appellate court, which ruled that, without compensation to developers, the denial of a project by a regional planning council (or a local government) represented an illegal taking of property; see "Florida Laws Construed," *National Wetlands Newsletter*, December 1979, p. 10.

50 See Nancy Stroud, "Legislative Action on Natural Resources Management," *Florida Environmental and Urban Issues*, October 1979, pp. 2–3.

51 Steve Chontos, *The Death of Dover, Vermont* (New York: Vantage Press, 1974). See also "German Firm Stops Vermont Uranium Plans, Citing Development Laws 'Burdens,'" *Land Use Planning Report*, April 30, 1979, p. 139.

52 See Myers, *So Goes Vermont*, p. 24.

53 See, for example, the statement of Walter Heine, Associate Deputy Secretary for Mines and Land Protection in the Pennsylvania Department of Environmental Resources, p. 59 of the *Report of the Committee on Interior and Insular Affairs, House of Representatives, on the Surface Mining Control and Reclamation Act of 1974* (Washington: Government Printing Office, 1974).

54 See Bruce Ackerman et al., *The Uncertain Search for Environmental Quality* (New York: The Free Press, 1974), p. 325 n. 27.

55 For the information in this paragraph, see Sabatier, "The Use of Technical Information in Land Development Review," pp. 21–27.

56 The poll was taken and the results provided me by State Senator William Doyle of Washington County, Vermont.

57 South Florida Regional Planning Council, *Developments of Regional Impact in Region 10* (Miami: SFRPC, 1975), pp. 9–10.

58 Tampa Bay Regional Planning Council, *Annual Report, 1974* (Tampa: TBRPC, 1975), p. 6.

59 Withlacoochee Regional Planning Council, *Annual Report, 1974* (Ocala: WRPC, 1975), p. 11.

60 California Coastal Commission, *Biennial Report, 1977–1978* (San Francisco: CCC, 1979), p. 18.

61 See Paul Sabatier, Dan Ray, and David Lambert, "The Development of the California Coastal Plan: Influence, Information, and Inter-Regional Variation," unpublished manuscript, available from Sabatier at the Division of Environmental Studies, University of California, Davis.

62 See, for example, Paul Sabatier, "State Review of Local Land-Use Decisions: The California Coastal Commissions," *Coastal Zone Management Journal*, Volume 3, Number 3, 1977; Mogulof, *Saving the Coast*, pp. 41–53; and Myers, *So Goes Vermont*, p. 22.

63 California Coastal Commission, *Biennial Report, 1977–1978*, p. 18.

64 See Mogulof, *Saving the Coast*, pp. 46–47.

65 California Coastal Commissions, *Local Coastal Program Status Chart: June 22, 1979* (San Francisco: CCC, 1979), pp. 3, 1.

66 Ibid. See also "Schedule for Local Coastal Plan Completion," *Coastal News* (San Francisco: California Coastal Commission), October 1978, p. 7. For more critical examinations of the relations between the coastal commissions and the localities, see Thomas Dickert and Jens Sorensen, *Collaborative Land-Use Planning for the Coastal Zone: Volume 1, A Process for Local Program Development* (Berkeley and La Jolla: University of California, Institute of Urban and Regional Development and Institute of Marine Resources, 1978), and Lenard Grote, "Coastal Conservation and Development: Balancing Local and Statewide Interests," *Public Affairs Report*, February 1978. Grote, a teacher and former councilman and mayor of Pleasant Hill, California (a noncoastal city near Oakland), was then a member of the San Francisco area coastal commission, and later chaired the state coastal commission.

67 "Vermont Governor Salmon to Press for Land Use Planning with Reduced State Role," *Land and the Environment*, May 16, 1975, p. 78.

68 Adirondack Park Agency press releases, February 22, 1978, and November 10, 1978.

69 Ibid.

70 Telephone interview, Adirondack Park Agency, August 1979. See also Adirondack Park Agency, *Evaluation of Adirondack Park Agency Local Planning Assistance Program, July 1979* (Ray Brooks, New York: APA, 1979).

71 See Myers, *Slow Start in Paradise*, pp. 20–26.

72 See ibid.; Healy, *Land Use and the States*, pp. 112–18; and Carter, *The Florida Experience*, pp. 228–63.

73 See Florida Department of Administration, Division of State Planning, *Annual Progress Report on State and Regional Planning, 1976–1977*, pp. 28–29.

74 See Florida Department of Administration, Division of State Planning, *Annual Progress Report on State and Regional Planning, 1977–1978*, p. 33.

75 Carter, *The Florida Experience*, p. 342.

76 Gallop, "The Florida Environmental Land and Water Management Act of 1972," p. 18.

77 Carter, *The Florida Experience*, p. 342, and Florida Department of Administration, Division of State Planning, *Annual Progress Report on State and Regional Planning, 1975–1976* (Tallahassee: Department of Administration, 1976), pp. 48–49.

78 For some examples, see Healy, *Land Use and the States*, pp. 123–24, 126–29.

79 See Thomas Muller and Kathleen Christensen, *State-Mandated Impact Evaluation: A Preliminary Assessment* (Washington: Urban Institute, 1976), pp. 34–35, 38–39, 44–46.

80 Healy, *Land Use and the States*, p. 129.

81 Ibid.

82 See, for example, "Oregon Imposes Farmland Protection, State Policy Order on Reluctant Locality," *Land Use Planning Report*, October 2, 1978, p. 317.

83 See minutes of the meeting of the California Coastal Commission, May 31, 1977, p. 4, available from the commission in San Francisco.

84 See Florida Department of Administration, Division of State Planning, *Florida State Comprehensive Plan* (Tallahassee: Department of Administration, 1977).

85 Florida Department of Administration, Division of State Planning, *Florida State Comprehensive Plan: Land Development Element* (Tallahassee: Department of Administration, 1977), p. 23.

86 Ibid., pp. 23, 24.

87 For what material there is on their implementation, see ibid., pp. 131–33.

88 Ibid., pp. 125–28; the quotation is from p. 125.

89 For an argument that the regulatory experience was primarily responsible for the strength of the plan, see Healy, "The Role of the Permit System in the California Coastal Strategy," in Healy, ed., *Protecting the Golden Shore*. On the preparation of the plan, see Duddleson, "How the Citizens of California Secured Their Coastal Management Program," ibid., pp. 32–48.

90 California Coastal Zone Conservation Commissions, *California Coastal Plan*, pp. 42–43.

91 Ibid., pp. 173–420.

92 For this section, see California Office of the Attorney General, *California Public Resources Code, Division 20: California Coastal Act* (Sacramento: COAG, 1976), Section 30233, p. 364.

93 For discussion of these defeats, see Heeter, "Almost Getting It Together in Vermont," pp. 356–71.

94 See "First Environmental Board Chairman Changes Mind, Says No Land Use Plan in 1975," *Vermont Watchman*, February 1975.

95 "Vermont Abolishes Statewide Land Use Plan," *Adirondack Defender*, Winter 1978, p. 1.

96 For an interesting exposition of this aversion, see A. Lawrence Chickering, ed., *The Politics of Planning: A Review and Critique of Centralized Economic Planning* (San Francisco: Institute for Contemporary Studies, 1976).

97 Victor Yannacone, Jr., "The Origins of Our National Environmental Policy," in Burchell and Listokin, eds., *Future Land Use*, p. 185. See also Strong, *Private Property and the Public Interest: The Brandywine Experience*, pp. 164–69.

98 The text's account is largely drawn from the sources listed in note 6 to Chapter 5, above, and from my interviewing.

99 See "100 Local Governments, Statewide Organizations Pass Resolutions: Abolish APA," *Adirondack Defender*, Summer 1976, and Evelyn Outcalt, "Area Priests Stand by Anti-APA Resolution," *Adirondack Daily Enterprise*, June 23, 1976.

100 See "Appendix: Abstract of Testimony at Citizen Speak-Outs Sponsored by Adirondack Park Local Government Review Board," pp. 10–20 in the *Supplement* to the *Lake Placid News*, December 18, 1975.

101 See "The Truth about Operation Survival," *Adirondack Defender*, Fall 1977, p. 18.

102 For a case of another state land-use agency with similar problems, see Jaffe, "Regional Planning Comes of Age on Martha's Vineyard," p. 22.

103 For Hickey's own account of his troubles, see "Appendix: Abstract of Testimony at Citizen Speak-Outs Sponsored by Adirondack Park Local

Government Review Board," p. 18. See also Lewis, "New York's Adirondacks," pp. 9–10.

104 See John Kinney, "A Backfire in the Catskills," *Empire State Report*, September 1975.

105 Robert Flacke, "Statement to Be Given at 75th Anniversary Luncheon Meeting of the Association for the Protection of the Adirondacks, August 20, 1976" (Ray Brook, New York: APA, 1976). See also Flacke, "The Adirondack Park Agency Comes of Age," *New York State Environment*, February 1977, which reprints the APA's 1976 *Annual Report*, also available from the agency in Ray Brook.

106 Harold Faber, "Adirondack Wilderness Is Focus of Land-Use Controversy," *The New York Times*, August 23, 1976, p. 26.

107 See, for example, Kathryn Roberts, "Summer Veto—Winter Test," *Lake Placid News*, March 4, 1976, p. 1.

108 APA, *A Citizen's Guide to Adirondack Park Agency Land Use Regulations* (Ray Brook, New York: APA, 1979).

109 APA press releases, November 10, 1978; July 29, August 12, September 14, and November 18, 1977; and March 18, 1978. The report of the advisory committee is *Citizens Advisory Task Force on Adirondack Hamlet Restoration and Development* (Ray Brook, New York: APA, 1978).

110 APA press releases, January 10, January 21, and August 15, 1977; February 22, April 21, and August 28, 1978; and January 26 and June 15, 1979.

111 APA press release, March 30, 1979.

112 APA press release, March 22, 1979. See also "Carey Approves 'Model' Procedures for APA Which Will Cut Permit Time," *Land Use Planning Report*, July 23, 1979, p. 234.

113 Adirondack Park Local Government Review Board, *Sixth Annual Report* (Long Lake, New York: APLGRB, 1978), p. 1.

114 "Short Takes by the Editor," *Adirondack Life*, March–April 1979, p. 4. See also Graham, *The Adirondack Park*, pp. 262–63.

115 Myers, *Slow Start in Paradise*, p. 33.

116 For some examples of regulatory bargains, see Myers, *So Goes Vermont*, pp. 21–23; Mogulof, *Saving the Coast*, pp. 13–14; Myers, *Slow Start in Paradise*, pp. 20–26; and Healy, *Land Use and the States*, pp. 42–45, 75–78, 112–18, 122–32.

117 California Coastal Commission, *Biennial Report, 1977–1978*, p. 18.

118 See p. 3 of the special supplement on the APA published by the *Lake Placid News*, March 4, 1976.

119 Vermont Environmental Board, *Statistics on Act 250 Program Applications, June 1, 1970–July 1, 1978* (Montpelier: VEB, 1978), p. 1. See

also Myers, *So Goes Vermont*, p. 21, and Heeter, "Almost Getting It Together in Vermont," pp. 371–72.

120 Personal communication, Donald Zutlas, Chief of Licensing and Bonding Division, Bureau of Surface Mine Reclamation, May 10, 1976.

121 For Florida's program, see Florida Department of Administration, Division of State Planning, *Annual Progress Report on State and Regional Planning, 1977–78*, p. 38. On Maryland's program, see pp. 6–7 of Maryland Public Service Commission, *Report of the Public Service Commission of Maryland, 1973* (Baltimore: MPSC, 1974), which is the most recent such report available. For some similar figures elsewhere, see Hawaii Department of Planning and Economic Development, *1976 Annual Report* (Honolulu: HDPED, 1976), p. 24, and Delaware Coastal Zone Industrial Control Board and Delaware State Planning Office, *Coastal Zone Act Administration, June 28, 1971–June 30, 1976* (Dover: DCZICB and DSPO, 1976), pp. 11–45.

122 This list of California coastal conditions is drawn from Mogulof, *Saving the Coast*, pp. 109–10. See also Healy, *Land Use and the States*, pp. 75–88; Healy, "An Economic Interpretation of the California Coastal Commissions," in Healy, ed., *Protecting the Golden Shore*, pp. 145–64; and Sabatier, "State Review of Local Land Use Decisions." For some south Florida DRI conditions, see Muller and Christensen, *State-Mandated Impact Evaluation*, pp. 36–37.

123 See Myers, *So Goes Vermont*, pp. 21–23, and Healy, *Land Use and the States*, pp. 40–41.

124 Vermont Environmental Board, *Act 250 Program Statistics, June 1, 1970–April 1, 1976* (Montpelier: VEB, 1976), p. 1.

125 See, for example the presentation of Robert Marcotte, Vermont Representative of the National Association of Home Builders, to the Environmental Board's public hearing of June 26, 1974. The presentation is available from Mr. Marcotte in Essex Junction, Vermont.

126 For a typical set of conditions put on a Maryland power plant, see Maryland Public Service Commission, *Report of the Public Service Commission of Maryland, 1973*, pp. 58–59.

127 For an energy-development case where killing by conditions may actually have occurred, see Healy, "The Role of the Permit System in the California Coastal Strategy," p. 78, and "An Economic Interpretation of the California Coastal Commissions," pp. 146–48.

128 Myers, *So Goes Vermont*, p. 25. The cited study is Walke, "Report on Problems in the Practice of Environmental Law in Vermont," p. 4. Governor Salmon's remark was part of a 1972 speech to a Council of State Governments symposium at Rosslyn, Virginia.

129 Daniel Mandelker, "Putting Together the Policy and Legal Decisions,"

in Soil Conservation Society of America, *Land Use: Tough Choices in Today's World*, p. 426.

130 For some other such cases in state land-use regulation, see Malcolm Rivkin, *Negotiated Development: A Breakthrough in Environmental Controversies* (Washington: Conservation Foundation, 1977), pp. 14–19, and Francis Murray, ed., *Where We Agree: Report of the National Coal Policy Project* (Boulder, Colorado: Westview Press, 1978).

131 See Rosener, *Environmentalism vs. Local Control*, pp. 8–9, and Rosener, "A Coastal Commissioner's Perspective: Choosing between What the Law Says and What the Law Allows," *Coastal Zone Management Journal*, Volume 4, Numbers 1/2, 1978.

132 For some particularly obvious cases involving California and Florida energy facilities, see Healy, *Land Use and the States*, pp. 83–87, 126–27. For a similar case involving a Hawaiian residential development, see Myers, *Zoning Hawaii*, pp. 23–24.

Chapter 8: The Bureaucratic Implementation Struggle

1 See, for example, any issue of the *Vermont Watchman*, published in Concord by the Vermont Conservative Caucus.

2 For a similar opinion, see National Association of Home Builders, *Transcript, Conference on State Land Use Legislation*, p. 88.

3 See Muller and Christensen, *State-Mandated Impact Evaluation*, pp. 19–20. For further documentation, see the Orange County Cost of Housing Committee, *A Study of the Cost of Housing in Orange County* (Santa Ana, California; OCCHC, 1975); the *Supplement* to the *Lake Placid News*, December 18, 1975, "Appendix: Abstract of Testimony at Citizen Speak-Outs Sponsored by the Adirondack Park Local Government Review Board"; Goldsmith, "Delays in Initiating Construction of Energy Facilities in the United States Due to Environmental Review Procedures"; Myers, *Slow Start in Paradise*, pp. 28–34; Myers, *So Goes Vermont*, p. 24; Healy, *Land Use and the States*, pp. 173–74; and Tucker, "Environmentalism and the Leisure Class."

4 See article 2, paragraph 27420 of the 1972 Coastal Act, available on pp. 126–27 of Mogulof, *Saving the Coast*.

5 Healy, *Land Use and the States*, p. 174.

6 Urban Land Institute, *The Economic Benefits of Coastal Zone Management: An Overview* (Washington: Department of Commerce, Office of Coastal Zone Management, 1976), p. 23.

7 Healy, "An Economic Interpretation of the California Coastal Com-

missions," p. 172. For a lower estimate, see Franklin James and Thomas Muller, "Environmental Impact Evaluation, Land Use Planning, and the Housing Consumer," *Journal of the American Real Estate and Urban Economics Association*, Fall 1977.

8 Urban Land Institute, *The Economic Benefits of Coastal Zone Management*, pp. 19–20.

9 For some outstanding examples, see the *Supplement* to the *Lake Placid News*, December 18, 1975, "Appendix: Abstract of Testimony at Citizen Speak-Outs Sponsored by the Adirondack Park Local Government Review Board," pp. 10–20.

10 See Florida Department of Administration, Division of State Planning, "Development of Regional Impact Application for Development Approval" (Tallahassee: DSP, 1976).

11 Florida Department of Administration, Division of State Planning, *Development of Regional Impact: Guidebook for the Preparation of the Application for Development Approval* (Tallahassee: DSP, 1976).

12 See South Florida Regional Planning Council, "Development of Regional Impact Process and Procedures for Filing a Development of Regional Impact Application and Information Required for an Application for Development Approval" (Miami: SFRPC, undated), and Tampa Bay Regional Planning Council, "DRI Application Clarification Sheet" (Tampa: TBRPC, undated).

13 Gallop, "The Florida Environmental Land and Water Management Act of 1972," p. 8.

14 See Illinois Institute of Environmental Quality, *Power Plant Siting in the State of Illinois, Part II—Environmental Impacts of Large Energy Conversion Facilities*, pp. 144–45; Baldwin, "Socio-Economic Impact of Power Plant Construction: A Case History," p. 2; and Myer Kutz, "Nuclear Industry Reviews Troubled Year," *Planning*, January 1978, p. 7.

15 See the *Supplement* to the *Lake Placid News*, December 18, 1975, "Appendix: Abstract of Testimony at Citizen Speak-Outs Sponsored by the Adirondack Park Local Government Review Board."

16 Heeter, "Almost Getting It Together in Vermont," p. 383 n. 175.

17 Milton Nadworny, "Some Economic Impacts of Water Pollution and Land Development Controls in Vermont" (Montpelier: Vermont Natural Resources Council, 1971), pp. 33–34.

18 For some estimates, see Healy, *Land Use and the States*, pp. 47, 173–74.

19 Myers, *So Goes Vermont*, pp. 20–21. For similar Vermont cases, see Healy, *Land Use and the States*, pp. 42–44, 47.

20 Healy, *Land Use and the States*, pp. 123–24, 174. For some further

figures, see Brooks, *Housing Equity and Environmental Protection*, p. 32.

21 For a list of federal, state, and local permits required for nuclear and fossil-fuel power plants, see Goldsmith, "Delays in Initiating Construction of Energy Facilities in the United States Due to Environmental Review Procedures," pp. 9–12. For a good discussion of this diversity as it shows up in strip mining of western coal, see National Academy of Sciences, *Rehabilitation Potential of Western Coal Lands*, pp. 13–14. See also John Quarles, *Federal Regulation of New Industrial Plants* (Washington: New Plants Report, 1979).

22 For some examples, see Fred Bosselman, Duane Feurer, and Charles Siemon, *The Permit Explosion: Coordination of the Proliferation* (Washington: Urban Land Institute, 1976), pp. 83–84.

23 For poll data, see Rosenbaum, "Private Property and the Public Interest: Citizen Involvement in State Land Use Control," pp. 31–35.

24 John Gamman, Shavaun Towers, and Jens Sorensen, *State Involvement in the Coastal Zone* (La Jolla, California: Institute of Marine Resources, 1975), p. i. See also Mogulof, *Saving the Coast*, p. 37.

25 Oregon Land Conservation and Development Commission, *Preliminary Draft: Oregon Coastal Zone Management Program* (Salem: OLCDC, 1975), pp. 18–21, 85–89.

26 Maine State Planning Office, "Summary of Principal Environmental Legislation that Relates to Coastal Management" (Augusta: MSPO, undated).

27 Joe Sizer, "Land Use Planning," paper presented to Minnesota Horizons Conference in 1975, quoted in Council of State Governments, *State Planning: Intergovernmental Planning Policy Coordination* (Washington: Department of Housing and Urban Development, 1975), p. 18.

28 For documentation, see American Institute of Planners, *Survey of State Land Use Activity*. For some studies of other states, see Betty Hawkins, "Patchwork Land-Use Planning in New York," *Empire State Report*, April 1975; Thomas Schmidt and Helen Cordell, *Laws Which Regulate Land Use in Pennsylvania* (Pittsburgh: Western Pennsylvania Conservancy, 1975); and Montana Department of Community Affairs, *Land Use Planning and Management in Montana: A Summary of Selected State Laws* (Helena: MDCA, 1977).

29 For some further examples, see Healy, *Land Use and the States*, pp. 167–68. For examples from the federal coastal zone program, see Comptroller General of the United States, *Report to the Congress: The Coastal Zone Management Program: An Uncertain Future* (Washington: General Accounting Office, 1976). For some examples

from California, see Rasa Gustaitis, "The Coastal Gamble: Who Wins under the New Law?" *New West*, January 17, 1977; Connie Cheney, "Let the Owner Beware: Examples of Government Land Use Regulation," in Institute of Contemporary Studies, *No Land Is an Island*; and Orange County Cost of Housing Committee, *A Study of the Cost of Housing in Orange County*. For examples from Vermont, see "Gallant Peru Selectmen Win Titanic Battle with Environmental Board," *Vermont Watchman*, February 1976, p. 11, and John McClaughry, "Supreme Court Rebukes Environmental Board," *Vermont Watchman*, May 1976, p. 15; from the Adirondacks, see the *Supplement* to the *Lake Placid News*, December 18, 1975, "Appendix: Abstract of Testimony at Citizen Speak-Outs Sponsored by the Adirondack Park Local Government Review Board," pp. 10–20; and from Maryland, see Goldsmith, "Delays in Initiating Construction of Energy Facilities in the United States Due to Environmental Review Procedures."

30 See National Association of Home Builders, *Transcript, Conference on State Land Use Legislation*, pp. 138–41.

31 Home Builders Association of Vermont, *Act 250 Analysis* (Essex Junction: HBAV, 1974), p. 2.

32 For an amusing and well-publicized California coastal case, see Calvin Tomkins, "Running Fence," *The New Yorker*, March 28, 1977.

33 For some examples, see Frank So, "Tips on Cutting the Delays of Regulation," *Planning*, October 1978; Greg Longhini, "How Three Cities Fared in One-Stop Permitting," *Planning*, October 1978; Urban Land Institute, *Large-Scale Development: Benefits, Constraints and State and Local Policy Incentives* (Washington: ULI, 1977), pp. 71–75; and Bosselman, Feurer, and Siemon, *The Permit Explosion*, pp. 32–37.

34 See the *Supplement* to the *Lake Placid News*, March 4, 1976, "APA Self Study: Law 'Sound' but 'Misunderstood,'" p. 8.

35 Urban Land Institute, *Large-Scale Development*, p. 71.

36 For a discussion of prehearing conferences in the New Jersey coastal zone program, see Rivkin, *Negotiated Development*, pp. 14–19.

37 For an example of similar restrictions in the Hawaii land-use program, see Myers, *Zoning Hawaii*, footnote on p. 26.

38 For some examples, see Urban Land Institute, Annette Kolis, ed., *Thirteen Perspectives on Regulatory Simplification* (Washington: ULI, 1979), especially Kenneth Senecal, "Regulatory Simplification in Vermont," and James May, "Regulatory Simplification: The Florida Experience"; Urban Land Institute, *Large-Scale Development*, pp. 59–94; Bosselman, Feurer, and Siemon, *The Permit Explosion*, pp. 19–37; Robert Healy, "Coordination: The Next Phase in Land Use

Planning," *Journal of Soil and Water Conservation*, July/August 1976; the May 1976 issue of *Environmental Comment* on "Coordination of Development Regulation: Untangling the Maze"; and the May 1977 issue of *Environmental Comment* on "Conflict Resolution."

39 For example, all but one of the references on simplification cited in note 38 were published by the Urban Land Institute, a Washington-based research and education organization of large builders.

40 California Senate Committee on Natural Resources and Wildlife, Subcommittee on Land Use Planning, "A Brief Summary of the California Coastal Act of 1976," pp. 2–3.

41 See Healy, *Land Use and the States*, pp. 80–83, 167–68; Mogulof, *Saving the Coast*, pp. 55–57; Scott, *Governing California's Coast*, pp. 202–17; and Banta, "The Coastal Commissions and State Agencies," in Healy, ed., *Protecting the Golden Shore*, pp. 125–27.

42 For the quotes, see "California Coastal Commission Proposes to 'Substantially Change' Its Authority," *Land Use Planning Report*, April 9, 1979, p. 114. For the opponents' legislation, see "California Panel Okays Cut in Coastal Zone Boundaries," *Land Use Planning Report*, March 26, 1979, p. 97, and "California Senator Seeks Compromise on Coastal Zone Boundary Controversy," *Land Use Planning Report*, April 2, 1979, p. 105.

43 See Herman Boschken, "Interorganizational Considerations in Coastal Management: The 1976 California Legislative Experience," *Coastal Zone Management Journal*, Volume 4, Numbers 1/2, 1978. For a more general argument of this sort, see Robert Hawkins, Jr., "Local Land Use Planning and Its Critics," in Institute of Contemporary Studies, *No Land Is an Island*.

44 See Healy, *Land Use and the States*, p. 41; Myers, *So Goes Vermont*, p. 18; and Heeter, "Almost Getting It Together in Vermont," p. 378.

45 Healy, *Land Use and the States*, p. 132. See also Gallop, "The Florida Environmental Land and Water Management Act of 1972," p. 8, and Muller and Christensen, *State-Mandated Impact Evaluation*, p. 40.

46 For some examples from coastal zone programs, see Sorensen, *State-Local Collaborative Planning*.

Chapter 9: The Economic Effects of the Programs

1 See David Ervin, James Fitch, R. Kenneth Godwin, W. Bruce Shepard, and Herbert Stoevener, *Land Use Control: Evaluating Economic and Political Effects* (Cambridge, Massachusetts: Ballinger, 1977), and

Robert Kneisel, *Economic Impacts of Land Use Control: The California Coastal Zone Conservation Commissions* (Davis, California: University of California, Davis, Institute of Governmental Affairs and Institute of Ecology, 1979).

2 Healy, "An Economic Interpretation of the California Coastal Commissions," pp. 174, 175.

3 See, for example, Healy, ibid.; Healy, *Land Use and the States*, pp. 168–75; Kneisel, *Economic Impacts of Land Use Control*; Urban Land Institute, *The Economic Benefits of Coastal Zone Management*; Institute for Contemporary Studies, *The California Coastal Plan*; Real Estate Research Corporation, *Business Prospects under Coastal Zone Management* (Washington: U.S. Department of Commerce, Office of Coastal Zone Management, 1976); Benjamin Stevens, *Potential Economic and Fiscal Impacts of a Land Use Policy for the Commonwealth of Pennsylvania* (Pittsburgh: Pennsylvania Land Policy Project, 1975); California Legislative Analyst, *Review of California Coastal Plan* (Sacramento: Office of Legislative Analyst, 1976); Economics Research Associates and Alvin Baum and Associates, *Economic Impacts of the Proposed Coastal Plan* (Sacramento: Joint Rules Committee, California Legislature, 1975); George Goldman and David Strong, *Governmental Costs and Revenues Associated with Implementing Coastal Plan Policies in the Half Moon Bay Subregion* (Berkeley: University of California, Cooperative Extension Service, 1976); and George Goldman, David Strong, Darryl McLeod, and A. T. Nakazawa, *Private Sector Economic Impacts Associated with Implementing Coastal Plan Policy in the Half Moon Bay Subregion* (Berkeley: University of California, Cooperative Extension Service, 1977).

4 See Kneisel, *Economic Impacts of Land Use Control*, pp. 17–40.

5 See Construction Industry Research Board, *Economic Analysis: California Coastal Zone Conservation Act* (Los Angeles: CIRB, 1976). For a similar California analysis, see California Council for Environmental and Economic Balance, *An Economic Profile of the California Coastal Zone* (San Francisco: CCEEB, undated).

6 Healy, *Land Use and the States*, p. 169.

7 Ibid.

8 See, for example, Florida Department of Commerce, *Dade County Labor Market Trends* and *Hillsborough County Labor Market Trends* (Tallahassee: FDOC, November 1975).

9 Adirondack Park Agency, *Adirondack Park Economic Profile, Phase Two: Recent Trends and Factors Affecting the Adirondack Real Estate Market* (Ray Brook, New York: APA, 1976), p. 6.

10 Ibid., pp. 2–7.
11 Ibid., pp. 6–9.
12 Ibid., pp. 9–19.
13 Ibid., p. 9. No comparable study has been done for nonrecession periods. Nor has much research been done on sales, construction starts, or sales prices comparing the Adirondacks with other areas on a more disaggregated basis—that is, by counties, municipalities, actual land uses, or areas where similar land uses are permitted—rather than by entire multicounty regions. See, however, Robert Anderson and Roger Dower, "Land Price Impacts of the Adirondack Park Land Use and Development Plan," *American Journal of Agricultural Economics*, forthcoming, and New York State Board of Equalization and Assessment, *Adirondack Park Real Property Tax Base Study: Fiscal Report* (Albany: NYSBEA, 1978), pp. 6–8. Both these references caution against drawing any firm conclusions from the data presented.
14 Letter quoted in Healy, *Land Use and the States*, pp. 130–31.
15 On the details of this technique and its alternatives in Pennsylvania, see Maneval, "Coal Mining vs. Environment," pp. 17–23, and Skelly and Loy Engineers–Consultants, *Economic Engineering Analysis of U.S. Surface Coal Mines and Effective Land Reclamation* (Washington: U.S. Department of the Interior, Bureau of Mines, 1975), pp. 3–55 to 3–92.
16 See, for example, Stephen Seidel, *Housing Costs & Government Regulations: Confronting the Regulatory Maze* (New Brunswick, New Jersey: Rutgers University Center for Urban Policy Research, 1978); Urban Land Institute and Gruen Gruen & Associates, *Effects of Regulation on Housing Costs: Two Case Studies* (Washington: Urban Land Institute, 1977); Frieden, *The Environmental Protection Hustle*, pp. 139–56; and Richardson, *The Cost of Environmental Protection*, pp. 107–38.
17 H. Frech III and Ronald Lafferty, "The Economic Impact of the California Coastal Commissions," in Institute for Contemporary Studies, *The California Coastal Plan*, pp. 84–85.
18 Security Pacific Bank, *California Coastal Zone Economic Study* (Los Angeles: SPB, 1975), p. 10–1.
19 Quoted in Healy, "An Economic Interpretation of the California Coastal Commissions," p. 166.
20 Ibid. See also Healy, *Land Use and the States*, pp. 88–90, and Michael Peevey, "The Coastal Plan and Jobs: A Critique," in Institute for Contemporary Studies, *The California Coastal Plan*, p. 99.
21 See Mayer, *The Builders*, pp. 354–60, and Frieden, *The Environmental Protection Hustle*, pp. 150–52.

22 Milton Nadworny, "Some Economic Impacts of Water Pollution and Land Development Controls in Vermont," p. 34.

23 Muller and Christensen, *State-Mandated Impact Evaluation*, pp. 21–28. See also p. 15.

24 Richardson, *The Cost of Environmental Protection*, p. 127.

25 Muller and Christensen, *State-Mandated Impact Evaluation*, p. 27.

26 Richardson, *The Cost of Environmental Protection*, p. 127.

27 Ibid., p. 49.

28 Ibid., p. 126.

29 Ibid.

30 Ibid., p. 131.

31 On the Pennsylvania studies, see Robert Evans and John Bitler, *Coal Mining Reclamation Costs: Appalachian and Midwestern Coal Supply Districts* (Washington: U.S. Department of the Interior, Bureau of Mines, 1975). See also Franklin Persse, David Lockard, and Alec Lindquist, *Coal Surface Mining Reclamation Costs in the Western United States* (Washington: U.S. Department of the Interior, Bureau of Mines, 1977); George Dials and Elizabeth Moore, "The Cost of Coal," *Environment*, September 1974, reprinted in *Appalachia*, October– November 1974; Pete Charton and E. A. Carr, "A Stock Answer to Reclamation of Surface Mined Lands," *Appalachia*, February–March 1977; University of Tennessee Appalachian Resources Project, *The Economic Impact of Back to Contour Reclamation of Surface Coal Mines in Appalachia: The TVA Massengale Mountain Project* (Knoxville: UTARP, 1976); and William Doyle, *Strip Mining of Coal: Environmental Solutions* (Park Ridge, New Jersey: Noyes Data Corporation, 1976). These studies, however, generally do not count in their calculations of reclamation costs any redressing of the damage stripping does to the value of adjoining property, to roads that serve the mines, and to the treasuries of nearby localities that must bear the public-service costs produced by the stripping.

32 See Thomas Muller and Franklin James, *Environmental Impact Evaluation and Housing Costs* (Washington: Urban Institute, 1975).

33 Muller and Christensen, *State-Mandated Impact Evaluation*, p. 29.

34 Myers, *Slow Start in Paradise*, p. 32.

35 For some documentation on Hawaii, see Myers, *Zoning Hawaii*, pp. 80–86, and Lowry and McElroy, "State Land Use Control: Some Lessons from Experience," pp. 18–21.

36 Healy, "An Economic Interpretation of the California Coastal Commissions," pp. 155–56.

37 Ibid., pp. 156–57.

38 See Myers, *Slow Start in Paradise*, p. 33.

39 Nadworny, "Some Economic Impacts of Water Pollution and Land Development Controls in Vermont," p. 35.

40 Shown in Reilly, ed., *The Use of Land*, p. 247.

41 Center for Science in the Public Interest, *The Enforcement of Strip Mining Laws in Three Appalachian States*, pp. 84–89.

42 Healy, *Land Use and the States*, p. 174.

43 Heeter, "Almost Getting It Together in Vermont," p. 383.

44 Letter from Robert Kuehn, Great Eastern Building Company in Cambridge, Massachusetts, to Donald Webster, August 15, 1975. I was given a copy by a member of the Vermont Environmental Board.

45 *Florida Trend*, September 1973, p. 20, quoted in Myers, *Slow Start in Paradise*, p. 34.

46 For a discussion of this issue as it applies to air and water pollution, see A. Myrick Freeman III, *The Benefits of Environmental Improvement: Theory and Practice* (Baltimore: Johns Hopkins University Press, 1979).

47 For an excellent example from state land-use regulation, see Institute for Contemporary Studies, *The California Coastal Plan*.

48 For some data on these points, see Douglas Costle, "Dollars and Cents: Putting a Price Tag on Pollution," *Environment*, October 1979, and Joseph Seneca and Peter Asch, *The Benefits of Air Pollution Control in New Jersey* (New Brunswick, New Jersey: Rutgers University Center for Coastal and Environmental Studies, 1979).

49 Since 1977, the Florida Division of State Planning (now the Bureau of Land and Water Management) has published a *DRI Bi-Weekly List* that contains a brief description of each DRI under review in the state, including the project's name, type, location, size, and regulatory status.

50 For some estimates of the economic benefits of limiting sprawl, see Real Estate Research Corporation, *The Costs of Sprawl*. For some estimates of the benefits of reducing air and water pollution, see Council on Environmental Quality, *Environmental Quality, 1978*, pp. 418–49.

51 William Toner, personal communication, October 1978.

52 See Council on Environmental Quality, *Environmental Quality, 1976*, pp. 152–54; Council on Environmental Quality, "Pollution Control and Employment," pp. 2–4, and the studies these two documents cite.

53 For the two estimates, see Council on Environmental Quality, *Environmental Quality, 1976*, pp. 153–54. For the $10 billion figure, see ibid., p. 167.

54 Kenneth Leung and Jeffrey Klein, "The Environmental Control Industry" (Washington: Council on Environmental Quality, 1975).

55 See Chase Econometrics, Inc., "The Macroeconomic Effects of Fed-

eral Pollution Control Programs: 1976 Assessment" (Washington: Council on Environmental Quality and Environmental Protection Agency, 1976).

Chapter 10: The Environmental Effects of the Programs

1 For some examples, see Maryland Power Plant Siting Program, *Power Plant Cumulative Environmental Impact Reports* (Annapolis: MPPSP, 1975 and 1978) and Pennsylvania Bureau of Water Quality Management, *Commonwealth of Pennsylvania 1977 Water Quality Inventory* (Harrisburg: Department of Environmental Resources, 1977).

2 Mogulof, *Saving the Coast*, pp. 105–6. See also Healy, *Land Use and the States*, pp. 76–88.

3 Myers, *So Goes Vermont*, p. 23. See also Heeter, "Almost Getting It Together in Vermont," p. 382, and Healy, *Land Use and the States*, p. 47.

4 Healy, *Land Use and the States*, p. 128.

5 For typical California conditions, see Banta, "The Coastal Commissions and State Agencies: Conflict and Cooperation," and Healy, "An Economic Interpretation of the California Coastal Commissions," pp. 45–165. For some south Florida data on DRI conditions, see Muller and Christensen, *State-Mandated Impact Assessment*, pp. 36–37. See also Adirondack Park Agency, *Comprehensive Report, Adirondack Park Agency, Volume 2, Appendix: A Comprehensive Statistical Review of the Adirondack Park Agency Program* (Ray Brook, New York: APA, 1976), p. 9.

6 See Appeal No. 279–74, minutes of state commission meeting of January 8, 1975, available from the commission in San Francisco.

7 See Maryland Public Service Commission, *Report of the Public Service Commission of Maryland for the Year 1973*, pp. 58–60.

8 Construction Industry Research Board, *Economic Analysis*, p. 8. For a more detailed analysis of these figures for the Los Angeles–Orange County area, see ibid., p. 7.

9 Rosentraub, Warren, and Gould, *Coastal Zone Development and Coastal Policy in Southern California*, p. 12. See also Robert Warren, Louis Wechsler, and Mark Rosentraub, "Local-Regional Interaction in the Development of Coastal Land-Use Policies: A Case Study of Metropolitan Los Angeles," *Coastal Zone Management Journal*, Volume 3, Number 4, 1977.

10 Rosentraub, Warren, and Gould, *Coastal Zone Development and Coastal Policy in Southern California*, pp. 21, 62, 64.

11 See Bernard Siegan, "Controlling Other People's Property through Covenants, Zoning, State and Federal Regulation," *Environmental Law*, Spring 1975, p. 445, and *Other People's Property*, p. 68.

12 Sabatier, "State Review of Local Land-Use Decisions," p. 265.

13 Ibid., p. 264.

14 Healy, *Land Use and the States*, p. 47. For a more technical and ambiguous endorsement of the environmental effects of Act 250, see Darby Bradley and Richard Mixer, "Act 250 and the Control of Soil Erosion and Sedimentation in Developing Areas of Vermont."

15 Adirondack Park Agency, *Comprehensive Report, Adirondack Park Agency*, Volume 2, *Appendix*, p. 17.

16 H. T. Sipe, "The Impact of Environmental Conditions on Plant Siting," unpublished paper presented to the National Conference of Regulatory Utility Commission Engineers in San Francisco in June 1975, especially pp. 6–7. For another instance of anticipatory design, see Constantini and Hanf, *The Environmental Impulse and Its Competitors*, pp. 46–47.

17 For similar conclusions reached in 1976 by a group of policy researchers (including myself) studying state land-use programs, see the *Minutes, State Land Use Policy Conference*, p. 2. These minutes are available from the Conservation Foundation in Washington, which held the conference.

18 Healy, *Land Use and the States*, p. 128.

19 Ibid., pp. 125–26. See also INFORM, *Promised Lands*, Volume 2, *Subdivisions in Florida's Wetlands*, pp. 346–83.

20 See Maneval, "Recreational Development on Reclaimed Land."

21 For further documentation, see *Citizens' Presentation to the Citizens Advisory Council* (Harrisburg: Pennsylvania Department of Environmental Resources, Citizens Advisory Council, 1975), which appears in the minutes of the council meeting on September 17, 1975, in Uniontown, Pennsylvania; Larry Margasak, "Old, New in Restoration Sit on the Same Hill," *Uniontown Morning Herald*, January 17, 1973; and Center for Science in the Public Interest, *The Enforcement of Strip Mining Laws in Three Appalachian States*, pp. 75–94.

22 See Healy, "The Role of the Permit System in the California Coastal Strategy," pp. 77–79. For further case studies of particular California permit cases of the kind described, see Healy, "An Economic Interpretation of the California Coastal Commissions," pp. 145–65, and Healy, *Land Use and the States*, pp. 76–88. For a somewhat less positive evaluation of the environmental effects of the Washington State coastal zone management program, see Maureen McCrea and James Feldmann, "Interim Assessment of Washington State Shoreline Man-

agement," *Coastal Zone Management Journal*, Volume 3, Number 2, 1977. For a favorable evaluation of the environmental effects of other states' coastal zone management programs, see U.S. Department of Commerce, Office of Coastal Zone Management, *The First Five Years of Coastal Zone Management: An Initial Assessment* (Washington: OCZM, 1979), pp. 19–42.

23 Quoted in Farney, "Whether Coloradoans Hate Pollution or Red Tape More Vehemently May Decide Governorship Race," p. 48.

24 Healy, "Environmentalists and Developers," pp. 7–8. See also Healy, "The Role of the Permit System in the California Coastal Strategy," p. 86–93.

25 Steven Brown and James Coke, *Public Opinion on Land Use Regulation* (Columbus, Ohio: Academy for Contemporary Problems, 1977), p. 10.

26 Ibid., pp. iii, 9. See also James Coke and Steven Brown, "Public Attitudes about Land Use Policy and Their Impact on State Policy-Makers," where the authors' initial expectations are discussed on p. 112 n. 3. For a similar argument and data from Wisconsin, see Charles Geisler and Oscar Martinson, "Local Control of Land Use: Profile of a Problem," *Land Economics*, August 1976. For somewhat contradictory data, see Constantini and Hanf, *The Environmental Impulse and Its Competitors*, pp. 3–26. This study was, however, conducted in 1970, a few years earlier than the other studies cited.

27 See *Minutes, State Land Use Policy Conference*, p. 1.

28 In 1973, there was one woman on the state coastal commission. By 1978, there were six—half the commission's membership.

29 Vermont Department of Budget and Management, *1975 Vermont State Budget* (Montpelier: VDBM, 1975), p. 237.

30 Flacke, "The Adirondack Park Agency Comes of Age," p. 6. For some similar instances from state coastal programs, see Sorensen, *State-Local Collaborative Planning*.

31 Lewis, "New York's Adirondacks," p. 15. See also Gallop, "The Florida Environmental Land and Water Management Act of 1972," p. 8.

32 See Paul Bergman and Franklin Bush, "The Community Impact Statement Ordinance of Clearwater, Florida: A 'Before the Fact' Impact Assessment as Part of a Municipal Growth Management Strategy," an unpublished paper presented to the 1975 annual conference of the American Institute of Planners, held at San Antonio.

33 See, for example, Alan Gold, "Dade County's Entry into the Quiet Revolution," *Land Use Law & Zoning Digest*, January 1978.

34 Heeter, "Almost Getting It Together in Vermont," p. 382. Emphasis in original.

35 See John DeGrove, "Florida's Legislature: The 1979 Session, An Introduction," *Florida's Environmental and Urban Issues*, October 1979, p. 1. For a similar turnabout in Oregon, see Richmond, "Unique Public Interest Law Group Supports Oregon Land Use Program," p. 8.

36 See Duddleson, "How the Citizens of California Secured Their Coastal Management Program," pp. 52, 224–25 n. 177.

Chapter 11: Making Land-Use Reform Work Better

1 For similar verdicts on the movement, see *Minutes, State Land Use Policy Conference*, p. 6, and Daniel Mandelker, "The Quiet Revolution Reconsidered," *Land Use Law & Zoning Digest*, August 1979.

2 See also Arthur Davis, "State Land Use Programs: Reality or Illusion?" (Cambridge, Massachusetts: Lincoln Institute of Land Policy, 1979).

3 "Slants and Trends," *Land Use Planning Report*, April 16, 1979, p. 117. See also "Impact of CZM Program Disputed in House Hearings," *Land Use Planning Report*, October 15, 1979, p. 527. On the final suspension of the Georgia program, see "Georgia Governor Withdraws State from Federal Coastal Zone Program," *Land Use Planning Report*, July 9, 1979, p. 218, and "OCZM Terminates Georgia's Program, Hopes to Recoup Unspent 305 Funds," *Land Use Planning Report*, July 16, 1979, p. 226.

4 See "California Governor Backs Bill to End TRPA; Rural Officials Score CTRPA Regulations," *Land Use Planning Report*, October 29, 1979, p. 345.

5 For an argument similar to the one in this paragraph, see Healy, *Land Use and the States*, p. 197.

6 For further discussion of this point, see Popper, "Ownership." For a specific example, see "Land Use Planning Hottest Utah Controversy," *Urban Growth*, October 31, 1974, supplement entitled *Political Report*, p. 1. For more on the Utah contest, see Dean, "How to Kill a Land Use Bill."

7 On the resistance to zoning, see the zoning literature cited in Chapter 3, note 94. On the resistance to air and water pollution controls generally, see J. Clarence Davies III and Barbara Davies, *The Politics of Pollution* (Indianapolis: Bobbs-Merrill, second edition, 1975). For specific local and regional studies of the resistance to air pollution controls, see Matthew Crenson, *The Un-Politics of Air Pollution: A Study of Non-*

Decisionmaking in the Cities (Baltimore: Johns Hopkins University Press, 1971); Ann Friedlander, ed., *Approaches to Controlling Air Pollution* (Cambridge, Massachusetts: MIT Press, 1978); George Hagevik, *Decision-Making in Air Pollution Control* (New York: Praeger, 1970); Henry Jacoby and John Steinbruner, *Clearing the Air* (Cambridge, Massachusetts: Ballinger, 1973); Charles Jones, *Clean Air*; James Krier and Edmund Ursin, *Pollution and Policy: A Case Essay on California and Federal Experience with Motor Vehicle Air Pollution, 1940–1975* (Berkeley: University of California Press, 1978); Ralph Nader's Study Group on Air Pollution, John Esposito, Project Director, *Vanishing Air* (New York: Grossman, 1973); Ralph Nader's Study Group on DuPont in Delaware, *The Company State*; Ralph Nader's Study Group on the Pulp and Paper Industry in Maine, *The Paper Plantation*, pp. 101–28; and Esther Schachter, *Enforcing Air Pollution Controls* (New York: Praeger, 1974). For specific local and regional studies of the resistance to water pollution controls, see Bruce Ackerman et al., *The Uncertain Search for Environmental Quality*; Ralph Nader's Study Group Report on Water Pollution, David Zwick and Marcy Benstock, Project Directors, *Water Wasteland* (New York: Grossman, 1971); Ralph Nader's Study Group on Industry and Environmental Crisis in Georgia, James Fallows, Project Director, *The Water Lords* (New York: Grossman, 1971); Ralph Nader's Study Group in DuPont in Delaware, *The Company State*; and Ralph Nader's Study Group on the Pulp and Paper Industry in Maine, *The Paper Plantation*, pp. 5–100.

8 For a discussion both of how zoning serves these ends and of how ownership interests have come to understand that it does so, see Perin, *Everything in Its Place*, pp. 129–62.

9 The text's account of the Brandywine failure comes from Strong, *Private Property and the Public Interest: The Brandywine Experience*. I reviewed this book in "How a Great Idea Bombed," *Planning*, May 1976, and further analyzed some of its implications in "Ownership: The Hidden Factor in Land-Use Regulation." The text's account draws heavily on these sources.

10 Strong, *Private Property and the Public Interest: The Brandywine Experience*, pp. 57, 169.

11 See ibid., p. 57.

12 Healy, "Rural Land: Private Choices, Public Interests," *Conservation Foundation Letter*, August 1977, p. 2.

13 Healy, *Land Use and the States*, p. 53.

14 See Strong, *Private Property and the Public Interest: The Brandywine Experience*, p. 167, which contains the quote.

15 Ibid., pp. 198–99. Emphasis in original. See, however, Strong's Dennis O'Harrow Memorial Lecture, "Needed: National Land Use Goals and Standards," given at the American Society of Planning Officials meeting in San Diego in April 1977, available from ASPO (now the American Planning Association) in Chicago.

16 See, for example, Carter, *The Florida Experience*, pp. 317–37; Council of State Governments, *Land: State Alternatives for Planning and Management*; Healy, *Land Use and the States*, pp. 191–208; Dickert and Sorensen, *Collaborative Land Use Planning for the Coastal Zone*, Volume 1, *A Process for Local Program Development*, pp. 67–75; Sorensen, *State-Local Collaborative Planning*, Chapter 9; Frank Popper, "Land Use Reform: Illusion or Reality?" *Planning*, September 1974; and Reilly, ed., *The Use of Land*, pp. 19–31.

17 For a discussion of the same reorientation as it applies to environmentalism as a whole, see Frank Popper, "Putting New Life into the Environmental Movement," *Planning*, May 1979. The text's argument draws heavily on this source. For alternative approaches to the reorientation, see Brooks, *Housing Equity and Environmental Protection*, pp. 77–120, and Conservation Foundation, *Conservation and New Economic Realities: Some Views of the Future* (Washington: CF, 1978).

18 See Corbin Harwood, *Using Land to Save Energy* (Cambridge, Massachusetts: Ballinger, 1977); the July 1977 issue of *Environmental Comment* on "Energy Conservation and Land Development"; Duncan Erley, David Mosena, and Efraim Gil, *Energy-Efficient Land Use* (Chicago: American Planning Association, 1979); Robert Byrne, "The Impact of Energy Costs and Supply Prospects on Land Development Practices," *Urban Land*, September 1979; Conservation Foundation, *Conservation and New Economic Realities*, pp. 33–54; Robert Rooney, "An Economic View of the Coastal Plan," *Cry California*, September 1976; and Rooney, *Dollars and Sense: The Economic Context of the California Coastal Plan* (Sacramento: Planning and Conservation League, 1976). Rooney, interestingly, is a former chairman of the Los Angeles area regional coastal commission who voted against the coastal initiative in 1972.

19 See, for example, John Rosenberg, "Land-Use Coverage: A Connecticut Sampler," *Columbia Journalism Review*, May/June 1978, and Jane Silverman, "The Communications Gap in Growth Management," *Environmental Comment*, September 1979, p. 11.

20 See National Consumer Congress, *Analysis of People's Counsels and RUCAG's* (Washington: NCC, 1975).

21 For a similar idea, see Nina Gruen, "Housing Consumer Effects: The

Neglected Land Use Impact," in Soil Conservation Society of America, *Land Use: Tough Choices in Today's World*, and Nina Gruen, "In the Land Use Game . . . Who Gets the Monopoly on the Good Life?" *Urban Land*, September 1977.

22 See, for example, Healy, *Land Use and the States*, p. 61 n. 16, and Heeter, "Almost Getting It Together in Vermont," pp. 372–73. For some similar data, see Adirondack Park Agency, *Comprehensive Report, Adirondack Park Agency*, Volume 2, *Appendix*, p. 9. See also Seidel, *Housing Costs & Government Regulations*; Frieden, *The Environmental Protection Hustle*; Urban Land Institute and Gruen Gruen & Associates, *Effects of Regulation on Housing Costs*; National Association of Home Builders, *Fighting Excessive Government Regulations* (Washington: NAHB, 1976); and U.S. Department of Housing and Urban Development, *Final Report of the Task Force on Housing Costs* (Washington: HUD, 1978).

23 Mayer, *The Builders*, p. 13.

24 For an attempt by the Florida Home Builders Association to produce a list of unnecessary technical requirements, see "Nice But Not Necessary," *FHBA Facts*, November 1975 (published in Tallahassee). See also the Urban Land Institute, *Cost Effective Site Planning: Single Family Development* (Washington: ULI, 1977).

25 For a similar suggestion in the specific field of energy development, see Twentieth Century Fund Task Force on United States Energy Policy, *Providing for Energy* (New York: McGraw-Hill, 1972), p. 26.

26 For further discussion of these various property-tax devices, see George Peterson, ed., *Property Tax Reform* (Washington: Urban Institute, 1973).

27 For studies of some of the existing state experiments, see American Land Forum, *Land & Food: The Preservation of U.S. Farmland* (Washington: ALF, 1979); Council on Environmental Quality, *Untaxing Open Space: An Evaluation of the Effectiveness of the Differential Assessment of Farms and Open Space* (Washington: Government Printing Office, 1976); Council on Environmental Quality, *A Survey of State Programs to Preserve Farmland* (Washington: Government Printing Office, 1979); Robert Coughlin, *Saving the Garden: The Preservation of Farmland and Other Environmentally Valuable Open Space* (Philadelphia: University of Pennsylvania, Regional Science Research Institute, 1977); National Association of Counties Research Foundation, *Disappearing Farmlands: A Citizen's Guide to Agricultural Land Preservation* (Washington: NACRF, 1979), pp. 9–14; William Toner, *Saving Farms and Farmlands: A Community Guide* (Chicago: Ameri-

can Planning Association, 1978); Leonard Wilson, *State Agricultural Land Issues* (Lexington, Kentucky: Council of State Governments, 1979); and the January 1978 issue of *Environmental Comment* on "Preservation of Prime Agricultural Land."

28 For a similar idea, see Healy, "Rural Land," p. 8. For some suggestions on how the environmental damage might be calculated, see Charles Thurow, William Toner, and Duncan Erley, *Performance Controls for Sensitive Lands: A Practical Guide for Local Administrators* (Chicago: American Society of Planning Officials, 1975).

29 See Peterson, ed., *Property Tax Reform.*

30 See National Council for Urban Economic Development Information Service, *Tax Base Sharing* (Washington: Municipal Finance Officers Association, 1976).

31 See William Matuszeski, "Trends in State Land Use Legislation," *Environmental Comment*, September 1976, p. 2, and Council on Environmental Quality, *Untaxing Open Space*, pp. 303–29.

32 For more on the Vermont tax, see Healy, *Land Use and the States*, pp. 57–59, 224. On the enactment of such a tax in Washington, D.C., see "D.C. Council Passes Antispeculation Measure," *Planning*, August 1978. See also Lee Webb, "Tax Reformers Go After Land Speculation," *Ways and Means*, July–August 1978.

33 See California Office of Planning and Research, *An Urban Strategy for California* (Sacramento: COPR, 1978), and Massachusetts Office of State Planning, *Toward a Growth Policy for Massachusetts* (Boston: MOSP, 1976).

34 See Leonard Wilson, "Public Investment Planning: A New State Imperative," *Environmental Comment*, September 1976.

35 See Council on Environmental Quality, *Environmental Quality, 1976*, p. 72.

36 Duddleson, "How the Citizens of California Secured Their Coastal Management Program," p. 224 n. 177. For further evidence from California, see Ed Salzman, "The Pendulum of Power," *California Journal*, July 1977.

37 Brown and Coke, *Public Opinion on Land Use Regulation*, p. iii. See also Clifford Weaver and Richard Babcock, "City Zoning: The Once and Future Frontier," *Planning*, December 1979, as well as their forthcoming book of the same title, to be published by the American Planning Association in Chicago.

38 For arguments of this sort, see Keith Honey, "Land Use Planning," *Practicing Planner*, June 1978, and Devon Schneider, "Can Cities and Counties Do the Job?" *Practicing Planner*, December 1978.

39 See Rosenbaum, *Land Use and the Legislatures*, pp. 18–29. Florida's 1975 Local Government Comprehensive Planning Act, which requires only local planning rather than zoning and subdivision regulations, is a step in this direction, but its results are at present uncertain. For a more general examination of the issues such laws pose, see the debate between Daniel Mandelker and Lawrence Susskind, "Should State Government Mandate Local Planning?" *Planning*, July 1978.

40 See Gerald Mylroie, "The Coastal Energy Impact Program," *Practicing Planner*, December 1978.

41 See Council of State Governments, *Coal Severance Taxes and Distribution of Income* (Lexington, Kentucky: CSG, 1976). On the Montana tax in particular, see Toole, *The Rape of the Great Plains*, pp. 80–125.

42 For the beginnings of such a federal program, which was later defeated in Congress, see "Boomtowns to Get $150 Million a Year in Administration Impact Aid Program," *Land Use Planning Report*, May 8, 1978, p. 149. For a similar program in Kentucky, see "Kentucky Begins Aid Program to Energy-Impacted Areas to Improve 'Serious Housing Deficiencies,'" *Land Use Planning Report*, August 13, 1979, p. 258. For a similar idea in Maryland power plant siting, see Maryland Power Plant Siting Program, *Long Range Plan* (Annapolis: MPPSP, 1975), p. 6.

43 See Gallop, "The Florida Environmental Land and Water Management Act of 1972," p. 9.

44 See Council of State Governments, *Financing Family Farms in Minnesota* (Lexington, Kentucky: CSG, 1979).

45 "California Flirts with Growth Control," *Planning*, August 1977, p. 7.

46 For a recent survey of efforts along these lines, see Robert Healy and John Rosenberg, "Nibbling Away at Problems in State Land Use," *Resources*, January–March 1979. In a spectacular example of this sort, in 1979 New Jersey established a Pinelands Commission to regulate and plan development in the state's million-acre, largely undeveloped Pine Barrens in the south-central part of the state. The commission has many similarities to the Adirondack Park Agency and the California–Nevada Lake Tahoe Regional Planning Agency. See "Pinelands Bill Becomes Law," *Land Use Law & Zoning Digest*, August 1979, p. 2. For a description of the Pinelands, see John McPhee, *The Pine Barrens* (New York: Farrar, Straus and Giroux, 1968).

47 For a contrary opinion for California coastal zone planning, see Healy, "The Role of the Permit System in the California Coastal Strategy."

48 For a similar idea in Florida, see Myers, *Slow Start in Paradise*, p. 33. See also Healy, *Land Use and the States*, p. 199. The U.S. Department

of Commerce's National Oceanic and Atmospheric Administration, the Department of the Interior's Fish and Wildlife Service, and the Council on Environmental Quality are now jointly making maps showing those coastal areas least environmentally suitable for large energy and industrial facilities and therefore most in need of protection.

49 See James Jarrett and Jimmy Hicks, *Untangling the Permit Web: Washington's Environmental Coordination Procedures Act* (Lexington, Kentucky: Council of State Governments, 1978); Charles Roe, Jr., "Simplifying Regulatory Procedures: A Commendable Washington State Approach," in Urban Land Institute, *Thirteen Perspectives on Regulatory Simplification*; and Healy, "Coordination," p. 145. The Council of State Governments has endorsed model legislation based on the Washington law; see its *Suggested State Legislation* (Lexington, Kentucky: CSG, 1978), pp. 24–30.

50 See Heeter, "Almost Getting It Together in Vermont," p. 379.

51 See also Kneisel, *Economic Impacts of Land Use Control*, pp. 34–39.

52 For existing examples of such handbooks, see Alaska Departments of Environmental Conservation and Commerce and Economic Development, *Directory of Permits* (Juneau: ADEC and ADCED, 1978); California Office of Planning and Research, *State Permit Handbook* (Sacramento: COPR, 1979); Connecticut Department of Environmental Protection, *Developer's Handbook* (Hartford: CDEP, undated); Delaware Department of Community Affairs and Economic Development, *Guide to Delaware Permit Regulations* (Dover: DDCAED, 1979); Hawaii Department of Planning and Economic Development, *Hawaii Coastal Zone Program: A Register of Government Permits Required for Development* (Honolulu: HDPED, 1977); Maine Department of Conservation, *Land Use Handbook for Maine* (Augusta: MDC, 1978); Montana Environmental Quality Council, *Environmental Permit Directory* (Helena: MEQC, 1978); Oregon State Permit Center, *1979 Regulatory Permits Inventory* (Salem: OSPC, 1979) Pennsylvania Department of Environmental Resources, *A Users Guide to DER Permits* (Harrisburg: PDER, 1977).

53 Mogulof, *Saving the Coast*, pp. 98, 99. See also Dean Misczynski, "The Awkward Economics of Coastal Planning," *Southern California Law Review*, May 1976, pp. 740–41.

54 For further elaboration of the compensation approach, see Jan Krasnowiecki and Ann Strong, "Compensable Regulations for Open Space: A Means of Controlling Urban Growth," in Institute for Contemporary Studies, *No Land Is an Island*, and John Costonis, Curtis Berger, and Stanley Scott, *Regulation v. Compensation in Land Use Control: A*

Recommended Accommodation, a Critique, and an Interpretation (Berkeley: University of California, Institute of Government Studies, 1977). For the beginnings of such an approach in Florida, see Robert Rhodes, "The Florida Property Rights Law," *Land Use Law & Zoning Digest*, January 1979, and Rhodes, "Compensating Police Power Takings: Chapter 78–85, Laws of Florida," *Florida Environmental and Urban Issues*, October 1978.

Chapter 12: Afterword: The Lessons for Other Fields

1 Paul MacAvoy, "The Existing Condition of Regulation and Regulatory Reform," in Institute for Contemporary Studies, *Regulating Business*, p. 4. See also MacAvoy, *The Regulated Industries and the Economy* (New York: Norton, 1979).

2 See Council on Environmental Quality, *Environmental Quality, 1978*, pp. 174–314.

3 See, for example, Donald Van Meter and Carl Van Horn, "The Policy Implementation Process: A Conceptual Framework," *Administration and Society*, February 1975; Eugene Bardach, *The Implementation Game: What Happens after a Bill Becomes a Law* (Cambridge, Massachusetts: MIT Press, 1977); Erwin Hargrove, *The Missing Link: The Study of the Implementation of Social Policy* (Washington: Urban Institute, 1975); Walter Williams and Richard Elmore, eds., *Social Program Implementation* (New York: Academic Press, 1976); Walter Williams, "Implementation Analysis and Assessment," *Policy Analysis*, Summer 1975; Martin Rein and Francine Rabinovitz, *Implementation* (Cambridge, Massachusetts: Harvard-MIT Joint Center for Urban Studies, 1977); Harold Luft, "Benefit Cost Analysis and Public Policy Implementation," *Public Policy*, Fall 1976; Paul Sabatier and Daniel Mazmanian, *The Implementation of Regulatory Policy: A Framework of Analysis* (Davis, California: University of California, Davis, Institute of Government Affairs, 1979); Sabatier and Mazmanian, "The Conditions of Effective Implementation," *Policy Analysis*, Fall 1979; Paul Sabatier, "Regulatory Policy-Making: Toward a Framework of Analysis," *Natural Resources Journal*, July 1977; and Jeffrey Pressman and Aaron Wildavsky, *Implementation* (Berkeley: University of California Press, 1973).

4 For a comparable argument, see Paul Sabatier, "Social Movements and Regulatory Agencies: Toward a More Adequate—and Less Pessimistic—Theory of 'Clientele Capture,'" *Policy Sciences*, September 1975.

5 For national poll evidence, see Robert Mitchell, "Environment: An Enduring Concern," *Resources*, January–March 1978, and Mitchell, "The Public Speaks Again: A New Environmental Survey," *Resources*, September–November 1978. For poll evidence on statewide attitudes toward the California coastal zone, see Duddleson, "How the Citizens of California Secured Their Coastal Management Program," p. 53.

Selected Bibliography

Books

Adirondack Park Agency. *Adirondack Park Land Use and Development Plan*. Ray Brook, New York: Adirondack Park Agency, 1973.

Adirondack Park Local Government Review Board. *1976 Annual Report, "A Local Perspective."* Long Lake, New York: Adirondack Park Local Government Review Board, 1976.

American Enterprise Institute for Public Policy Research. *Government Regulation: What Kind of Reform?* Washington: American Enterprise Institute for Public Policy Research, 1976.

American Institute of Planners. *Survey of State Land Use Activity*. Washington: Department of Housing and Urban Development, 1976.

American Law Institute. *Model Land Development Code: Official Draft*. Philadelphia: American Law Institute, 1976.

American Society of Planning Officials. *Subdividing Rural America: Impacts of Recreational Lot and Second Home Development*. Washington: Government Printing Office, 1976.

Andrews, Richard, ed. *Land in America: Commodity or Natural Resource?* Lexington, Massachusetts: Lexington Books, 1979.

Babcock, Richard. *The Zoning Game: Municipal Practices and Policies*. Madison: University of Wisconsin Press, 1966.

Bosselman, Fred, and Callies, David. *The Quiet Revolution in Land Use Control*. Washington: Government Printing Office, 1972.

Bosselman, Fred; Feurer, Duane; and Siemon, Charles. *The Permit Explosion: Coordination of the Proliferation*. Washington: Urban Land Institute, 1976.

Brooks, Mary. *Housing Equity and Environmental Protection: The Needless Conflict*. Washington: American Institute of Planners, 1976.

Brown, Steven, and Coke, James. *Public Opinion on Land Use Regulation*. Columbus, Ohio: Academy for Contemporary Problems, 1977.

Burchell, Robert, and Listokin, David, eds. *Future Land Use: Energy, Environmental, and Legal Constraints*. New Brunswick, New Jersey: Rutgers University, Center for Urban Policy Research, 1975.

303

California Coastal Zone Conservation Commissions. *California Coastal Plan*. Sacramento: State of California Documents and Publications Branch, 1975.

Carter, Luther. *The Florida Experience: Land and Water Policy in a Growth State*. Baltimore: Johns Hopkins University Press, 1974.

Center for Science in the Public Interest. Albert Fritsch, Director. *The Enforcement of Strip Mining Laws in Three Appalachian States: Kentucky, West Virginia, and Pennsylvania*. Washington: Center for Science in the Public Interest, 1975.

Comptroller General of the United States. *Report to the Congress: The Coastal Zone Management Program: An Uncertain Future*. Washington: General Accounting Office, 1976.

Construction Industry Research Board. *Economic Analysis: California Coastal Zone Conservation Act*. Los Angeles: Construction Industry Research Board, 1976.

Council of State Governments. *Land: State Alternatives for Planning and Management*. Lexington, Kentucky: Council of State Governments, 1975.

Council of State Governments. *State Growth Management*. Lexington, Kentucky: Council of State Governments, 1976.

Davis, G. Gordon, and Liroff, Richard. *Conflict in the North Country: A Study of the Implementation of Regional Land Use Controls by the Adirondack Park Agency*. Washington: Environmental Law Institute, 1979.

DeGrove, John. *Land Management: New Directions for the States*. Columbus, Ohio: Academy for Contemporary Problems, 1976.

Dickert, Thomas, and Sorensen, Jens. *Collaborative Land-Use Planning for the Coastal Zone: Volume 1, A Process for Local Program Development*. Berkeley and La Jolla: University of California Institute of Urban and Regional Development and Institute of Marine Resources, 1978.

Doyle, John, Jr. *State Strip Mining Laws: An Inventory and Analysis of Key Statutory Provisions in 28 Coal-Producing States*. Washington: Environmental Policy Institute, 1977.

Finkler, Earl; Toner, William; and Popper, Frank. *Urban Nongrowth: City Planning for People*. New York: Praeger, 1976.

Frieden, Bernard. *The Environmental Protection Hustle*. Cambridge, Massachusetts: MIT Press, 1979.

Friedman, Milton. *There's No Such Thing as a Free Lunch*. La Salle, Illinois: Open Court, 1976.

Friedman, Milton, and Friedman, Rose. *Capitalism and Freedom*. Chicago: University of Chicago Press, 1962.

Graham, Frank, Jr. *The Adirondack Park: A Political History*. New York: Knopf, 1978.

Healy, Robert. *Land Use and the States*. Baltimore: Johns Hopkins University Press, 1976. Second edition, co-authored with John Rosenberg, 1979.

Healy, Robert, ed. *Protecting the Golden Shore: Lessons from the California Coastal Commissions*. Washington: Conservation Foundation, 1978.

Institute for Contemporary Studies. *The California Coastal Plan: A Critique*. San Francisco: Institute for Contemporary Studies, 1976.

Institute for Contemporary Studies. *No Land Is an Island: Individual Rights and Government Control of Land Use*. San Francisco: Institute for Contemporary Studies, 1975.

Kaplan, Samuel. *The Dream Deferred: People, Politics and Planning in Suburbia*. New York: Seabury, 1976.

Kneisel, Robert. *Economic Impacts of Land Use Control: The California Coastal Zone Conservation Commissions*. Davis, California: University of California, Davis, Institute of Government Affairs and Institute of Ecology, 1979.

Land Use Planning Report. *A Summary of State Land Use Controls*. Silver Spring, Maryland: Land Use Planning Report, 1976 and 1977.

Linowes, R. Robert, and Allensworth, Don. *The States and Land Use Control*. New York: Praeger, 1975.

Little, Charles. *The New Oregon Trail: An Account of the Development and Passage of State Land-Use Legislation in Oregon*. Washington: Conservation Foundation, 1974.

Little, Charles. *Shifting Ground: New Priorities for National Land Use Policy*. Washington: Library of Congress, Congressional Research Service, 1976.

Lowi, Theodore. *The End of Liberalism: Ideology, Policy, and the Crisis of Public Authority*. New York: Norton, 1969. Second edition, subtitled *The Second Republic of the United States*, 1979.

Lyday, Noreen. *The Law of the Land: Debating National Land Use Legislation, 1970–75*. Washington: Urban Institute, 1976.

Mandelker, Daniel. *Environmental and Land Controls Legislation*. Indianapolis: Bobbs-Merrill, 1976. Supplement, 1978.

Mayer, Martin. *The Builders: Houses, People, Neighborhoods, Governments, Money*. New York: Norton, 1978.

Mogulof, Melvin. *Saving the Coast: California's Experiment in Intergovernmental Land Use Control*. Lexington, Massachusetts: Lexington Books, 1975.

Muller, Thomas. *Fiscal Impacts of Land Development: Employment, Housing, and Property Values*. Washington: Urban Institute, 1976.

Muller, Thomas, and Christensen, Kathleen. *State-Mandated Impact Evaluation: A Preliminary Assessment.* Washington: Urban Institute, 1976.

Myers, Phyllis. *Slow Start in Paradise: An Account of the Development, Passage, and Implementation of State Land-Use Legislation in Florida.* Washington: Conservation Foundation, 1974.

Myers, Phyllis. *So Goes Vermont: An Account of the Development, Passage, and Implementation of State Land-Use Legislation in Vermont.* Washington: Conservation Foundation, 1974.

Myers, Phyllis. *Zoning Hawaii: An Analysis of the Passage and Implementation of Hawaii's Land Classification Law.* Washington: Conservation Foundation, 1976.

Nader, Ralph; Green, Mark; and Seligman, Joel. *Taming the Giant Corporation.* New York: Norton, 1976.

Nader, Ralph, Study Group. *See* Ralph Nader's Study Group on Land Use in California.

National Association of Home Builders. *Transcript, Conference on State Land Use Legislation.* Washington: National Association of Home Builders, 1973.

National Commission on Urban Problems. *Building the American City.* Washington: Government Printing Office, 1968; and New York: Praeger, 1969.

Natural Resources Defense Council. Elaine Moss, ed. *Land Use Controls in New York State: A Handbook on the Legal Rights of Citizens.* New York: Dial Press/James Wade, 1975.

Natural Resources Defense Council. Elaine Moss, ed. *Land Use Controls in the United States: A Handbook on the Legal Rights of Citizens.* New York: Dial Press/James Wade, 1977.

Nelson, Robert. *Zoning and Property Rights: An Analysis of the American System of Land-Use Regulation.* Cambridge, Massachusetts: MIT Press, 1977.

Pelham, Thomas. *State Land-Use Planning and Regulation: Florida, the Model Code, and Beyond.* Lexington, Massachusetts: Lexington Books, 1979.

Perin, Constance. *Everything in Its Place: Social Order and Land Use in America.* Princeton, New Jersey: Princeton University Press, 1977.

Ralph Nader's Study Group on Land Use in California. Robert Fellmeth, Project Director. *Politics of Land.* New York: Grossman, 1973.

Reilly, William, ed. *The Use of Land: A Citizens' Policy Guide to Urban Growth.* New York: Crowell, 1973.

Richardson, Dan. *The Cost of Environmental Protection: Regulating Housing Development in the Coastal Zone.* New Brunswick, New Jersey: Rutgers University Center for Urban Policy Research, 1976.

Rosenbaum, Nelson. *Citizen Involvement in Land Use Governance: Issues and Methods*. Washington: Urban Institute, 1976.

Rosenbaum, Nelson. *Land Use and the Legislatures: The Politics of State Innovation*. Washington: Urban Institute, 1976.

Rosener, Judy. *Environmentalism vs. Local Control: A Study of the Voting Behavior of Some California Coastal Commissioners*. Claremont, California: Claremont Graduate School, 1977.

Rosentraub, Mark; Warren, Robert; and Gould, David. *Coastal Zone Development and Coastal Policy in Southern California: A Two-Year Analysis of the South Coast Regional Commission*. Los Angeles: University of Southern California, Sea Grant Program, 1975.

Sabatier, Paul, and Mazmanian, Daniel. *Can Regulation Work? The Implementation of the 1972 California Coastal Initiative*. Davis and Claremont: University of California, Davis, Institute of Government Affairs, and Pomona College, Program in Public Policy Analysis, 1979.

Scott, Stanley. *Governing California's Coast*. Berkeley: University of California, Berkeley, Institute of Governmental Studies, 1975.

Seidel, Stephen. *Housing Costs & Government Regulations: Confronting the Regulatory Maze*. New Brunswick, New Jersey: Rutgers University Center for Urban Policy Research, 1978.

Siegan, Bernard. *Land Use without Zoning*. Lexington, Massachusetts: Lexington Books, 1972.

Siegan, Bernard. *Other People's Property*. Lexington, Massachusetts: Lexington Books, 1976.

Soil Conservation Society of America. *Land Use: Tough Choices in Today's World*. Ankeny, Iowa: Soil Conservation Society of America, 1977.

Sorensen, Jens. *State-Local Collaborative Planning: A Growing Trend in Coastal Zone Management*. Washington: Department of Commerce, Office of Coastal Zone Management and Office of Sea Grant, 1978.

Stigler, George. *The Citizen and the State: Essays on Regulation*. Chicago: University of Chicago Press, 1975.

Strong, Ann. *Private Property and the Public Interest: The Brandywine Experience*. Baltimore: Johns Hopkins University Press, 1975.

United States Department of Commerce, Office of Coastal Zone Management. *The First Five Years of Coastal Zone Management: An Initial Assessment*. Washington: Office of Coastal Zone Management, 1979.

Urban Land Institute. Annette Kolis, ed. *Thirteen Perspectives on Regulatory Simplification*. Washington: Urban Land Institute, 1979.

Urban Land Institute and Gruen Gruen & Associates. *Effects of Regulation on Housing Costs: Two Case Studies*. Washington: Urban Land Institute, 1977.

Urban Systems Research and Engineering. *The Growth Shapers: The Land*

Use Impacts of Infrastructure Investments. Washington: Government Printing Office, 1976.

Ward, Benjamin. *The Ideal Worlds of Economics: Liberal, Radical, and Conservative Economic World Views*. New York: Basic Books, 1979.

Articles and Pamphlets

Babcock, Richard. "On Land-Use Policy." *Planning*, June 1975.

Babcock, Richard, and Feurer, Duane. "Land as a Commodity 'Affected with a Public Interest.'" *Urban Land*, November 1977.

Coke, James, and Brown, Steven. "Public Attitudes about Land Use and Their Impact on State Policy-Makers." *Publius*, Winter 1976.

Davis, Arthur. "State Land Use Programs: Reality or Illusion?" Cambridge, Massachusetts: Lincoln Institute of Land Policy, 1979.

Environmental Comment. Issue of May 1976 devoted to "Coordination of Development Regulation: Untangling the Maze."

Environmental Comment. Issue of May 1977 devoted to "Conflict Resolution."

Gallop, Earl. "The Florida Environmental Land and Water Management Act of 1972: A Partially Fulfilled Expectation." *Florida Environmental and Urban Issues*, November/December 1978.

Healy, Robert. "Coordination: The Next Phase in Land Use Planning." *Journal of Soil and Water Conservation*, July/August 1976.

Healy, Robert. "Environmentalists and Developers: Can They Agree on Anything?" Washington: Conservation Foundation, 1977.

Healy, Robert, and Rosenberg, John. "Nibbling away at Problems in State Land Use." *Resources*, January–March 1979.

Johnson, M. Bruce. "A Critique of the Concept of Federal Land Use Regulation." *Environmental Law*, Spring 1975.

Lewis, Sylvia. "New York's Adirondacks: Tug of War in the Wilderness." *Planning*, September 1976.

McClaughry, John. "The Land Use Planning Act—An Idea We Can Do Without." *Environmental Affairs*, Volume 3, Number 4, 1974.

Mandelker, Daniel. "The Quiet Revolution Reconsidered." *Land Use Law & Zoning Digest*, August 1979.

Mandelker, Daniel, and Susskind, Lawrence. "Should State Government Mandate Local Planning?" *Planning*, July 1978.

Maneval, David. "Coal Mining vs. Environment: A Reconciliation in Pennsylvania." *Appalachia*, February–March 1972.

Meyer, Peter. "Land Rush." *Harper's*, January 1979.

Nadworny, Milton. "Some Economic Impacts of Water Pollution and Land Development Controls in Vermont." Montpelier: Vermont Natural Resources Council, 1971.

Popper, Frank. "Land Use Reform: Illusion or Reality?" *Planning*, September 1974.

Popper, Frank. "Putting New Life into the Environmental Movement." *Planning*, May 1979.

Popper, Frank. "We've Got to Dig Deeper into Who Owns Our Land." *Planning*, October 1976.

Preate, Ernest, Jr. "A New Law for an Old Problem." *Appalachia*, February–March 1972.

Rosenbaum, Nelson. "Private Property and the Public Interest: Citizen Involvement in State Land Use Control." Washington: Urban Institute Working Paper, 1977.

Rosenbaum, Nelson. "The State Role in Wetlands Protection." *Environmental Comment*, July 1978.

Sabatier, Paul. "Social Movements and Regulatory Agencies: Toward a More Adequate—and Less Pessimistic—Theory of 'Clientele Capture.'" *Policy Sciences*, September 1975.

Sabatier, Paul. "State Review of Local Land-Use Decisions: The California Coastal Commissions." *Coastal Zone Management Journal*, Volume 3, Number 3, 1977.

Sullivan, Fred. "Adirondack Zoning: A National Experiment in Land-Use Control Faces Local Challenge." *Empire State Report*, December 1975.

Tucker, William. "Environmentalism and the Leisure Class." *Harper's*, December 1977.

Walke, Judy. "Report on Problems in the Practice of Environmental Law in Vermont." Boston: Conservation Law Foundation of New England, 1973.

Weaver, Clifford, and Babcock, Richard. "City Zoning: The Once and Future Frontier." *Planning*, December 1979.

Index

311

DESIGNED BY IRVING PERKINS ASSOCIATES
COMPOSED BY THE NORTH CENTRAL PUBLISHING CO.
ST. PAUL, MINNESOTA
MANUFACTURED BY BANTA DIVISION
GEORGE BANTA COMPANY, INC., MENASHA, WISCONSIN
TEXT IS SET IN TIMES ROMAN
DISPLAY LINES IN SERIF GOTHIC AND TIMES ROMAN

Library of Congress Cataloging in Publication Data
Popper, Frank.
The politics of land–use reform.
Bibliography: pp. 303–309
Includes index.
1.   Land use—Law and legislation—United States.
2.   Regional planning—Law and legislation—United States.
3.   Land use—United States.   I.   Title.
KF5698 P66   346.7304'5   80-23255
ISBN 0-299-08530-9
ISBN 0-299-08534-1 (pbk.)